PRAISE FOR KENNY MacASKILL

PRAISE FOR *GLASGOW 1919*

"As the Great War ended, a century ago, revolutions broke out all over Europe. In this thrilling book, Kenny MacAskill pilots us down Red Clydeside to the brink of its Niagara – a real revolution – and shows why it didn't go over the edge. This is the story of Glasgow as a great city awakening to its own strength – the incredible power of mobilising hundreds of thousands of working men and women to defy authority and battle for justice."

NEAL ASCHERSON, JOURNALIST AND WRITER

"A new and thoughtful insight into a vital part of our history."

HENRY McLEISH, FORMER FIRST MINISTER OF SCOTLAND

"MacAskill is at his best as a writer when getting to grips with the detail of events; set-pieces such as the fracas in George Square are portrayed in great depth and with an eye for the dramatic moment."

SCOTTISH LABOUR HISTORY

"This is a terrific popular history by Kenny MacAskill, setting the imagination alive as the decades flash before us."

PAUL LAVERTY, SCREENWRITER OF *THE WIND THAT SHAKES THE BARLEY* AND *I, DANIEL BLAKE*

RADICAL SCOTLAND

UNCOVERING SCOTLAND'S RADICAL HISTORY
FROM THE FRENCH REVOLUTIONARY ERA TO THE 1820 RISING

KENNY MacASKILL

Ian

Best wishes for your next book and great work on "Shreddded". Truth will out.

Kenny MacAskill

\Bᵇ\
Biteback Publishing

First published in Great Britain in 2020 by
Biteback Publishing Ltd
Westminster Tower
3 Albert Embankment
London SE1 7SP
Copyright © Kenny MacAskill 2020

ISBN 978-1-78590-570-4

10 9 8 7 6 5 4 3 2 1

A CIP catalogue record for this book is available from the British Library.

Set in Adobe Garamond Pro and Bell Gothic

Printed and bound in Great Britain by
CPI Group (UK) Ltd, Croydon CR0 4YY

*To the memory of those who sacrificed
their lives for the cause of the people*

CONTENTS

1	The Monument	1
2	In Search of the Revolutionary Story	13
3	A Discontented Land	27
4	The King's Birthday Riots and Other Disturbances	37
5	The Friends of the People and the Trees of Liberty	47
6	The First National Convention and Repression Unleashed	57
7	Muir and Palmer Stand Trial	75
8	The British Convention Meets and the Other Martyrs Stand Trial	89
9	A Change in Tactics and the Pike Plot	109
10	George Mealmaker and the Society of the United Scotsmen	121
11	The Militia Act Riots	149
12	The Massacre of Tranent	175
13	Foreign Armies and the Dutch Invasion	197
14	A Legacy Remains and the Fate of the Other Martyrs	215
15	Radicalism Reignited	241
16	Events in England	259
17	The 1820 Rising	275
18	Aftermath and Epilogue	291
	Appendices	305
	Bibliography	325
	Acknowledgements	329
	Notes	331
	Index	339

CHAPTER 1

THE MONUMENT

Tall and bleak in the heart of Edinburgh stands a 90ft obelisk. Visible from the Old Town and far beyond, it is sited in Old Calton Cemetery, at the east end of Princes Street and on the very edge of Calton Hill. Resting in its lea is the mausoleum of David Hume, a founding father of the Scottish Enlightenment, and alongside it lie the graves of other leading citizens. Only 100 yards east lies St Andrew's House, the headquarters of the Scottish Government, all of which testify to the area's importance.

But whilst its silhouette is recognised by many, its history and purpose are sadly known by few. The Duke of Wellington, whose statue stands a few hundred yards along the road, and Admiral Nelson, whose column sits on Calton Hill, are both far more well known. The Battles of Waterloo and Trafalgar, which these statues commemorate, are likewise better remembered than the struggles the obelisk recalls, although they occurred during the same period.

This is partly as a result of the passage of time, but mainly because a narrative has been established, from which the individuals and their cause were marginalised, if not written entirely out. The difficulties faced in the monument's construction reflect the efforts that were made to try and obscure the memory of those it commemorates.

As the knowledge of the individuals and their cause have faded, so has the monument itself. As it is made from grey sandstone it has been blackened over the years by the smoke that once billowed throughout the city, which led to Scotland's capital being affectionately known as 'Auld Reekie'. But the monument's story is the prelude to the tale of forgotten revolutionary years in Edinburgh and Scotland.

Simple and austere in its design, the memorial bears just two inscriptions.

On one side of its base the following epitaph is etched:

TO

THE MEMORY OF

THOMAS MUIR

THOMAS FYSHE PALMER

WILLIAM SKIRVING

MAURICE MARGAROT

AND

JOSEPH GERRALD.

—

ERECTED BY

THE FRIENDS OF PARLIAMENTARY REFORM

IN ENGLAND AND SCOTLAND

1844

On another base there are inscriptions from speeches made by two of those commemorated:

I HAVE DEVOTED MYSELF TO THE CAUSE OF THE PEOPLE. IT IS A GOOD CAUSE — IT SHALL ULTIMATELY PREVAIL — IT SHALL FINALLY TRIUMPH.

SPEECH OF THOMAS MUIR IN THE COURT OF

JUSTICIARY ON THE 30TH OF AUGUST 1793

Beneath that is inscribed:

I KNOW THAT WHAT HAS BEEN DONE THESE TWO DAYS
WILL BE RE-JUDGED.

SPEECH OF WILLIAM SKIRVING IN THE COURT OF

JUSTICIARY ON THE 7TH OF JANUARY 1794

This is the Political Martyrs' Monument, which commemorates Thomas Muir, Reverend Thomas Fyshe Palmer, William Skirving, Maurice Margarot and Joseph Gerrald, whose names are inscribed upon it. They are heroes of Scotland's reform movement, although what is less well known is that three of them were actually English. Who were these martyrs of Scottish radicalism?

Thomas Muir was born into a successful merchant family in Glasgow in 1765, and later moved to the large Huntershill House in nearby Bishopbriggs. Forsaking early thoughts of joining the ministry, he studied law initially in Glasgow before falling out with the university authorities and completing his studies in Edinburgh. Following his graduation, he became an advocate and quickly gained a reputation for representing the poor, sometimes without a fee. But he also took to radical politics and his reputation in this field, as in the legal profession, soon flourished. He quickly became the leading figure in the cause for reform and a man marked out by the establishment.

Muir has been rightly celebrated and remains a hero to many on the left in Scotland as well as to those supportive of progressive causes. Books about him and related activities recording his memory have made his name recognisable, though still not as extensively as he deserves. However, the other political martyrs are far less widely known, if they are known at all.

Thomas Fyshe Palmer was born in Bedfordshire and educated at Eton and Cambridge, before becoming a Church of England curate; not the background normally associated with a Scottish radical. Growing disillusioned with the English established church he first joined, he then became an evangelist for the Unitarian Church. After moving to Scotland, he assisted in Montrose, before taking charge of a church that was established in Dundee in 1785. Preaching there and more widely across the area, he soon became known for his radical sermons and writings. His involvement in radical societies likewise followed.

William Skirving was a farmer's son born in Liberton, then a village near Edinburgh, in 1745. Attending Edinburgh University, he had intended to become a minister before he changed his mind, and instead became a tutor. His marriage to a farmer's daughter from Fife saw him obtain land at Strathruddy. Subsequently, upon returning to Edinburgh, he began farming his father's land and pursued academic interests, including publishing a book on farming. During this period he was becoming more active in the capital's radical circles.

Maurice Margarot, born in Devon in 1745, was the son of a wine merchant. Travelling extensively with his father, he ended up studying at university in Geneva. Moving thereafter to France, he was there when revolution broke out in 1789, which meant that he personally met many of the leading participants. After returning to England in 1792 he became involved in radical politics and was elected chairman of the London Corresponding Society (LCS), which was then the leading radical organisation in England.

Joseph Gerrald was born in St Kitts, West Indies, the son of a wealthy Irish planter. Following his father's death when he was still a child, Gerrald travelled to England. He later went back to the West Indies before moving to the United States, where he became a lawyer in Philadelphia. After returning to England he moved to Bath where he too became involved in radical politics and the LCS in particular.

All five individuals were members of or delegates to the First National Convention of the societies of the Friends of the People, which were groups that in the early 1790s sought universal suffrage and parliamentary reform in Scotland. For this was a time when the right to vote was possessed by only a few, with the government chosen by an oligarchy of the rich. The major land-owning elite held the power in the land and Scotland was governed in their interests.

It has been argued with good reason that another name should be inscribed on the memorial. George Mealmaker was born in 1768 into a weaving family in Seagate, Dundee. He became a weaver and was an elder in a dissenting church, as well as a leading radical in the area. He had a wide political agenda. As with some other radicals, he expressed his objection to the subjugation of the highlands and showed solidarity against the landowners. He accepted responsibility for writing the seditious document that Palmer was sentenced for, but even this proved insufficient to save the minister from his fate and he was convicted of distributing it anyway. Five years later in 1798, Mealmaker was himself condemned for distributing and writing further pamphlets, as well as for his leading involvement in a clandestine organisation known as the Society of the United Scotsmen.

The establishment was so alarmed by the cause of the martyrs that the authorities moved quickly and ruthlessly to crush it. Thomas Muir's arrest and trial at the High Court in August 1793 heralded an intense period of state repression that saw the other radicals join him in facing persecution, not just prosecution.

Thomas Muir is now celebrated and the impassioned speech that he delivered from the dock is rightly venerated by lawyers, as well as radicals. However, all five men faced a legal system that openly connived with the state, thus ensuring their conviction on charges of treason and sedition. Justice most certainly was not done and the sentences were harsh even for those days. Transportation to Botany Bay was their sentence and all were given fourteen years bar Palmer, who was sentenced to seven years. Mealmaker was also given a fourteen-year punishment. Only one of the six individuals made it home alive from their enforced exile on the other side of the world.

Their real crime, as far as the ruling elite was concerned, lay in supporting the cause of democracy and the rights of the people. It was a cause taken up by many and had considerable support across the land. Many less-celebrated individuals also endured varying degrees of punishment and many less high-profile incidents also took place in the fight for democracy. The severe sentences that were meted out reflected the fear the authorities had of the fledgling reform movement.

For in 1789 the French Revolution had ignited a demand for radical change that rapidly spread across Scotland as elsewhere in Britain and Ireland with the publication in 1791 of Thomas Paine's book *Rights of Man*. Radical pamphlets, books and newspapers began to proliferate, along with debating clubs and other societies. The toast 'Liberty, Equality and No King', and other radical and republican sentiments began to be espoused. At meetings of Friends of the People and other groups, the French revolutionary anthem 'Ça ira' could often be heard ringing out. Trees of liberty were planted as a symbol of reform and support for the French Revolution, as they had for the American Revolution a decade before.

This then is also the story of the revolutionary years that followed the momentous events in France and where the revolutionary ripples on the continent lapped upon Scottish shores, from the early 1790s until 1820. It straddles both the French Revolutionary Wars and the Napoleonic Wars, as well as the cycles of poverty and unemployment that afflicted Britain in the last decade of the eighteenth and the early decades of the nineteenth century.

These were tempestuous times as urbanisation accelerated with people moving or being displaced from the land, literacy increased and technology advanced. Scotland mirrored some developments and indeed led the way in others. The country's early inception of a public education system created a more literate society than most. Moreover, in Europe no other territory apart from Poland experienced 'such rapid rate of urban expansion as Scotland between 1750 and 1850'.[1]

As society and the economy transformed with the Industrial Revolution, trade unionism and Chartism replaced previous radical agitation. The authorities soon realised that other tactics beyond brute force and suppression were required. Some political powers would need to be ceded to allay the demands of both moderate reformers and radicals alike. The first Reform Act was therefore invoked in 1832, though it would not be until 1918 that the demands of the Friends of the People were finally met when the right to vote was extended to all men over the age of twenty-one.

Soft power was also used alongside the threat of repression, persuasion and banishment, and it was to be as key to the strategy as new laws or other government actions. History, as is said, is written by the victors and this was the case following these revolutionary years in Scotland. Such narratives glorify the Empire and the establishment, and create a mystique of prestige and power. Some of this history is selective or simply presented from the perspective of the authorities, other aspects have almost been mythologised or are just patently untrue. Most accounts have written the radicals out of the story and built up a picture of a compliant people governed by enlightened rulers. This was all part of the historical charm offensive launched after 1820.

At this time Edinburgh's New Town was being developed, with streets laid out and statues erected to honour the town's grandees. It was also an opportunity to celebrate Tory success and power. The first part of the New Town was constructed by 1820 and statues quickly followed. Henry Dundas's monument, which was erected in 1823, dominated St Andrew Square with the statue staring imperiously down at passers-by. On George Street, named after George III, who had reigned from 1760 until 1820, a statue of his son George IV was erected. Further down the road, a monument for William Pitt the Younger was installed, who was premier for much of this tumultuous period. Other towns and communities in Scotland saw a similar celebration of the rich and powerful. This was not the case for the radicals or their struggles.

The new narrative detailing recent events was formally launched when the newly crowned King George IV came to visit Scotland in 1822, which was the first visit from a reigning monarch in nearly 200 years, since Charles I's coronation in 1633. This itself gave lie to the myth of a royalty that was devoted to its subjects and a public that in return offered loyal support. For many, the King was not God given, but a Hanoverian imposter, and a figure for whom there was little warmth, let alone loyalty. Republican sentiment in Scotland was far greater than accepted history has led us to believe. The Jacobite song 'The Wee, Wee German Lairdie' had been written for George I a century before, but it was a sentiment still felt by many towards the monarchy. This perhaps explains why it has been suggested that a new tune was written for the song during that later period.

Sir Walter Scott choreographed the royal visit, and he used his novelistic skills to craft a romanticised, if not almost mythological Scotland. The event offered an opportunity to try and unite the highlands and lowlands with a common culture and presented the Hanoverian dynasty with a chance to 'tartanise' their image, and disguise their foreign roots. For the Scottish elite it was also an opportunity to emphasise their 'Scottishness' despite being tied to a union controlled from London, where many such individuals had relocated.

The trip lasted for over a fortnight and it was in effect a huge open-air tartan pageant. The Royal Company of Archers acted as the monarch's ceremonial bodyguard, a function they still perform to this day, and now as then, the company is made up of members from the upper echelons of the Scottish establishment. The group has perhaps come to represent the embodiment of the 'North Briton' some were hoping to create during this time. Events took place within Edinburgh and far beyond; the King paraded around in his tartan finery and the modern kilt was born. The clothing that is now viewed as quintessentially Scottish was in fact far from it at this time, with the original plaid kilt having been banned following the Battle of Culloden in 1746 and the defeat of Bonnie Prince Charlie and the Jacobite cause. Repression then followed in the highlands, which brought with it the subjugation of a people and their culture.

However, these draconian measures were quietly forgotten and instead a new narrative was peddled depicting the monarch in the supposed Scottish 'national costume' showing his respect for the nation and his subjects. Other invitees were equally garishly attired and many were reluctant and no doubt embarrassed by being forced to wear such dress. Nonetheless, the establishment obsequiously ingratiated themselves with His Royal Highness and the military dutifully obeyed the royal command. Needless to say, the poor were uninvited, unwelcome and did not take part in the events, except when providing service.

Highland games also followed on from this part of the trip, and were an attempt by major landowners to show a supposedly benevolent disposition and defuse discontent amongst tenants. By this time across the highlands the nature of this relationship had changed from a familial bond to one of owner and tenant. Clearances had begun as sheep started to supplant people, which led to opposition and even open rebellion in Ross-shire.

There was a need to manufacture an image of landowners as being from and for the people, though nothing could have been further from the reality. A report in the *Caledonian Mercury* on the Highland Society in January 1798 evidenced the power of the elite by listing the president as the Duke of Argyle and the vice-presidents as the Duke of Buccleuch, Lord Balgonie, the Earl of Kinnoul and the Earl of Cassilis.[2] A mythology portraying clan chiefs as being loyal to their people was spun during this time and it sadly lingers with some to this day, when in fact they were often the perpetrators of a shameful betrayal. Others were lowland landowners who simply cultivated a highland image.

These same landowners, from the highlands and lowlands, who had acquired their land, often in dubious circumstances or with little legal

entitlement, were positively encouraged to use soft power to molli-
fy discontent, whilst attempting to establish a more benign image.
As with the kilt, the highland games continue to this day and have
become accepted as a traditional part of the Scottish calendar in many
parts. They are enjoyed by many and are viewed as being distinctively
Scottish but their creation was far less straightforward.

So, to trace the story of these revolutionary years we begin with the
memorial that stands in Old Calton Cemetery. Its erection was an
attempt to counteract a narrative that exuded loyalty and patriotism,
yet excluded those who had struggled for radical change. The monument's tale is symbolic of the establishment's glorification of its own
success and the efforts made to bury the memory of the opposition.

The planning for the tribute did not commence until the late 1830s
when things had calmed down and some rights had been won. But
the sacrifice that had been made by those early radicals had to be
acknowledged. Both the debt of gratitude owed and the need to preserve their memory was felt by many. The memorial was funded by
public subscription, which demonstrates the widespread support that
it gained, and its genesis lay with Peter Mackenzie, a Glasgow radical
and editor of the *Reformers' Gazette*. As well as seeking to build upon
the modest gains in the first Reform Act, he also sought to preserve
radical memory through books and memorials.[3]

This led to a desire to see actions taken across the country and not
just in the capital. The first statue erected to the martyrs of 1820 was in
Glasgow and, as would be the case in Edinburgh, its construction faced
a number of challenges. The council refused permission for it to be
sited near where a radical had been executed in 1820. However, another
leading Glasgow radical agreed that it could be placed on his land near
Royston, then outside the city, and where a huge gathering had taken
place in 1816. Unveiled in 1832, the monument was later destroyed but
replaced by another, which was funded by the Scottish Chartist movement and still stands to this day in Sighthill Cemetery, Glasgow.

Following this, Mackenzie's thoughts then turned to the construction of a memorial to Muir, whose grave he had visited in France, and those others who had first begun the battle for political reform. Committees were established both north and south of the border and indeed a similar but smaller obelisk to the one now standing in Edinburgh was finally unveiled in London in Nunhead Cemetery in 1852, which was backed by those who campaigned for the memorial in Edinburgh.

Mackenzie's plan was supported by the radical MP Joseph Hume, who pursued it in Parliament over many years, and who also obtained support from the Irish MP Daniel O'Connell, known as 'the Liberator' for his support for Catholic emancipation. An Edinburgh lawyer, William Moffatt, who had been both a friend of Thomas Muir and a legal adviser at his trial, was also active in its backing.[4]

The memorial was designed by a leading nineteenth-century architect, Thomas Hamilton, which again testified to its importance. Hamilton also designed the nearby Old Royal High School and the adjacent memorial to Robert Burns, as well as George IV Bridge and the Royal College of Physicians. Along with the obelisk, Hamilton's constructions now make up part of Edinburgh's famous cityscape.

However, the construction of the Political Martyrs' Monument, as in Glasgow, was not without controversy or resistance. The original plan had been to site it on top of Calton Hill, ensuring that it would dominate the city's skyline and be visible from all around. This proposal was vehemently opposed by Tories on the city council who were aware of its radical symbolism and therefore refused permission. This was an early portent, perhaps, for later refusals to countenance positioning the Scottish Parliament in the nearby Old Royal High School, for fear of creating a nationalist totem.

When a site in the adjacent burial ground was obtained further protests were raised and arguments were even made that it would disturb the dead, ludicrous as this now may seem. The objections were only finally overruled following court action. It was clear that the issue was not the location, but the symbolism it evoked. Radicals were neither to be recorded nor allowed to form part of Scotland's history, as far as some in the establishment were concerned.

The foundation stone was eventually laid in 1844 and a crowd of 3,000 people gathered to pay their respects. As well as fittingly memorialising the individuals and their cause, the unveiling of the obelisk was also an opportunity to counterpose an alternative history to what was being recorded. Many involved, such as the lawyer Moffatt, had lived through the events and knew that the truth was vastly different from that which had been propagated. As they continued their struggle, it was vital to maintain the memory of those who had gone before and to understand what had actually happened.

So this is the story of the monument. Sadly, the establishment version has largely predominated in popular history, which explains why so few know about the martyrs and the revolutionary years during which they lived. The tartanry, statues and street names are now acknowledged and in many instances have been assimilated and are enjoyed. But there is an alternative narrative in Scotland's history that is largely unrecorded, much of which remains unknown or unheralded.

This book is therefore an attempt to right that wrong and tell their tale; this is the story of radical Scotland.

CHAPTER 2

IN SEARCH OF THE REVOLUTIONARY STORY

I was born in Edinburgh and grew up in a small town not far from it. Yet, although I visited the city often and invariably saw the obelisk on the skyline, I did not know about the story of the martyrs until much later. Wellington and Nelson were well recounted, whether at school or in the media, but the story of those who had fought and suffered for the cause of reform was absent. Peterloo was mentioned but events in Paisley and the Rising of 1820 were not. Although Manchester was nearly 240 miles from my home, I was aware of what happened there in 1819, whereas Tranent was less than forty miles from my house but the massacre there was neither taught in school nor mentioned in the media.

My experience was not unusual and most people who grew up in Scotland when I did would have been similarly unaware of this radical history. Sadly, whilst there has been a great deal of progress in teaching Scottish history, much of the country's radical tradition still remains untold. This is not simply a product of the education system but is symptomatic of wider society and especially the influence of the media. The culture and perspective of the establishment has been the prism through which much of history has been recounted as the authorities controlled and influenced most of the media both then and now. Of course, some individuals have made valiant efforts to tell the story and both local and oral histories often tell a different tale.

An orthodoxy has developed that has lingered alongside the statues and street names in Edinburgh, which has celebrated the glories or success of the elite. In Scotland this was not done by some invading foreign army building its monuments and forcing its narrative upon a subjugated people. Instead it has been the Scottish establishment who have constructed the statues, set the syllabus and more importantly set the tone that has been echoed in the media down the years.

Following the union there was initially a great deal of assimilation as the establishment headed south and even those who remained sought to reject their 'Scottishness'. The practice of the landowning elite sending their children to public schools in England began, which was then followed by the founding of similar institutions in Scotland. Such privileged members of the society were embarrassed by what they perceived to be the coarseness and poverty of their native land and many readily sought to embrace an upper-class English identity and accent, despite being rebuffed or laughed at by those with whom they sought to integrate and emulate.

This was followed by the creation of a supposed new Scottish identity in the early decades of the nineteenth century. Whilst this identity may have been initially ridiculed, it soon became not just accepted but embraced and it exists to this day with members of the ruling elite 'lording' it over highland games or clan societies. However, it did at least lead to a Scottish history being somewhat rediscovered.

Nevertheless, what was then emphasised was highly romanticised and often purely focused on famous figures. The glories of the Scottish past have frequently been characterised by the tales of Bruce and Wallace, as well as Mary Queen of Scots and other such renowned individuals. In this way, genealogy and heraldry became popular and the Jacobites were sentimentalised. The people's story it most certainly was not, and even less was it the story of the Scottish radicals who fought for a different society.

Later in the nineteenth century, as the British Empire was expanding and with many Scots flourishing, there was a change in attitude.

Many unionists began emphasising their Scottishness and taking pride in their country's achievements. The union was unquestionably a good thing as far as they were concerned, as was the British Empire. Popular opposition to the union and the cruelty and crimes of colonialism were frequently ignored. Renouncing political nationalism, such individuals sought to maintain distinctive institutions, as well as recording their own version of history.

The twentieth century and the two world wars helped to foster a British identity, which was developed as a result of other social changes that came about from urbanisation and industrialisation through to the mass media. Notwithstanding the rise of political nationalism, the received history that was passed on became the accepted view. Moreover, as distances became smaller and communication advanced, Scotland was pulled ever closer into the British bosom. TV and radio became the medium through which a shared culture was created and a view of history aired. In some ways Scottish radical history was subsumed and the Tolpuddle Martyrs and Wat Tyler became better known than the 1820 martyrs or Thomas Muir. Much of this was understandable as the radical histories of England and Scotland became entwined and a British labour movement evolved, but the distinctive nature of Scottish radicalism and its separate roots have largely been forgotten.

Over recent years both academics and others have made a concerted effort to provide a more accurate analysis of past events in an attempt to help to change how much of Scottish history is perceived. The work done on some topics, such as the Highland Clearances, has been outstanding in its depiction of the brutality and cruelty of events, even though it has rightly been acknowledged that most Scots emigrated voluntarily and in order to pursue a better life. A more nuanced understanding of Jacobitism has also been developed, moving it away from being regarded as a civil war, which it was but only in part, and providing a more objective understanding of events in comparison to the romanticism of the past. For example, Murray Pittock's work on both

Culloden and the Jacobite rebellions has been critical in allowing for a more accurate understanding of what happened during this period, as well as offering an insight into why the received accounts about these events were created by the establishment.[1] More recently, great work has been done on Thomas Muir and other radicals who rose to the fore as industrialisation and modern political movements developed.

In many ways perceptions rather than a concrete historical narrative have set the tone. A great deal of radical history has been recorded by historians, who have their own perspectives and opinions, and many of whom, though by no means all, would have subscribed to the prevailing Tory orthodoxy or that of the Whig/Liberal opposition. This is perfectly understandable but it means that the radical viewpoint has rarely been given a voice.

Like many, I have been inspired by reading about Muir, even if this came about long after my formal education ended. Tom Johnston's *The History of the Working Classes in Scotland* was hugely influential, alongside other similar works.[2] Modern-day activists have raised my awareness about Scotland's radical history and provided pointers to other sources that I have avidly read. I felt ashamed when one day I stood beneath the Political Martyrs' Monument, the purpose of which I had been unaware of for so long, and read the poignant yet defiant epitaphs. This led me to want to find out more about those who were involved in the radical cause during Scotland's revolutionary years.

This then is the story of what I discovered about the Friends of the People through the United Scotsmen to the 1820 Rising; brave people who gave their lives or liberty for the cause of universal suffrage. Much information used to research this book was readily available in academic publications. Other information was offered by local histories in libraries from Paisley to Perth, and far beyond, which provided historical records, often written from within living memory.

Many aspects of these events are undisputed, but some interpretations are different. For example, some historians concur on key dates and events, but disagree on the extent that the French Revolution had an effect on Scotland. Some argue that it had a near-seismic effect and others that it had little effect at all. Nonetheless, the consensus seems to be that it had a clear impact on many, as a vision of a different society became a reality. Support for radicalism was greater and popular loyalism weaker in Scotland than in England. But even south of the border historians have begun to challenge the suggestion that there was little support for revolution. Roger Wells has stated that 'the notion that the French were the potential liberators rather than enemies was frequently articulated from within the British working class, until at least disillusionment at the rise and early career of Bonaparte began to undermine – though not to destroy before 1803 – popular Francophilia'.[3]

Whatever the perspective of historians, this is still vastly different to how France is perceived in the media, where the country is frequently portrayed as being a mortal enemy. Popular culture largely reaffirms this idea and marginalises any radical view. Literature and even TV shows such as *Hornblower* and *Sharpe* depict France as being Britain's constant adversary throughout history. This has been less of a theme in Scotland where the 'Auld Enemy' has traditionally been England and a knowledge of the 'Auld Alliance', between Scotland and France, still remains. So, what was the mood of ordinary people and what were the reactions of radicals to the early years of the French Revolution?

It is more problematic to assess later years as many of the disturbances and most of the groups involved were located within communities that were clannish and closed off from outsiders. Even if some groups did not support the actions that were being planned, they most certainly were not going to tell strangers this, let alone representatives of the government that they despised. Such actions are replicated to this day in occupied areas, on oppressed lands and even in some deprived housing schemes in urban areas. Notwithstanding government efforts to insert spies and agent provocateurs, the information obtained and recorded by the authorities was often limited; frequently it could be ascertained that actions were being planned but not what, when or by whom.

The orthodox historical analysis of such radicalism has been that it occurred almost spontaneously and any coordination, let alone coop-eration, has been downplayed. Riots and disturbances have often been explained as being the result of localised objections to conscription or economic grievances. This has been challenged by later works and also by new perspectives on incidents that occurred in England at the same time. Could multiple incidents across numerous communities and over such a short space of time simply be a local response to wider grievances? The Militia Act riots in 1797 mushroomed across the country over a very short time-frame; was this really just a coincidence? Or were such expressions of unrest part of a wider radical response when constitutional means had either failed or been closed down, and insurrection was planned?

Likewise, it is clear that much of the radicalism during this era was part of a wider push across Britain for reform. However, nationalist sentiment was far from absent. An article published in the spring of 1792 and reprinted as a pamphlet that September by the columnist James Thomson Callender offered a scathing assessment of the consti-tutional situation. He described 'Scotland as a conquered province of England and claimed that Scottish MPs (who were well aware of their situation) behaved accordingly as the servile tools of English misman-agement'.[4] Some of the histories of the 1820 Rising have suggested that it was a nationalist rising, portraying it as a Scottish insurrection. In addition, the words of one of the banners carried, 'Scotland; Free or a Desert', have entered the nationalist lexicon.

Yet, James Thomson Callender was, if not a lone voice, then cer-tainly a minority one. Three of the original political martyrs were English. Later the cause of reform was again revived and even electri-fied by visits from leading English radicals. The violent response to the massacre at Peterloo demonstrated that sympathies transcended the border. Organisations such as the Friends of the People or the United

Scotsmen cooperated with their English and Irish counterparts. Yet distinct, if not entirely separate, organisations operated in Scotland. As ever, different interpretations have developed between nationalist and socialist camps. Were they just separate organisations or were they advocates for the same cause, or could it have been a mixture of both?

Although these were questions that would need an answer, other details were accepted by all historical interpretations. It was accepted that the French Revolution was the successor to events that had started elsewhere, which had been the spark for desires that had been developing. For before the French Revolution there was the American Revolution that commenced in 1773 with the Boston Tea Party and the War of Independence until 1783, when peace was declared and the United States of America was officially recognised.

France was pivotal in the victory of the United States over Great Britain yet it came at a great cost to the French, and would come back to haunt them. The majority of the costs for continental involvement were borne by the poor rather than the rich, and yet they gained little from it. Resentment against the monarchy festered and grew as support for many of the ideas articulated in the newly formed United States of America increased. The winds of revolution were blowing across the Atlantic towards Europe.

In Scotland, meanwhile, as throughout the rest of Britain, the reaction to the American Revolution had initially been one of opposition, if not hostility. It was a threat to trade and the economy, let alone social order and stability. However, as the war dragged on popular opinion turned against the government and sympathy for the American states grew. Failure to defeat the rebellion highlighted the incompetence of the administration and raised questions about the ability to govern much closer to home. As in France, the cost of the war and its effect on the economy influenced opinion, but so too did the ideas that inspired the revolution. Calls for liberty and equality began to be made along with support for American independence.

Initially, interest in and support for the unrest in America was primarily found amongst what were called the 'middle ranking' people. Social classes as defined in later years had not yet developed, with the Industrial Revolution still to fully take hold. However, for the purposes of this book the term 'working class' will be used as it is less patronising or insulting than the term 'ordinary' or 'common people', or the more abusive term 'lower orders' that was common parlance during this era. Those who were mobilised by events in America were the wealthier and better-educated people, who were flexing their political muscles and seeking the right to vote, to reflect their new-found prosperity and status. However, their demands were made for them and their ilk only, and not for working people nor even their own spouses.

As in America, the Scottish people wanted their say and the right to vote, which they felt they now deserved. Whilst 'no taxation without representation' did not ring out in Scotland as it did across the Atlantic, its sentiment most certainly existed. The 1780s saw calls in Scotland for changes to be made to the burgh and county election system along with greater accountability and scrutiny for the electoral system. Burgh reformers were principally drawn from amongst the wealthy burgesses, whilst county reformers were predominantly drawn from independent freeholders, small shopkeepers and artisans.

Scotland at this time was for all intents and purposes ruled by an oligarchy, largely representing or comprised of the major landowners. Power was vested in the Lord Advocate, who reported to the British Home Secretary. The position of Scottish Secretary had not been established and control was exercised through the legal office, which was the power within the land. Under this system a handful of people dictated the lives of hundreds of thousands, even millions, of working people. The right to vote was possessed by few, indeed it is estimated that only 4,500 men could vote in a country that had a population of 1.6 million according to the census of 1801.

A review of Scottish parliamentary constituencies conducted in

1788 revealed that 'thirty county Members of Parliament were elected by a mere 2,662 voters'. 'The remaining fifteen MPs were chosen by the self-perpetuating and corrupt town councils of the royal burghs'.[5] In reality, the situation was even worse; it has been suggested that almost half of the electors were fictitious and that in Perthshire, for example, there were just 161 voters. This meant that elections could often be farcical and that corruption was rampant.

The radical editor Peter Mackenzie recounted an election for the constituency of Bute, Ross and Cromarty in his book *Reminisces of Glasgow and the West of Scotland*.[6] He reckoned that there were fewer than fifty electors for this widespread and extremely large constituency. Bad weather made travel to Rothesay on the Isle of Bute, where the election was being held, impossible. As a result, only one candidate was on the island when the contest took place. However, not only was he the only candidate, but the only voter on the island. Without either any sense of shame or legal impediment he proceeded to nominate himself before the Sheriff. Seconding the nomination, in his apparently distinct role as chairman of proceedings, he then voted for himself. He went on to administer the oath of office to himself and even declared himself duly elected. Such was democracy at that time and this tale was no doubt replicated across the country, though perhaps not as starkly.

The burgh elections were equally corrupt and almost dynastical and have been described by the historian W. L. Mathieson as being 'self-selecting, almost self-electing'.[7] Mathieson went on to explain how the Earl of Bute had been Provost of Rothesay for forty years and that during that period the Duchess of Argyll had governed Dumbarton through supposedly elected councillors. This system extended the length and breadth of the country, with Whithorn and Wigtown run by acolytes of the Earl of Galloway, who was also a member of both, and 'the oldest inhabitant of Stranraer, which was managed by the Earl of Stair, could not recall a resident Provost'.

Rules that were supposed to ensure that there was some turnover of members on councils were easily circumvented. The Earl of Eglinton who held sway in Irvine avoided the law of rotation, which was meant to ensure that some members stood down on a regular basis, by always having two other candidates available to stand. It is no wonder that the landed gentry or their nominees could stay in office throughout their lives but then also pass down the position to their heirs: 'The Provost of Lanark, though still young, had been in power for ten or twelve years and his father and grandfather had each officiated for thirty-five years.'[8]

Not only were there few rules in place, but those that existed were designed to make control by those in charge almost absolute.

> Where a proportion of the council had to be chosen from lists submitted by the incorporated trades, the merchant councillors, who were self-elected, contrived to perpetuate their supremacy by making it a rule that the minority of their own members at any private meeting, should always concur with the majority in public.[9]

Dissent was therefore restricted to those who were able to challenge the rules.

It is not surprising that the perversion of democracy led to misrule and corruption. 'Wigtown had assigned to its patron, the Earl of Galloway, for £16 of feu duty land which now yielded £400. The heirs of eleven Provosts of Dumfries owned property which had once belonged to the Burgh.'[10] These areas of patronage and control were termed 'pocket boroughs', though 'rotten burghs' might have been more appropriate, even if that was a name that was first used elsewhere and later on. Whatever names such areas were given, a shameful situation existed across the land.

The façade of democracy was tightly controlled not just in councils but in Parliament by the overlord Henry Dundas, on behalf of the ruling elite. He was himself the scion of a landholding and legal elite as he was the son of Lord Arniston, who was both a judge and a Tory MP and possessed a large estate. The Dundas family and Henry in particular are excoriated by Tom Johnston in his book *Our Scots Noble Families*.[11] The family dynasty began with a former governor of Berwick who moved north and he was followed by future generations of MPs for Edinburgh and Lord Advocates almost as if such positions were a birthright.

Henry Dundas's influence over the supposedly elected Scottish politicians was all pervasive. By 1784 he was able to deliver to the Tory Party under Pitt 'twenty-two of the forty-five Scottish seats', which would rise to thirty-four by 1790.[12] By 1802 the Tories had almost absolute control, with 'forty-three out of the forty-five' being either nominees or under his sway.[13]

Dundas was a Scottish lawyer and Tory politician who was elevated to Viscount Melville in 1802. He was a close ally of William Pitt the Younger and was Lord Advocate for Scotland between 1775 and 1783. Dundas subsequently served as Home Secretary between 1791 and 1794 and would later also become Secretary of War and First Lord of the Admiralty. His promotion to a position in London did not detract from the power and influence he held in Scotland, and despite the distance he maintained his dominance and it was with good reason that he acquired nicknames such as 'King Harry the Ninth', 'The Grand Manager of Scotland' and even 'The Uncrowned King of Scotland'.

Henry's nephew Robert Dundas served as Solicitor General, the deputy position to the Lord Advocate, between 1784 and 1789 before succeeding to the principal position himself in 1789 when aged only thirty-one. He held the position until 1801 when he became Chief Baron of the Exchequer. Robert's sinecures continued in the political as well as legal world, as he also succeeded his uncle as Tory MP for Midlothian in 1790, but he was to be far less able than his uncle and both deferred to him and took instructions from him. Control therefore remained effectively firmly in the grasp of Henry Dundas for much of this period.

Despite the fact that Henry Dundas ultimately fell from grace, he managed to suitably enrich himself during the time he was in power.

Suspicions were raised about his financial management of the Admiralty and a commission of inquiry was established in 1802, which resulted in him being impeached in 1806. He was ultimately acquitted and then retired from public life; he died in 1811.

This was the political situation that led to calls for reform, which were inspired by the American Revolution. Despite gathering considerable support amongst the 'middle ranks', reform was still vehemently opposed by Dundas and the Tories, for whom it was just the thin edge of the political wedge, and a bill in Parliament was soon defeated.

But all this was forgotten when the French Revolution broke out in 1789, and the political dynamic quickly changed. No longer was the demand for suffrage made by the middle ranks, but now it was the franchise for all, with calls coming from not just the better-off members of society, but from amongst the working classes. This meant that the threat to the established order was even greater, and as a result the establishment would oppose it even more violently.

As mentioned previously, historians disagree over the extent of public support in Scotland for the French Revolution but it is hard not to believe that it had a seismic effect. The revolution's impact on other parts of Britain and across other lands in Europe was massive. The events most certainly resonated with many and the raising of political consciousness amongst many ordinary people was huge. This was the impetus for change and it gave hope that previously had not existed. Such a sense of awakening would come about again in later centuries with the Bolshevik Revolution and other earth-shattering events. Such a change is reminiscent of Fergal Keane's vivid description of the effect of the Easter Rising that led to the revolutionary events in Ireland more than a century later: 'The impossible became imaginable and then possible and they saw a chance of belonging to something larger than themselves.'[14] Similar sentiments must have been felt in Scotland in 1789.

Just as the American Revolution opened possibilities for the middle-ranking people to achieve political power equivalent to their wealth and growing influence, the French Revolution ignited hopes amongst working people not just for the vote but for further change. It was no longer the case that a better world was only available following death and in heaven. As Henry Cockburn, a Whig lawyer and later a High Court judge, stated at the time: 'Everything rung, and was connected with the Revolution in France ... Everything, not this or that thing, but literally everything, was soaked in this one event.'[15] The country was awakening and the working class was stirring.

'The ordinary people of Scotland began to show an active interest in political reform. The events in France were followed assiduously in the newspapers.'[16] New publications were springing up across the country and even existing ones such as the *Caledonian Mercury* and *The Scots Magazine* were fascinated by events; the former turned one of its four pages over to reports from France and the latter published essays and poems in support of the revolution. Newspapers from London were also eagerly scanned for any news.

Initially, the revolution was largely welcomed across the political spectrum, even if Edmund Burke had warned of its effect on social order. There was no love lost between the British elite and their former French foe and it was regarded as a vindication of the British model of governance. The supposed 'Glorious Revolution' of 1688 made the crown answerable to Parliament, which was lauded as a form of British liberalism, rather than the monarchical absolutism as existed in France. In Britain, Parliament and not the monarch was in charge, albeit a Parliament still controlled by and run in the interests of the few.

There were no doubt some who hoped that a British type of system would follow in France and all would be well. The disturbances at the Bastille in 1789 reduced French power and influence, but did not disturb the established social order. The events were not initially seen to be a threat, except by Burke, and certainly not a threat to the power and status of the elite. But all that was to change.

As the monarchy in the form of Louis XVI was first toppled and then ultimately executed in January 1793, a mixture of revulsion, fear and rage spread across the establishment and much, if not most of the ruling class. Panic and anger gripped the elite classes not just in Britain but across all of Europe. The *'sans-culottes'* had risen and the rich and powerful had fallen. If it could happen in France, then it could happen anywhere. The establishment began to prepare themselves to defend their interests, just as radicals sought to achieve change.

The French Revolution demonstrated that a new world was possible in a country that had been slumbering politically for several generations. As was noted by Kenneth Logue, there was a 'bulk of the poorer sections of society, for whom the French Revolution was a revelation. There existed in Scotland a deep-rooted egalitarianism and, with the example of France before them, many Scots saw that this could be translated into political democracy.'[17] The progressive ideas that the French Revolution popularised captured the imagination of idealists and reformers of every class. This was even recorded in poetry by Robert Burns who in 1795 penned 'A Man's a Man for a' That' with the immortal lines:

> It's coming yet for a' that,
> That man to man the world o'er,
> Shall brothers be for a' that.

A spark had been lit and ideas exploded within the minds of many. 'Liberty, Equality, Fraternity' resonated as loudly in Scotland as it had for many of the poor and dispossessed across the English Channel. The revolutionary years in Scotland had begun.

CHAPTER 3

A DISCONTENTED LAND

The Scotland that awoke to the clarion call of the French Revolution was a country that was slowly changing. The urbanisation and industrialisation that marked later generations was in its infancy and would not accelerate until the revolutionary years had passed. But the movement of people from country to town was discernible in the lowlands, as well as the highlands. Other changes were becoming noticeable as technology was advancing and a highly literate people began to reconsider the world about them. Yet, again the real story belies an image that has been created of a country beholden to its masters and in thrall of its Kirk.

According to the 1801 census Scotland had a population of 1.6 million at a time when Great Britain (excluding Ireland) had a population of 10.9 million. This figure was slightly lower in the 1790s, but increased over the next two decades and had reached 1.8 million by 1811 and was just under 2.1 million by 1821. However, this was still primarily a rural population and only 20 per cent of Scots lived in towns. In 1791 Glasgow had a population of 61,945 and even by 1801, only seven towns in Scotland had a population over 10,000.[1]

The weaving industry, which was the principal employment for many and the occupation that was most politically engaged, was undergoing reform. At this time, weaving was the bastion of industrial militancy until the trade declined and the mantle was picked up

27

by the miners. The nature of the weaving business was beginning to change, even though the work was still being completed at the residences of workers and not in the factories that would later be built. Larger producers started supplying individual weavers with their yarn and collecting the finished product from them after it was completed. Whilst this was a long way from the factory process it was still a significant change, which meant that a weaver could become more of a wage earner than an independent operator. By the 1790s this change was happening not just in the Glasgow and Paisley areas, but across much of central Scotland from Ayrshire, Renfrewshire and Lanarkshire into Stirlingshire, Perthshire, Angus and Fife.

A consequence of this transition was the formation of associations for protection from exploitation. Although these were not as structured as trade unions – and indeed many of the weavers would have renounced unionisation, as they regarded themselves to be independent craftsmen rather than direct employees – the organisations they formed operated in a similar fashion. Committees were created, mass meetings in support of strikes were called and even picketing and the intimidation of blackleg workers took place. In 1787 the 'Clyde Valley Weavers General Association formed to resist wage cuts'.[2]

Organisation within the weaving industry was replicated in other trades, as artisans realised the importance of cooperating to protect their rights and to advocate their cause. Other industries such as shoemakers followed suit. In this way, industrial changes were driving political thought and organisation even before the effects of the French Revolution could be felt. 'To these men the struggle was not one between employers and employees, but one between the wealth producing sections of the community "the people", who were excluded from the political process, and the non-producers "the aristocracy", who dominated that process.'[3] These developments were led by skilled tradesmen and artisans much more than the labouring classes or agricultural workers, who were rarely organised and whose lives would have been consumed by the daily grind of living and surviving.

Other occupations were also affected by industrial and agricultural changes. Cotton spinners and colliers were becoming politicised, evidenced by reports on activities in Dunbartonshire and Ayrshire. The ability of such workers to become actively engaged in politics was constrained by their employment, which lacked the independence of action of weavers and other trades. Likewise, tenant farmers were also becoming more involved; there were reports of Bastille Day in 1792 being celebrated by many in East Lothian and this was no doubt replicated elsewhere. In Roxburghshire there were accounts detailing how landowners were becoming alarmed by the radical spirit developing amongst their tenantry.

Though these organisations were at most proto-trade unions they indicated that there was growing appreciation of the need for unity and mutual support. This was highlighted not just by the creation of trade organisations but also in the establishment of 'friends' societies. For example, there were ten such societies in Hamilton by 1791, the most important of which were the two weaver societies, which had a combined membership of 180. One year later eighty societies were recorded in Glasgow, many of which were organised on a trade basis.[4] This was of course still a long way from a fully fledged working-class movement but it was a sign of the growing recognition of the need for unity and cooperation amongst ordinary working people.

The growing discontent was framed in terms of power. 'When discussing the rights of labour, the Scottish radicals identified their "class enemies as the landed classes" and that was because "the land-owning classes bestrode eighteenth-century Scotland like colossi."'[5] Scottish animus towards the landed gentry was therefore deep-rooted and existed not just in the highlands where the clearances, which saw the removal of people to be replaced by sheep, had commenced but also in agricultural lowland areas and across the entire country. The clearances were something that would linger long in the memory of ordinary people and help explain not just Tom Johnston's evisceration of the land-owning gentry more than a century on, but also antagonisms over landownership that continue to this day.

The Treaty of Union had protected Scotland's distinct institutions of church, education and law. These entities had largely remained unaltered since the Act was passed in 1707 and their operation was ordinarily beyond the influence of working people. There were few openings for poorer people within the legal profession, which remained the prerogative of the wealthy, though the middle ranks were advancing within it. Education was used by people of all classes for self-improvement and economic betterment and had not become a social or political battleground.

But the church most certainly was an area where social debate had been ongoing. Even if such conflict was of an ecclesiastical rather than political tenor, it certainly had class undertones. For long before the disruption that saw a schism in the Kirk in 1843 significant internal debates had been ongoing. The Church of Scotland was at that time divided between a 'Moderate' faction which predominated and an evangelical wing known as the 'Popular' faction which opposed it, though many members showed their distaste for both groups by leaving for dissident or secessionist churches.

Ostensibly, disagreements occurred over patronage and the right to appoint ministers. Despite a growing number of the ruling elite becoming irreligious as Enlightenment thinking developed, this did not seem to prevent them interfering in the appointment of ministers. Irrespective of faith this became an important instrument of social control. This is a tale that undermines much of the perceived democratic structure of the then Presbyterian Church and highlights the influence that the wealthy landowners and aristocracy possessed. Despite the intentions of the founders of the Reformed Church, patronage had existed for landowners and other wealthy individuals for many years and internal struggles had been ongoing. In 1733 there was what has been described as the 'First Secession' as members left the Church of Scotland following the Act of the General Assembly. The Act gave preferment to property owners where the landholder had not exercised his right to nominate the minister, rather than to the congregation as a whole. The Reverend Ebenezer Erskine from Stirling was at the forefront of dissenters during this time and he gave a sermon in which he stated: 'I can find no warrant from the word of God to confer the spiritual privileges of His House upon the rich beyond the poor, whereas by this Act, the man with the gold ring and gay clothing is preferred unto the man with the vile raiment and poor attire.'[6]

The Moderate faction were firm supporters of the status quo, both socially and politically, and were aligned with, if not cravenly obsequious to, the ruling elite. This allegiance was so obvious that the Kirk has been described as 'a willing bastion of loyalism' and was often close to functioning as an arm of the state.[7] The Moderates tended to predominate amongst the more affluent sections of society, with the poorer classes affiliating with the opposition or joining secessionist churches.

The Popular clergy tended to oppose the Moderates, largely on theological grounds relating to the independence of the Kirk from patronage, although they also more generally opposed political interference in ecclesiastical affairs, referring to the founding principles of the Reformed Church. Working people appeared to be more comfortable with the more orthodox Calvinism, which was closer to the intentions of the original Reformation. Although support for the Popular faction of the church predominated amongst the middle-ranking classes, it extended into the weaving communities that had not joined secessionist churches. This could be part of the reason why the Moderates often portrayed their Popular opponents as being on the side of the rabble. But whilst some Popular clergy expressed sympathy for the American colonists – though not for the calls for independence – support for the

French Revolution was a step too far and both the Moderate and Popular factions were united in opposition to the events in France.

It was for this reason that many of the most radical clergy left the country and either joined secessionist churches or went abroad, especially to Ireland but also to America. One of the most famous of these radical figures was Reverend John Witherspoon who, having been a leading opponent of the Moderate faction, eventually accepted entreaties to move across the Atlantic from his parish in Paisley. In America he became president of what is now Princeton University and was a signatory of the American Declaration of Independence.

For those who remained and disagreed with the church theologically or politically, there was a ready-made alternative. Much of Scottish history has portrayed the Church of Scotland as being almost omnipotent, if not being universally followed by a compliant people. But this was far from the situation; 'by 1792 there were 287' seceding churches and the Lord Advocate Robert Dundas estimated their membership numbered 150,000.[8]

By the 1790s, it was estimated that approximately 10 per cent of the population were members of seceding churches. This is a substantial figure given that the percentage would have been even higher in lowland Scotland as, at that time, this is the only area where the seceding churches were located. For example, Stirling had a population of 4,698 people, 2,795 of which were members of the Church of Scotland and 1,415 were aligned with dissenting churches.[9] The situation would have been similar in other lowland areas, particularly amongst weaving communities.

Although irreligion and rationalism were growing during this time, this was only amongst a small section of society, although it was not just the elite that were openly questioning or renouncing religion, but also some members of the working class. But many, if not most, radicals still had links to churches, particularly dissenting ones. However, whilst many radicals were dissenters, this did not mean that all dissenting churches were radical. For some, their radicalism was in their theology rather than their politics.

The martyrs had links to the dissenting churches through Palmer, who was a minister, Skirving, who had considered joining the church, and Mealmaker, who was an elder. The moral basis to reform was a key issue for the leadership of the church and their parishioners. This is an aspect of Scottish socialism that continued in future generations, as was seen with the Red Clydesiders in the twentieth century, who shared similar connections to dissenting churches.[10]

During this period many working people in communities across central and lowland Scotland were not just organising in their trades and forming associations, but were also establishing their own churches. This was a potentially volatile mixture. As noted by Bob Harris, 'the rise of religious dissent, together with explosive growth in semi-independent manufacturing villages in many parts of lowland Scotland, served to weaken traditional social controls in Scottish society'.[11] It is no surprise then that the archetypal radical was often portrayed as a 'seceding weaver'.

Towards the end of the eighteenth century the control of the landed aristocracy was weakening and a willingness to question authority was growing. On its own this situation was insufficient to light the revolutionary fuse, but into this mix the French Revolution and the works of Thomas Paine were added. They provided the final spark that would ignite the fire.

Thomas Paine was born in Norfolk, England, in 1737 and emigrated to America in 1774, at the start of the revolution. His pamphlet *Common Sense*, which advocated American independence, became a bestseller and indeed a weapon for the revolution as it helped popularise support. He subsequently moved to France where in turn he became a defender of the French Revolution. His work *Rights of Man* was published in 1791 and sought not just to defend the revolution but extolled a new vision of society.

Paine's activism caused fear and anger amongst the oligarchy in Britain, who tried and convicted him for sedition in absentia for his writing. He was subsequently imprisoned by Robespierre as the revolution turned on itself and was only freed following pressure from the United States. He died in the USA in 1809, but had already fallen from grace following the publication of his pamphlet the *The Age of Reason* in 1794, which was seen as an attack on Christianity. However, for the purpose of this book, these later events are irrelevant and it is the controversy of his earlier work that matters. Paine's conviction did also have a knock-on effect in Scotland, but by then *Rights of Man* had already set the revolutionary fuse.

By 1792 Paine's work had not simply reached Scotland but had hit almost every corner of the country. Cheap copies of his pamphlet were run off and immediately found an avid readership, despite the text having been proclaimed seditious in the summer of 1792. The government received reports that even in Dumfries his work was well known and that it was also available in Stornoway, having been translated into Gaelic.

Scotland by then was already a land primed for the arrival of the pamphlet. The reading culture that had arguably commenced with the Reformation – as people needed to be literate in order to read the word of God – meant that Paine's writing was widely read. By this time weaving communities were used to clubbing together to buy papers and books to be shared and distributed amongst themselves, long before public libraries existed. As a result, Paine's words spread like wildfire and the authorities had good reason to be worried.

Despite the incendiary effect of Tom Paine's work, many Scottish radicals did not see him as a spiritual or intellectual leader. His views on religion were concerning for many in what was still a deeply Calvinist country, and where radicalism, as we have seen, was often tempered by membership of dissenting churches. The intellectual basis of Paine's arguments, whilst not rejected entirely, were often ignored in preference of existing philosophies or political interpretations. For example, Scottish history offered historical and legal arguments of sovereignty as an alternative to the republican model that Paine promoted. Notwithstanding such influences, the explosive effect of Paine's work should not be underestimated.

Meanwhile, unrest had been growing throughout the second half of the eighteenth century. Disturbances had taken place, the majority of which related to food prices, particularly the cost of oatmeal, which was then a staple. Other issues also manifested themselves in discontent, which varied from anti-Catholicism, through patronage, to burgh and county reform and even the slave trade. Rioting had occurred in the late 1770s when legislation was proposed to improve the rights of Catholics.

Although some in Scotland benefited greatly from the odious slave trade, not just members of the elite but far beyond, there was also considerable opposition to it. Scotland had a disproportionally high number of petitions for the immediate abolition of the trade, which was justified by the population, though this may well have been offset by the disproportionate profits made by the few. As is the case with the erection of statues and the naming of streets after politicians, it is those who made their wealth through the slave trade who are re-called, rather than those who tenaciously opposed it. Such individuals spoke to the power of the establishment more than the sympathies of the people. However, as the trade expanded Scotland and the role played by many Scots increased and this shameful involvement must be acknowledged.

But it was still food prices that was the most contentious issue, and the first disturbance of the period came in December 1780 in Crieff. Shortly after this 'in the early spring of 1783 there were four distur-bances at Port Patrick, Port William, Kirriemuir and Lower Largo'.[12] The next year, these events were followed by distilleries being attacked at Edinburgh and Dalkeith. A cotton tax imposed by Pitt brought at least 7,000 striking weavers to Glasgow Green for a demonstration in 1787, with a similar event taking place in Paisley. This unrest lasted over two months during which blackleg workers were attacked and eight weavers were shot and killed by troops brought in to deal with the demonstrations and growing discontent.

A brief period of tranquillity followed, but tensions would rise again after 1789. However, during this period it was politics and the writing of Thomas Paine that were being cited as the reason for activism, as much as anger about food prices or other factors. In some areas specific local issues such as corruption led to protests, for example, there was a seamen's strike over wages in Aberdeen in December 1792. But the underlying driver for most unrest was the growth in revolutionary spirit and the demand for radical reform. An explosive cocktail was brewing that was further compounded by the weather in 1792. A very harsh winter meant that food and fuel were either scarce or expensive, which caused despair for many a poor family, if not entire communities. As Peter Hume Brown has astutely stated, 'the new doctrines of liberty found a ready soil' in Scotland.[13]

For even amongst those supporting parliamentary reform through constitutional means, agitation was taking place. Many who had been seeking burgh and county reform were energised, albeit peacefully, that summer by the events in France. This confirmed the view that for a long time the revolution was widely popular. From 'East Linton in the east to Kilmarnock in the west Bastille Day had been met with calls for Parliamentary Reform'.[14] The Whig Club in Dundee and the Burgh Reform Organisation in Aberdeen were both in communication with the French National Assembly. It appeared as though even the moderates were stirred by what was happening and wanted to show their support. Revolution was in the air.

CHAPTER 4

THE KING'S BIRTHDAY RIOTS AND OTHER DISTURBANCES

Summer and late autumn of 1792 saw significant discontent across the land, with the largest and certainly the highest profile disturbance occurring in Edinburgh at the very doors of the establishment. This revolutionary image is not one the capital has now, nor is it an aspect of its history that is widely known. The King's birthday riots, as they were called, would have shown the ruling elite their fate if matters were allowed to get out of hand.

At the same time as disturbances started taking place at home, the revolutionaries had declared the French Republic on the continent. 'Liberty, Equality and Fraternity' were the cries being echoed across Scotland. As fears mounted amongst the European establishment, Austrian and Prussian armies marched to put down the revolution in France, whilst at home fretful authorities prepared for repression.

The King's birthday was traditionally celebrated by the affluent with a reception at Parliament House, located off the High Street in Edinburgh. For working people, it was simply an opportunity for drinking and carousing, which was usually paid for by the wealthy elite as a sign of their apparent benevolence. Given that a monarch had not visited Scotland for nigh on 200 years and there was little warmth or support for the royal family in the country, it was understandable that it was the partying that mattered for most.

However, with the desperate social and economic situation and with passions roused by the French Revolution, things were about to change, but not as the authorities would have liked. The birthday celebrations became a demonstration against the authorities and Henry Dundas in particular. That the protest was clearly politically motivated was evidenced by the prelude to the event. In the weeks before the King's birthday, handbills were distributed within Edinburgh calling for people to take action. The printers and distributers of these documents were obviously motivated by the events in France and hoped to encourage their fellow citizens to take action. The types of pamphlets created were widespread and varied in nature, from anonymous letters calling for effigies of Dundas to be burned, to death threats against prominent individuals. One that was pinned to the door of the centrally located Tron Kirk declared:

Notice to the Public,

On Monday 4 June Being the King's Birthday, The Effigies of the Rt, H. H D----- M of P for this City will be Publicly burnt at the Cross of Edinburgh.

By order of the Magistrates

Dragoons we fear them not the Laws of our king.[1]

Handbills and placards started appearing in May 1792 and, having no doubt seen many himself and received reports of others, the Lord Provost of Edinburgh James Stirling sent out patrols to tear down and remove any found on the streets. But still material continued to appear, which meant that not only were they widespread but also that those involved were more than just a few disgruntled individuals. Trouble was clearly brewing as June approached. One pamphlet circulated the week before the disturbances even mentioned the Porteous Riots that had occurred decades before and had led to a law officer being killed. Some individuals were obviously seeking to ensure that not only would the King's birthday be a major demonstration but that it would be a confrontational affair. Further handbills appeared proclaiming the following:

NOW IS THE TIME
BURN THE VILLAIN
FEAR NOT – YOU WILL
BE SUPPORTED

Another read simply:

BURN THE VILLAIN
DUNDAS

The political temperature was rising as summer arrived. Although the authorities had experienced trouble before, they were caught off-guard this time. The speed at which events occurred left them entirely unprepared for what was to come. Trouble started in the evening of Monday 4 June and went on until the Wednesday night. Crowds of up to 2,000 people gathered on the High Street in Edinburgh and from there things quickly escalated. At 7.30 p.m. on that first night, as the great and the good were enjoying their festivities in the grander confines of nearby Parliament House, others were assembling a stone's throw away with vastly different intentions.

A sentry box was torn from the ground on the High Street and carried down the Royal Mile to the Netherbow Port. There it was burned and the crowd began setting off fireworks. Dragoons who were coming up the High Street were set upon and forced to retreat. The mood was beginning to turn ugly.

Anticipating potential trouble earlier that day, the Lord Provost had arranged for troops to be stationed in the town. They were soon called out as the authorities began to lose control and struggled to reimpose order. The Riot Act was read by the Sheriff, with the Lord Provost ordering the dragoons to confront the crowd. Mounted troops then rode their horses along the pavements to disperse the crowd but this just led many demonstrators to escape into stairwells or up closes where cavalry could not follow. Once the soldiers had passed the protesters reappeared, coming down either from the stairs they had sheltered in or from neighbouring ones having gone through connected back yards. Crowds remained gathered until late at night when the dragoons withdrew up the High Street towards Edinburgh Castle. However, the scene was set for further disorder, even though the official celebrations had ended.

The next day started quietly enough but there were plans for further demonstrations being devised. Some protesters were hurriedly assembling an effigy of Dundas from discarded clothing and hung it between two poles. A crowd of around twenty men, accompanied by women and children, then marched off to George Square with the effigy. This area had been constructed in the 1760s as the wealthier sections of the community moved away from the huddled masses in the Old Town tenements. Gathering outside the house of Lady Arniston, Henry Dundas's mother who lived in a grand building in the square, they set light to the effigy and began throwing missiles, which broke several windows. In the house that night Lady Arniston was joined by another son and Admiral Adam Duncan, who was soon to become celebrated for the Battle of Camperdown. The two gentlemen rushed forth to try to chase the crowd away, but were forced to ignominiously beat a retreat after being stoned by the protesters.

By this time the numbers in the square had swelled but the

gathering had also come to the attention of the Sheriff. Rushing over, he sought to quieten the growing disorder but his endeavours were only met with a hail of abuse, along with stones and even dead cats being hurled at him. Soldiers were also sent for and soon arrived to support the Sheriff. The Riot Act was again read out and the Sheriff also sought to intimidate the crowd by ordering the troops to prepare to fire. Attempts to move the crowd on failed, with missiles and abuse continuing to be hurled at the soldiers and the wealthy homes they were protecting. In an effort to break the stalemate, the Sheriff took a party of soldiers out through a street and back into George Square. This attempt to approach the rioters from behind initially seemed to work and the crowd dispersed from the area before a guard was posted outside Lady Arniston's house.

However, the calm did not last for long and trouble simply moved elsewhere. The crowd began pursuing the Sheriff and soldiers who were heading towards St Andrew Square, where there were rumours that another disturbance had broken out. It turned out that no disorder was found, but that trouble had once again broken out in George Square. A group of about fifty young men then returned to Lady Arniston's house and confronted the soldiers stationed there. Despite the military presence they proceeded to stone the house and broke all of its ground-floor windows. By this time the Sheriff had returned with the main body of his troops and the crowd were caught between the two sets of soldiers. Shots were fired into the air and the crowd retreated out of the square, into nearby Crichton Street.[2]

At this point things quickly escalated. It is not known whether the crowd simply did not believe that the troops would fire or if some were simply carried away by the events. The Sheriff gave the order and a first fusillade was fired in the air. No one was injured but the action did not have its desired effect, as the crowd continued to press. A second and more lethal volley was then fired, which killed one demonstrator and badly wounded several others. This put an end to the disturbances for the evening and the crowd quickly dispersed, taking their dead and injured with them. However, if the authorities thought that this would bring an end to the protests, they were badly mistaken.

Wednesday saw crowds gather for the third night in a row and this time they were even more numerous and ever more determined. In the evening, demonstrators started assembling in George Square at 6 p.m. and within a few hours the crowd numbered some 2,000. The troops who were guarding Lady Arniston's house moved towards the mob and as they were mindful of the actions of the night before the crowd quickly left the scene.

But rather than simply dispersing, they headed as a group towards St Andrew Square, where the Lord Provost's house was located. Stones were thrown and sentry boxes outside the house were ripped up and propped against the door in an attempt to start a fire. Although the attempt to burn the house down failed, every window was broken by a deluge of missiles, all whilst the Lord Provost's terrified wife and daughters sheltered inside.

Realising that they had lost control of the town, the authorities lit a beacon at Edinburgh Castle and fired guns from it. Troops were then marched from the citadel by the Sheriff to try and restore order. Perhaps fearing what had happened the night before, the crowd simply slipped away. This brought the disturbances in Edinburgh to an end, but the authorities sought to quickly find those responsible and bring them to account. A round-up was carried out on this final night of the riots and a few arrests made but it was basically only stragglers or drunks who were detained.

A full review into what had happened was carried out over the following weeks. But, attempts to identify the ringleaders were as unsuccessful as the initial round-up. The authors of the handbills remained unknown, as did the identities of the instigators. This was despite the fact that a sizeable reward of 150 guineas was offered for information, in addition to a pardon for anyone who was willing to testify.

The only arrests that were made were of marginal figures and even in these cases, successful prosecution was limited, with just three being brought to court. The first was a brewer's labourer accused of being the leader of the crowd in George Square on the final and most riotous night. He was charged with mobbing and rioting and it was evident that the authorities believed that he was a leading player, but this was a role he strenuously denied. Whilst accepting that he had been there at the time of the riots, he argued that he was a victim, having been taken there forcibly by the crowd and that he had ended up drinking away his sorrows. Despite this curious defence, the jury accepted his evidence and found the case not proven.

A few days later two others appeared at the High Court charged with different offences. A house servant admitted to throwing missiles but denied that they had been directed at the soldiers. Again, his pro-testations that he was simply caught up in events whilst being engaged on his master's business were accepted by the jury, and the charges were found not proven.

The final accused was a chaise driver who was faced with the sub-stantial charge of being involved in the riot, which he denied. He was represented by Thomas Muir, who was gaining a reputation not just for his advocacy of the revolutionary cause but for his representation of radicals in court. In the hearing, the accused stated that he had been in the Tron Kirk area as he was collecting his daughter and had simply been caught up in events. Although the jury found him guilty it was only for throwing one stone towards the soldiers. The verdict was challenged by Muir as that offence had not been specifically men-tioned in the more general charges laid. His objections, however, were rejected by the judge, as was the jury's obvious attempts to limit the extent of his guilt. As would become the pattern in the years to come, the individual was sentenced to fourteen years' transportation. Fortu-nately for the chaise driver, he was released the following year.

Edinburgh was neither alone nor the location of the last trouble in

Scotland that year. Attempts were made in Banff to turn the King's birthday celebration into a denunciation of the government. However, the organisers of the protest were both less efficient and less courageous than those in Edinburgh. Members of a reform club had gone through the town the Saturday before the birthday festivities encouraging people to burn effigies of Dundas. After catching wind of the planned event magistrates warned the public about the severe consequences for such activities and seized an effigy. They also armed some of their own servants and workers on the day of the birthday to ensure that there would be no trouble. In this they were proven to be correct, as the few young men who did gather, quickly dispersed.[3]

Given the distance between Banff and Edinburgh and yet the similarity of the protests that were organised in each of the towns suggests that there must have been some communication between the groups, and this is confirmed by incidents that occurred elsewhere. All of which demonstrated that collusion, if not organisation, was ongoing. In June 1792 'Aberdeen, Perth, Dundee and almost every village in the North of Scotland burned Dundas in effigy'.[4] However, events were not confined to being above the Tay, as Peebles saw likewise and Lanark 'was in a very disagreeable State of Tumult and disorder for eight days'.[5] In the Lanarkshire county town threats were made towards the provost and magistrates, pamphlets calling for action were distributed and shots were even fired at the provost's house. Issues with local corruption appear to have been an underlying cause leading to the events in Lanark but the timing and similarities with protests elsewhere suggest that the wider issues were also a factor.

Even in the highlands, discontent was growing, although it was not as directly related to the French Revolution as elsewhere in Scotland. The year 1792 had become known in the highlands as the year of the sheep. Tenant farmers were being replaced in Ross-shire by sheep and the farmers responded by driving the herds off of their community's land. At social events and after church, locals were told to organise and prepare. Eventually, over 400 men, some armed with guns or bludgeons, herded the sheep as far as Beauly, near Inverness, before they were intercepted. News of this and other confrontations that had taken place reached Dundas and the military were mobilised with the Black Watch deployed from Fort George. Six men were later prosecuted with two being sentenced to transportation for seven years. This was another portent of the severity of sentencing which was to follow as a new phase of the Highland Clearances commenced.

But, as the leading highland historian James Hunter has noted: 'Effigies of leading politicians had been burned in almost every village in the north of Scotland by men and women who, following French precedent, also planted so-called trees of liberty.'[6] Both the actions of some of the leaders of the protests and the reactions of the authorities, confirm an undercurrent of wider political agitation. The Ross-shire disturbances emanated from Strathrusdale just a few miles from Cromarty, where a tree of liberty was planted and radical publications, including those written by Paine, had been translated into Gaelic. Land was the primary issue for many of the protests, but radical sentiment was an underlying theme.

The revolutionary spirit was abroad across Scotland and this was captured by Robert Burns in his poem 'The Tree of Liberty'. The poem has been attributed to the bard, although its precise authorship is unconfirmed, and it provides a flavour of the feelings that would have been felt across Scotland at this time. Its first verse describes the radical beliefs that appealed to those who had worked long and hard for little reward 'to feed the titled knave'.

> Heard ye o' the tree o' France,
> I watna what's the name o't,
> Around it a' the patriots dance,
> Weel Europe kens the fame o't,
> It stands where ane the Bastille stood,

A prison built by Kings, man,
When superstition's hellish brood
Kept France in leading strings, man.

The tree of liberty was a symbol that soon sprouted up around the country, sometimes literally with trees being planted, and on other occasions with garlands being placed around constructions that were made to look like a tree. Although there was a brief period of quiet that followed the King's birthday riots and the protests in the summer of 1792, this was just the calm before the storm. The radicals were organising and discontent was growing. Trees of liberty were being planted.

CHAPTER 5

THE FRIENDS OF THE PEOPLE AND THE TREES OF LIBERTY

With revolutionary fervour spreading across the country it was only natural that radical organisations would begin to be established. Discussion and debate had been ongoing in coffee rooms and taverns, workplaces and on the street, but the time had come to unite behind a common cause. More formal organisation was required and as a result the Friends of the People was established in Edinburgh on 26 July 1792.[1]

A meeting was called by a group that called itself the Societies of Friends for General Reform. The gathering was advertised widely and brought groups together from all parts of the country, although those from Edinburgh were in the majority given the distance and cost of travel. The group intended to form an association supporting radical reform and thereafter promote it around the land. It was to be built on the burgh and county reform movements and the group's aims were kept very general. Equal representation for the people was the primary ambition, but beyond that little else was discussed.

Assembling in Fortune's Tavern on the Canongate in Edinburgh, the Friends of the People was inaugurated. This was not the only radical society in Scotland but it became by far the largest and best organised, and certainly had the highest profile and was therefore the group that would be targeted most by the authorities. The society brought together both former supporters of burgh reform and newer more radical individuals.

With the meeting called in the month following the King's birthday riots, there was also a desire amongst some members to defuse tensions and to take control of the direction of the radical movement. Concerned about the disturbances and the revolutionary calls being made, the gathering was also an attempt to shift the focus back onto change through peaceful reform with 'moderation and constitutionalism the hallmark'.[2] Most members came from the burgh and county reform movements, rather than the radicals who had been joining up with other groups, such as the weaving communities. For some individuals, the organisation was no doubt seen as an opportunity to temper if not corral the newer and wilder elements of discontent. Later this would create some tension between moderates and radicals, with many of those who had joined from previous reform movements deciding to leave as revolutionary events in France intensified.

The meeting in Edinburgh in July 1792 was attended by a much more diverse group than most societies that sprung up thereafter in the capital and across Scotland. At the gathering there were not just artisans and tradesmen, who were fired up by Paine and the French Revolution, but there were also lawyers and other liberal Whigs, especially those from the former burgh reform movement. Thomas Muir was also present. However, William Skirving, who was present at that first meeting, noted that the membership in Edinburgh was still predominantly made up of working people, even if the social make-up of the leadership did not reflect this.

The name 'Friends of the People' was taken from an existing organisation which was operating in England. However, although the name was taken from their English counterparts, the structure of the Scottish group was to be significantly different. Founded by Whigs, the English version of the society was largely aristocratic and very exclusive; it was also quite selective, having high subscription fees. So, despite the fact that it took the same name, the Scottish version of the society adopted a different model and sought a broader support base.

The model chosen was more akin to the London Corresponding Society, which was another radical grouping with which the Friends of the People had already been in communication. Ironically, the LCS was founded by the Scot Thomas Hardy who was from Larbert but had moved to London at an early age. Two of the other LCS founding members were Maurice Margarot and Joseph Gerrald.

As with the Friends of the People, the LCS sought universal male suffrage but the group operated differently. It had branches in other English cities, although it was largely London-based and provided a forum for discussion and debate. Split into divisions and smaller groups, its members were largely small independent craftsmen, with the group's lower membership fees reflecting both their limited wealth and the desire for wider support. It was the LCS that the Scottish Friends of the People would operate most closely with and it was their model of low subscription rates and mass membership that was emulated.

As a consequence, the appeal of the Friends of the People extended far beyond the middle-ranking classes, with artisans, working people and weavers making up the predominant part of its support base. The growth in membership proved to be explosive not just in Edinburgh, where around 200 people attended the next meeting a short while after the inaugural gathering, but across the country, which again reflected the impact of the French Revolution. By 30 September 1792 the *Caledonian Mercury* reported that 'societies are everywhere formed and clubs instituted for the sole purpose of political debate ... from Wick in the north to Wigton in the south and from Dunbar in the east to Dumbarton in the west.'[3] Membership of twelve such societies set up in Edinburgh was estimated to be between 2,000 and 3,000. One report received by government in late 1792 suggested that for the

nine societies in Glasgow and three others in the immediate vicini-
ty, membership had reached 1,200. It was estimated that there were
twelve groups in Perth, as was the case with Paisley in the west.

The class base of the membership of the new societies was also becoming evident at this time. In Glasgow members were exclusively
drawn from amongst the weaver and artisan communities, which
was largely replicated around the country. Whilst in Edinburgh, as
was highlighted by Skirving, the society had a similar demography
but also included some more radical well-to-do individuals, such as
lawyers like Muir. This no doubt caused concern for those who had
joined to moderate the radical cause and many soon began to distance
themselves from the organisation, if not leave completely.

This same report estimated that membership for the west was
between 40,000 and 50,000; although this may have been a slight
over-exaggeration it emphasises the fact that, across the country,
towns both large and small were beginning to organise. In larger towns
such as Paisley and Kilmarnock the total number of members of such
groups was considered to be between 500 and 800. Smaller villages
were also developing their own membership base, even if numbers
were considerably lower. Individual organisations were established
around Paisley, Lochwinnoch, Kilbarchan, Johnstone and Neilston.
Likewise, in Ayrshire communities such as Hurlford, Galston and
Kyle were developing networks and not just in the larger towns like
Ayr or Kilmarnock.

The same pattern appeared elsewhere in the country. Larger towns
may have had the most members but they often formed the hub for
spokes to smaller communities nearby. This linked Tayside around
Perth to the likes of Glamis, Strathmiglo and Auchtermuchty or
Dundee and places such as Forfar, Kirriemuir, Montrose, Arbroath
and St Cyrus.

This also applied in the east and central Scotland: in Lanarkshire,
Stirlingshire and the Lothians, communities were developing in

Hamilton or Shotts or in towns such as Linlithgow or Dalkeith. Even in more isolated parts associations were formed as the effect of the revolution was felt. On the Isle of Bute, Lord Bute noted that 'liberty and the rights of man are inscribed upon every door of the cotton mill in Rothesay and the general conversation of the working people tend that way'.[4]

Although societies sprang up across the country, they still predominated in the more industrial areas whether in the west or through the central belt into Perthshire and Angus. Perth was then primarily a weaving community; it is estimated that there were 1,500 looms in the city by 1794, which helps explain its radicalism at the time, in comparison to its more douce modern image.[5] Societies were also formed from or in addition to others that already existed. In Dundee, the Society of the Friends of the Constitution was formed in September 1792 and in the spring of 1793 the Friends of Liberty was established. In more rural areas such societies were less prevalent due to the power of large landowners and their ability to pressurise tenants. Hence why areas such as Caithness, Aberdeenshire and the Borders were far less fertile territory for organisation, although societies were formed in Wick and Selkirk.

The radical gospel was spread by word of mouth and disseminated through pamphlets and papers. This was partly helped by changes in the weaving industry, which provided a mobile workforce that moved between larger towns and the surrounding villages for work and trade. Such information was also carried by radicals who evangelised the message of reform. Thomas Muir toured the central belt to speak at meetings, help establish new societies and to encourage the formation of others.

As the membership and number of radical groups grew, it made sense to try and bring them together. Communication had been ongoing not just between groups in larger towns with neighbouring smaller communities, but more widely across the country, as organised events and the travel of Muir demonstrated. Discussions were also taking place with organisations in England and with societies abroad. The first contact between Scottish radicals and their Irish counterparts came about in 1792 and in the same year a few Scots even visited France.

It was only natural, having established a national society, that a national convention should be held. There was a desire to promote the radical cause and Muir had been in touch with the Society of United Irishmen, who were pushing for the Scots to hold a convention. The Irish counterpart had been established the year before, again following the publication of Paine's writing, and it had quickly grown in size and strength. Bringing the Scottish groups together offered members the chance to meet and mingle with kindred spirits and also provided an opportunity for solidarity as the authorities began to flex their muscles in response to what was happening. The First National Convention of the Scottish Friends of the People was therefore set to be held on Tuesday 11 December 1792.

As autumn turned to winter the reports that reached the authorities must have been concerning, as not only were societies spreading across the land, but discontent was growing. Opposition was coalescing and the strength and popularity of the radicals was increasing. A report from Perth mentioned that it was 'not uncommon to hear boys in the street crying "Liberty Equality and No King"'.[6] In early November there was a report that an effigy of Dundas had been seen and another government source stated that when news of the fall of Brussels was received the town had gone 'quite mad about liberty and equality', adding that:

> The Tree of Liberty was planted with great Solemnity in this town and a great bonfire with ringing of bells and a general illumination upon hearing that General Dumourier had entered Brussels. The Lower Class of People talk of nothing but Liberty and Equality

– No Dundas – No Bishops – and No King. Nothing but a Republic for us.[7]

Another report described how 'many People' were determined to bring about a revolution similar to that in France in Scotland, and dramatically depicting Edinburgh as having become 'the Paris of Scotland'.[8] Henry Dundas experienced some of the atmosphere for himself when he returned north in the autumn and was forced to abandon a visit to Perth due to the likelihood of demonstrations. The protests occurred in his absence, indicating that there was a groundswell of opinion and a willingness to challenge authority. This convinced Dundas that there was a threat of insurrection and that there was a need for repressive measures to quash the opposition.

It was also not surprising that disturbances returned with a vengeance as winter approached. Hardship increased as the effects of the bad weather were felt and anger began to mount. In addition to local climatic factors, the opposition were buoyed by events on the continent when French revolutionary forces defeated the Austrian Imperial Army and liberated Brussels. The revolution, far from being crushed, was growing in strength. Enthusiasm and belief would have only increased amongst radicals in Scotland in response to these events.

Lord Adam Gordon, the military Commander-in-Chief in Scotland, considered Perth to be a very dangerous place and was unhappy to deploy troops there, as he was concerned that they might either revolt or be suborned. This did not just apply in Perth but across the smaller neighbouring towns and in communities all across lowland Scotland. For trees of liberty were being planted in Stonehaven, Aberdeen, Fochabers, Auchtermuchty and Strathmiglo, and in many other towns across Scotland. Whilst in Newburgh a plan to burn effigies was only thwarted by a show of force by the town authorities: 'Although undocumented, the impression gained from the Government's reaction is that disturbances such as these were relatively widespread.'[9]

Meanwhile, over two weekends and on a number of weekdays, crowds gathered in Dundee and a tree of liberty was planted. It was almost immediately pulled down by some individuals described as 'young gentlemen'.[10] This merely incited the demonstrators, who quickly distributed pamphlets calling for people to avenge the insult and the following day a crowd of several hundred protesters gathered in the town centre. They burned effigies and marched to the houses where either those responsible lived or to others who had incurred their wrath. They then proceeded to the provost's house, where they took the keys to the bell tower and started ringing out the bells across the town, whilst building a bonfire and erecting another tree of liberty. Trouble continued in the following week with the tree once more being removed but yet again being replaced. Order was only restored when dragoons arrived to support the beleaguered provost. The concern of the authorities was evidenced by naval ships being dispatched from Newcastle.

A review by the authorities found that various factors were to blame for the unrest, from animosity towards an excise tax, to an insult made about the local Unitarian minister Reverend Thomas Fyshe Palmer. However, it is hard to see these occurrences as being inspired by anything other than revolutionary events, even if other factors may have also had an influence. For example, one of those attacked by the mob blamed it on radicals not just from within the town but also on weavers from nearby Forfar and Kirriemuir. This was similar to events in Aberdeen where a seamen's strike had been ongoing and during the associated protests a tree of liberty was reportedly planted.

So, as the First National Convention of the Scottish Friends of the People neared, concern amongst the authorities was mounting and Thomas Muir was already in their sights, as the main figurehead. Robert Dundas, when commenting that he was earnestly seeking the opportunity to prosecute him, described Muir as 'the most determined

Rebel in Scotland'.[11] The convention would soon provide him with the opportunity to do just that.

The use of the pejorative term 'rebel' was indicative of deep-rooted fears held by the establishment since the Jacobite rebellions, if not before. Riots and disturbances had been experienced before but the scale and the sophistication of this was new. The fear of revolution abroad was now matched by the fear of unrest closer to home. The establishment was being threatened as their order and control were challenged.

All this was unknown to the radicals who were in high spirits when the societies convened on 11 December, with the meeting scheduled to continue over the proceeding days. Approximately 170 delegates from eighty societies representing around thirty-eight towns attended James's Court in Edinburgh. The official minutes recorded that delegates from branches far and wide were in attendance, including numerous branches from Edinburgh, Glasgow, Paisley, Perth and Kilmarnock through to smaller towns such as St Cyrus in the northeast to Lochwinnoch and Kilbarchan in the west. Some societies that did not manage to send an official representative, such as those in Dundee and Leslie, arranged for Muir or Skirving to represent them (a list of delegates is included in Appendix A).

And so, the scene was set, but storm clouds were already gathering and would soon break.

CHAPTER 6

THE FIRST NATIONAL CONVENTION AND REPRESSION UNLEASHED

Delegates assembled on Tuesday 11 December 1792 for the First National Convention of the Scottish Friends of the People with opinion already hardening on all sides. As hope was being ignited amongst the poor, fear was increasing amongst the ruling elite. Steps had already been taken by the government to control the rising radicalism, such as declaring Paine's work as being seditious, and further actions were now being implemented. Loyal postmasters were called upon to report radical packages and suspicious mail, along with information on who was sending or receiving it. The army presence was increased and soldiers were deployed across the country.

Lord Adam Gordon made arrangements in Perth and elsewhere to guard against disturbances or insurrection. Troops were stationed where potential trouble might be faced and soldiers were brought down from Fort George, as the focus moved from the highlands to the lowlands. As well as two troops of dragoons going to Perth another was sent to Dundee. Troops were also dispatched to Hamilton and Kilmarnock whilst Stirling Castle was reinforced. Aberdeen, where the seamen's strike was ongoing, was also reinforced with additional soldiers.

Discussions about strengthening the military presence across the country had already taken place and further strategic actions were taken. Garrison building commenced in 1793 in the lowlands, mirroring what had happened in the highlands after the Jacobite rebellions. After the rebellions, Fort William, Fort Ruthven, Fort Rannoch and ultimately the citadel of Fort George were constructed, which provided strategic control over the highlands, and in 1793 this process was replicated in the lowlands.

Ostensibly this was due to the expansion in the size of the military, as war with revolutionary France loomed. The growth in the army was such that billeting with families or local hostelries simply was not possible. However, Lord Adam Gordon also stated that strategically it no longer felt safe to station troops within the community, given the spreading radical sentiment. Reports had been received of troops attending reform meetings and some even joining radical groups, and it was therefore deemed essential that they were segregated from the public. The strategy was focused on suppressing revolutionary Scots as much as it was aimed at repelling an invasion from revolutionary France.

The building of the Queen's Barracks in Perth and the Piershill Barracks in Edinburgh commenced in 1793 and they were completed shortly thereafter. Hamilton Barracks in South Lanarkshire followed in 1794 and the Gallowgate Barracks in Glasgow were finished the year after, alongside a base that was built in Ayr. Given that there were existing military installations at Stirling Castle and Edinburgh Castle and in Aberdeen, this was about ensuring control over areas where there was the potential for rebellion. As with the highlands the forces were strategically positioned. Nothing was left to chance, which was a clear indication of how fearful the authorities were.

As well as actions by the government, precautionary steps were taken by members of the wider establishment. Landowners and wealthy individuals funded loyalist newspapers and supported the distribution of anti-reform pamphlets. The majority of papers were supportive of the government but increased financial backing undoubtedly ampli-fied vitriol against radicals and augmented praise for the authorities. As Bob Harris noted: 'In late 1792, the *Glasgow Courier* printed a succession of anti-radical items aimed explicitly at the labouring classes, some of which purported to be written by men of their rank, while in 1793 its main political correspondent, who wrote under the pseudonym "Asmodeus", contributed a series of letters attacking local radicals.'[1] Pro-government writers and pamphleteers were also reward-ed for their efforts in an attempt to stem the rising revolutionary tide.

However, the challenges were not just limited to Scotland, as radi-cal societies were also springing up in England; popular loyalism was greater south of the border and the threats of violence against radicals was also greater. There were very few effigies of Thomas Paine burned in Scotland and it seems to have been a much more widespread tactic in England. This reflected not just a greater hostility to reform in England but more intimidatory actions against reformers generally. However, calls for reform could still be heard, particularly in the areas that were undergoing industrialisation.

Loyalist groups were established by the elite to counter the pro-liferation of radical groups and they were encouraged and actively supported by the government. The authorities recognised the need to target the so-called 'lower orders' to try to defuse unrest. According-ly, efforts to promote popular loyalism went into overdrive and the church in Scotland assisted with this effort.

As early as August 1792, landowners in Inverness began meeting to raise volunteer regiments from amongst their tenants and servants. November saw the establishment of an anti-reform organisation in London called the Association against Levellers and Republicans. Two Scots were delegated to attend from the Edinburgh establishment. A meeting was then held in Edinburgh the following month, which was attended by the supposed 'gentry of the city and county of Edin-burgh', who pledged to 'stand by the constitution with their lives and fortunes', which was perhaps indicative of the wealth they possessed. They committed to using 'their utmost endeavours to counteract all seditious attempts, and in particular, all associations for the publication or dispersion of seditious and inflammatory writings, or tending to excite disorders or tumults within this part of the kingdom'.[2] The document was left for individuals to sign at the Goldsmiths' Hall and thereafter the signatories became known by that name.

The Goldsmiths' Hall Association quickly acquired a membership of several hundred of the rich and well-to-do in Edinburgh, with the members of the association's management committee reflecting its elite status. Sir John Inglis of Cramond, a major landowner, was elected chairman and the committee consisted of six landowners, five lawyers, two bankers and a surgeon. Doubtless all individuals were keen to protect their assets, as much as they wished to oppose reform. This was all part of a campaign to demonise the opposition and bolster support for the status quo.

The authorities sought to secure support across the country and loyalism became organised into state-sponsored vigilante groups in a counter-revolutionary manner. Such an organisation was set up in Glasgow and a few were also created elsewhere. However, Scotland never had the same number of loyalist clubs or support for the cause as existed in England. North of the border there were never more than a handful of such groups, whereas in England estimates vary from several hundreds to perhaps even 2,000.

Although these counter-revolutionary groups were supposedly formed for working people, they were established by members of the elite and their influence and actions in Scotland cannot be ignored. Great efforts were made by churches and councils to have working people renounce reform and espouse loyalty. Petitions were circulated and calls to sign them were spread far and wide. Most such attempts appear to have been abject failures or were met with a sullen response and sometimes meetings calling to support loyalism would even be taken over by reform supporters and the resolutions they were presenting were changed to being supportive of reform.

The radical newspaper, the *Edinburgh Gazetteer*, carried a story about the village of Aberdalgie in Perthshire.[3] The Earl of Kinnoul, who was the landowner in Aberdalgie, summoned the village to a meeting to pledge support for a loyalist petition. Despite the local minister haranguing the attendees for quite some time, none were prepared to sign. Similar reports were received from elsewhere around the country.

Other forms of threat and coercion were also unleashed by the rich and powerful. These varied from the imposition of relatively minor inconveniences to much more explicit and harsher acts. Landowners refused to allow their tenants to attend Bastille Day celebrations and the Duchess of Buccleuch reportedly discharged her haberdasher for being a member of a reform society. However, the more insidious included the public identification of radicals and requests that wealthy people boycott their trade or business, and ministers informing landlords about any radical parishioners.

Across the country, shop owners were threatened with ruin, tradesmen with a loss of work and tenant farmers with eviction. Blacklisting was practised, which meant that work dried up and businesses closed as a result of even being perceived as having radical sympathies. Radical teachers were especially feared and were hounded in both schools and universities, and even lawyers who supported reform began to struggle. As radical societies noted at the time, attacks by the aristocracy and the church were relentless across the land.

Despite this backdrop, delegates to the First National Convention were in a buoyant mood. The boom in the number of societies must have been encouraging and the reports from France equally heartening. Procedures from revolutionary France were copied with preliminary discussions reflecting the egalitarian mood of the times. Delegates addressed each other as citizen and a decision was made to elect the president on a daily basis, though a permanent secretary and treasurer were appointed. Skirving succeeded to the former role and Muir was at the forefront of the movement from the outset. The proceedings on the first day of the convention were largely taken up with formalities and administration.

However, the following two days saw discussions that would provide the evidence the authorities were seeking: that seditious actions were being organised and that a revolution was being planned. On the second day an address from the Society of United Irishmen was the subject of a heated debate. The United Irishmen were already larger and stronger than any equivalent organisation in Britain. Their views were also far more radical and much more nationalistic than any Scottish group at that time. Then as now, Scottish and Irish nationalism were substantially different, particularly on religious issues. However, the Irish were eager to make contact with kindred spirits in both Scotland and in England. It also seemed that Muir and Skirving were equally keen to see alliances being forged and had encouraged them by being in communication with their Irish counterparts. Both men were firmly in the more radical camp and no doubt saw the United Irishmen as potential allies, if not an organisation to emulate.

Radicals led by Muir wished to have the United Irishmen address, sent by their chairman William Drennan and secretary Archibald Hamilton Rowan, read out and entered into the proceedings, whilst moderates feared that this could either be treasonous or construed as being treasonous. One paragraph in the document described Scotland as 'rising to distinction not by a calm, contented secret wish for a reform in Parliament, but by openly, actively, and urgently willing it, with the unity and energy of an embodied nation'. The tone of this statement is mild now, but most certainly was viewed as being inflammatory back then. Other phrases in the address were equally capable of being interpreted as supporting sedition.

Not only could this statement be interpreted as promoting sedition, it included phrases that seemed to challenge the Treaty of Union. In the debate the radicals prevailed and Muir formally read out the address from the United Irishmen. Further discussions then took place which led Muir to withdraw the statement and agree to return the document to the group and seek its amendment and moderation. By this point the damage had been done and the spies present at the meeting would have recorded the comments and tenor.

Despite the reading of the Society of United Irishmen's letter, the political aims of the First National Convention were not nationalist. The group wanted reform of the British Parliament. A few individuals, such as Muir, may have harboured nationalist views, but many others objected to any attack on the union. Muir did not demur from such a position at this point, even if his later statements were more explicitly nationalist.

It may be that either Muir recognised that the wider mood was different or that he simply felt that the timing was inappropriate. What is clear is that the overall intention of the First National Convention was to seek reform across Britain. This was not just a case of the group distancing itself from the United Irishmen but a core part of the developing radical ideology. This was perhaps a recognition of the religious, as much as the political landscape in Scotland. The monarchy was deeply tied to Protestantism and many people were hostile to Catholicism. Abjuring republicanism and overt links to Catholic countries was a pragmatic stance to adopt.

This was not just the view taken at the convention but was one that had applied since the establishment of the friendship societies: 'No society of the Friends of the People published resolutions either explicitly or implicitly criticising the union, while, with one exception, no radical handbills or pamphlets argued the nationalist case.'[4] It was the lack of democracy rather than rule from London that was the issue; the aristocracy rather than the Treaty of Union who were the enemy.

This is perfectly understandable given the circumstances that existed at that time. Of course, Parliament decided on taxes and war and remained vital to social reform. But with church, law and education protected by the Treaty of Union, in many ways Scotland and England operated as entirely distinct societies. This was compounded by the fact that travel was difficult, expensive and unavailable for most in society. The media was limited and entertainment was predominantly local, which meant that working people in England and Scotland lived in separate and quite different societies. The Scots were also confident in their own distinct identity, even if some were beginning to view themselves as being British.

The fact that London was the location for the seat of political power was of far less importance when compared to who actually exercised control. Power in Scotland lay with and was exercised by the land-own-ing elite. It was this elite that the radicals understandably viewed as being the enemy and, at this stage at least, reform in London was viewed by most as being the solution. This may have been different for a few individuals who sought the repeal of the Treaty of Union. But at that First National Convention it was reform of Scotland as a part of Britain that formed the political agenda; and this would remain the case for most individuals throughout this period.

On the third and final day of the convention, a resolution circu-lated by the loyalist Goldsmiths' Hall Association provoked debate. It was clearly intended to be critical of the radicals in general and to intimidate them specifically. However, after some debate, it was agreed that the terms of the resolution were actually wide enough to be acceptable. The document largely demanded loyalty to the Consti-tution and denounced violent disturbances and was similar in tone to other statements that had been distributed locally. Some delegates ex-plained how they had signed local resolutions without any objections or incidents and were eager that the convention did likewise, to either defuse hostility or suborn the resolutions.

After discussion it was concluded that there may be merit in delegates signing the resolution, although it was agreed that after their signature they should add 'delegate of the Friends of the People'. In this way they could defuse some of the hostility without compromising their principles. However, the Goldsmiths' Hall Association would not accept this and soon barred anyone from doing so. Names that had been added with this addition were swiftly deleted.

The establishment line towards the radicals was obviously hardening. Perhaps as a consequence of this, two further motions were agreed at the convention. One was an opposition to riot and sedition, and stated that any member involved in such actions would be expelled. Again, this was an attempt to appease the opposition and demonstrate the convention's peaceful intentions. The other motion, though, was indicative of growing concerns amongst the delegates and was designed to provide reassurance by stating that any member who was unfairly pursued by the authorities would be supported by the group.

The mood was still a mixture of buoyancy and defiance when the convention was finally concluded. Delegates on the final evening stood together and loudly swore the French revolutionary oath 'Live Free or Die', although there was still sufficient concern about this being viewed as seditious for it to be omitted from the official minutes. However, the spies present had recorded that the oath had been sworn and the damage had been done. This was compounded by an earlier comment made that morning about arming radicals, albeit in the context of quelling riot and disturbance. Again, as far as the authorities were concerned, this was a demonstration of not only seditious activity but revolutionary intent. Although this may have been taken out of context, the authorities were looking for any excuse to demonise the group.

The convention then adjourned until the following April. But as 1793 dawned, the authorities already had the evidence they required. Paine had been convicted *in absentia* in England, but north of the border those propagating his works were now also being pursued, as the authorities started to crack down on radical literature and other public dissent. Arrests had been made before the end of 1792 and summons had already been served. Court actions were due to commence in the first few days of the new year. The first to appear in court was due to be an apothecary from Edinburgh called James Tytler, who as well as editing the second edition of *Encyclopaedia Britannica*, was also the first Briton to fly in a hot-air balloon. He was charged with producing seditious literature.

Thomas Muir was due to represent Tytler and over Christmas and New Year, the radical advocate had returned home to Huntershill to prepare his case, as well as to enjoy the family festivities. However, the authorities were now starting to move against the radical leaders in addition to Tytler and the others who had already been charged. Robert Dundas was soon to get his wish and prosecute Muir.

On 2 January 1793 Muir was making his way back to Edinburgh on a coach. When it stopped at Holytown for a change of horses, King's messengers were waiting with a warrant for his arrest. Muir was escorted to Edinburgh and taken to the Tolbooth where prisoners were kept. There he was questioned by the Sheriff about whether he had attended radical meetings in Dunbartonshire and in particular whether he had read out the address from the Society of United Irishmen at the First National Convention. Muir declined to answer and questioned the basis of his arrest. Despite his protestations he was remanded in custody until bail could be posted, which was quickly done by his friend and fellow radical William Moffatt.

Following his release, Muir considered his next course of action. No date had been set for his trial but he did have other commitments, including Tytler's defence. However, it was becoming clear that a full crackdown was now underway and the radical cause was coming under attack. Muir's radical beliefs took precedence over his legal responsibilities. After a discussion with friends and fellow radicals, it was agreed that he depart immediately for London. Once there he could discuss what steps could be taken in defence of both individuals and the wider cause in Scotland with leading English radicals. A friend and colleague, James Campbell, took over responsibility for his affairs and arrangements were made to cover his court commitments, including Tytler's forthcoming trial.

The journey south took four days, but on his arrival, Muir was immediately made welcome by his radical friends. However, discussions with English reformers soon caused him concern. Events in France where the King had been arrested and tried had sent ripples of fear across many parts of society in England. No decision had been made about the French monarch's fate, but unease was growing. English radicals were already feeling the backlash and there were fears about the consequences of an execution, which had already been demanded by Robespierre. Muir worried about the effect on the English reform movement, and no doubt the consequences posed for the Scots. Muir's fears proved to be accurate as the execution and 'reign of terror' that followed had a huge impact on the radical cause in Scotland and Britain.

Accordingly, despite the lengthy journey he had already made to London, Muir decided to travel on to France. He intended to try and persuade the revolutionary authorities to spare Louis XVI's life, which would benefit the radical cause in Britain or at least limit the damage already being done to it. However, this was always a forlorn hope, if not an utterly madcap adventure. Tension was mounting in France and the mood was beginning to turn ugly. Foreign radicals were welcomed as allies but there was also a widespread fear of spies. After all, war was being waged on the continent, even if it was not yet with Britain. Arriving shortly after the King's conviction and just before his execution on the guillotine on 21 January 1793, Muir's pleas for leniency fell on deaf ears. He was still welcomed by many in France and whilst staying in Paris he met Paine and Mirabeau, amongst others.

Meanwhile, back in Scotland the first week of January had brought the prosecution of James Tytler and the trials of other radicals were set to follow over coming weeks and months. Potentially as a result of being frightened by Muir's arrest, Tytler fled and there was therefore no need for a replacement advocate to take his place. Tytler went first to Belfast, before moving to the United States. Many more would follow this path in the months and years to come, either at the start of their prosecution or as the authorities' net was closing in. In most cases outlawry would follow, which effectively prevented any return for the individuals, but no attempt was made by the authorities to pursue them. This was long before the enforcement of arrest warrants internationally, but it did lead to enforced exile.

Frequently such radicals would flee south. Distances and communications were such that they would be largely left alone by the Scottish authorities. After fleeing and leaving worldly possessions and sometimes even family behind, many individuals could start a new life in England and be unnoticed and untroubled. Others ventured even further and went abroad, especially to the new land of the United States of America as Tytler had done, which was regarded as a bastion of liberty and a place where their reformist views would be unchallenged.

Tytler was to be the first of many from the movement who sought sanctuary elsewhere. His trial was immediately followed by the trial of three Edinburgh printers, John Morton, James Anderson and Malcom Craig. Charged with sedition, their crime was not linked to the material they had produced but what they had suggested. They were accused of proposing the following toast: 'to George the third and last and damnation to all Crowned Heads'. The toast had allegedly been made in the presence of soldiers who the trio had invited to join them in the celebrations. The three also supposedly told the troops that their pay was too low and that they should support reform.

Although they denied committing the offence, they provided a letter of apology but denied being members of the Friends of the People. Despite this they were convicted and sentenced to nine months' imprisonment. The judge indicated that if they had gone any further they would have been guilty of high treason rather than sedition and that if they had committed any previous offences they would have been sent to Botany Bay rather than prison.

Just as this trial was ending another was beginning with the month of January not even half-way through. John Elder, another Edinburgh printer, and William Stewart, a Leith merchant, were charged with sedition for publishing 3,000 copies of Paine's *Rights of Man* for distribution in the west of Scotland. Stewart, as with other radicals awaiting prosecution, simply absconded rather than risk trial. The case against Elder continued but was finally dropped, with no reason given. He may have provided the authorities with information or it may have been that his assurances of future good conduct were accepted.

By the end of the month another Edinburgh publisher was on trial as the crackdown against seditious literature continued. Captain William Johnston was the publisher of the *Edinburgh Gazetteer* and a high-profile advocate for reform, having attended the Fortune's Tavern meeting. His crime along with another accused named Drummond who stood trial with him was not for reprinting Paine, but for the paper that they were publishing. He was imprisoned for three months and required to post funds to guarantee future good behaviour.

A similar fate befell Walter Berry and James Robertson in late January 1793. Both men were bookshop owners in the city, and were convicted of distributing seditious pamphlets. They were sentenced to six months' imprisonment. The next month saw the trial of yet another printer called Alexander Scott for publishing seditious material. He too fled and became an outlaw.

This crackdown was not just restricted to Edinburgh, as the first days of February saw the trial of James Smith and John Menzies in Glasgow. They were charged with sedition for attending reform meetings and forming an association in Partick known as the Sons of Liberty and the Friends of Man. Smith was a gunsmith in the Gorbals who fled before his trial and the case against Menzies did not proceed, although again it is not known why.

All of this was bad enough for the individuals involved but the situation in Scotland for radicals more generally was about to get a whole lot worse. On 21 January 1793 Louis XVI was sent to the guillotine and spasms of fear and revulsion were sent through the ruling elite across Europe. Britain reacted by dismissing the French Ambassador and on 1 February 1793 revolutionary France responded by declaring war on Britain.

The stakes had increased and turmoil had been unleashed, as a letter written by Dundas at the time confirmed: 'The bad news from the Continent, has been received in this place and in the West country, with a sincere joy, as we lament them; and I am sorry to say from the information we have received, that Paisley and the neighbourhood are in a very unpleasant situation.'[5] The situation was similar elsewhere in the country. In Tayside there were three public meetings in early January, with over 2,000 attending in Dundee. The state was right to be concerned and the repression that had already been unleashed was only going to become more severe.

Muir had failed to achieve his aims when travelling to France and his absence from Scotland would cost him dearly. The authorities decided to act quickly against him. Whether this was because they knew that he was absent is not known, although it does look as if it was done to make things more difficult for him. On 26 January an indictment was served at his home, which provided a date of 11 February for his trial. His friend James Campbell immediately sent it on to him but it did not arrive in Paris until 8 February, just three days before he was due to appear. The covering letter from his friend explained the situation, along with a document that provided details on the charge of sedition.

Not only did this allow insufficient time for Muir to return to Scotland, but by now France was also at war with Britain, which further complicated matters. Campbell managed to have the trial postponed when it was called on 11 February, even though Muir was absent. Pleas for additional time to both prepare and allow for his client to return from abroad led to the granting of an extension until 25 February. This was barely sufficient time to get notification to Muir in Paris, let alone allow for his return.

Accordingly, when the case was called once more on 25 February, Muir was again absent. Legal formalities were followed, albeit as a charade, and his name was formally called several times, despite his absence being known. Lord Braxfield was the presiding judge and he was to become the scourge of not just Muir but the other political martyrs. He was Lord Justice Clerk, Scotland's second-most senior judge, but he already had a reputation both for his use of broad Scots, but more worryingly as being a hanging judge. Humanity, let alone fairness, was seemingly absent from his approach to justice and he was very much part of the establishment and intent on defending the interests of the landowners. At the start of the year he had already delivered a violent denunciation of reformers that was printed in a pamphlet. It was no doubt with relish that he pronounced bail forfeited and granted a warrant for Muir's arrest.

At this time Muir was still in France. He had to decide what to do and it appears as if he was conflicted. He wrote to the *Edinburgh Gazetteer* in a letter published on 1 March and stated that he intended to return. However, information also suggests that he might well have been considering other options. There is some evidence that he thought about buying land and remaining in France, although the situation there was deteriorating and it seems unlikely that he would have stayed. It was more likely that he would head to the United States, where he could start a new life, as others had already done. Taking some time to mull it over, he remained in France, whilst mixing with other radicals in the ongoing milieu.

His inner conflict is understandable as his conviction was almost certain if he went back to Scotland. But he was also aware that, given his leading role, his failure to return could have a huge impact on both the organisation and the morale of reformers more generally. Yet, exile is never easy, despite the fact that others had gone before him to a land that he admired, which must have been tempting. Perhaps he thought that his legal skills might allow him to avoid conviction or at least to promote the radical cause during the trial, which he most certainly did. It has also been suggested that he chose martyrdom, although if he did, he certainly never anticipated the severity of the sentence that was ultimately handed down. Punishment may well have been anticipated and viewed as the price he would have to pay but no one would have predicted just how draconian it was to be.

Muir appears to have been weighing up his options until a very late stage, for his journey home was neither immediate nor direct. Given the circumstances and the risk, if he chose any other option it would have been understandable. His wayward return journey was partly due to the war but it also appears that he took time to discuss his options with others and particularly his friends in the United Irishmen. Departing France required him to obtain permission from the revolutionary authorities to both travel within the country and indeed to leave it. This was done relatively easily, although it did take some time. However, it was more difficult to find a passage on a ship. With the countries at war, Royal Navy ships were patrolling and a vessel from a neutral country would therefore be required, though they were far more scarce at this time than was normal.

Eventually, on 13 July 1793 he secured a berth on an American ship bound from Le Havre for Baltimore with a stop at Belfast on the way. After arriving in Belfast a few days later, Muir advised the captain that he was heading to Dublin whilst berthed. The vessel was not due to sail on for over a week as goods were loaded and unloaded and it appears that even at this stage Muir was keeping his options open. This Dublin visit seems to have been part of an attempt to reach a final decision, despite Muir's written protestations to the *Edinburgh Gazetteer*.

In Dublin he met with the United Irishmen to discuss the political situation not just in Scotland but across Britain and Ireland. Unrest was far greater in Ireland and would explode by the end of the decade. The United Irishmen were not only more clandestine in their activities but also far more revolutionary, although it would be a few more years before they became openly insurrectionary. The society was intent on mobilising for reform, and if need be revolution. Wolfe Tone was at the forefront of the group and Catholic emancipation was a major issue. Brave and determined, they referenced their ongoing struggle and belief that they could succeed. The Irish would have been eager for partners, as they planned their future actions.

It is not hard to see how this would have appealed to Muir, who was already far more sympathetic to the radical, rather than moderate position of his contemporaries. He appears to have been energised by his meetings in Dublin and stayed for a number of days and even travelled with Hamilton Rowan and others. It also appears that he formally became a member of the United Irishmen.

This visit apparently finally helped Muir to make up his mind. He did not want to take exile in America but wanted to return to Scotland, to face almost certain punishment, but also an opportunity to energise and mobilise the radical cause. Muir may have believed that his suffering could inspire others or maybe that it was his duty to stand his ground rather than run. His return also offered a platform to demonstrate his eloquence and his courage, which might also have influenced his decision.

And so, emboldened by his meeting, Muir set about returning to Scotland. He said his farewells to the United Irishmen and set off by coach for Belfast where he boarded a waiting ship. This time, though, he was not embarking for Baltimore but to be transferred to a regular mail ship that sailed from Belfast to Portpatrick. Muir was coming home to stand trial. But he was not going to be alone in his ordeal.

CHAPTER 7

MUIR AND PALMER
STAND TRIAL

After departing Belfast Lough on 30 July, Muir soon landed in Port-patrick, which was then the principal Scottish port for travel from Ireland, with ships going back and forth daily across the narrow North Channel. Government spies had been monitoring Muir's progress throughout his journey back to Scotland even though information about him had been limited in France and Ireland.

Officials were briefed to look out for him and as his profile was widely distributed, he was quickly spotted. By the time he stopped to rest overnight in Stranraer, the authorities were preparing to pounce. The following morning, Muir was awoken by the Sheriff and his officers and arrested. Steps were quickly taken to notify the Lord Advocate and seek further instructions on what was to be done with him. In the interim, he was kept in custody in Stranraer until court officers finally arrived to escort him to Edinburgh. Muir arrived in Edinburgh on 6 August, where he was again placed in the Tolbooth.

News of Muir's arrest spread like wildfire and his friends and colleagues were soon in touch. The first step was to seek to have him released on bail, which James Campbell arranged. For the bail application Muir was marched up the High Street to the court, flanked by red-coated soldiers with fixed bayonets, which left any bystanders in no doubt about the importance of the prisoner. The granting of bail was no mere formality either given that he had already broken one surety. But after some debate and opposition by the authorities it was finally granted with a trial fixed for 30 August 1793. This did not leave Muir with a great deal of time to prepare his case but this was the norm in those days.

And so, on 30 August Thomas Muir the radical advocate appeared in court as the accused. Choosing to represent himself, he was supported by his friend and solicitor William Moffatt. Five judges were on the bench with Lord Braxfield as senior judge. From the outset it was clear that this was not a trial but a state inquisition. As Peter Hume Brown has described, Muir's trial was 'prejudiced by the very atmosphere of the court, for almost to a man the members of the Bar shared the panic of the classes'.[1] The outcome was clear and only the sentence was unknown.

The jury was handpicked by the court, thus ensuring that all were members of the Goldsmiths' Hall Association. There were three main charges facing Muir. Firstly, exciting disaffection by seditious speeches. Secondly, circulating *Rights of Man* by Thomas Paine and some of his other subversive works. Finally, reading and defending the Society of United Irishmen's address at the First National Convention of the Scottish Friends of the People.

The first two charges were particularly weak although this did not trouble the court, nor did it unduly worry the jury. The alleged seditious speeches were references to reports from spies who had attended meetings at which Muir had spoken across the central belt of Scotland. The tone and tenor of his addresses emphasised that he was clearly arguing for parliamentary reform rather than sedition. Evidence that he had been circulating Paine's work came from a servant at Huntershill who looked suspiciously like an informant and whose evidence was flimsy to say the least. However, the final charge relating to the address from the United Irishmen did have substance, which explained the nervousness and concern of some individuals who attended the convention.

The evidence provided varied from factual reports, through jaundiced remarks to frankly absurd statements that simply attempted to paint a picture of a dangerous revolutionary. Unsubstantiated and prejudicial comments were permitted which stated that he was a 'French emissary', a member of an Irish society that was involved in radical activities in Ireland that were similar to those of the London Corresponding Society in England, and that he had a seal inscribed with the words 'Ça ira'. Most of these comments were not relevant to the specific charges but this did not matter and the court was willing to give the Lord Advocate a free rein. When addressing the jury, Robert Dundas described Muir in a variety of terms, the least offensive being 'demon of mischief' and 'pest of Scotland'. Both the court and the jury seemed to lap it up.

However, when it came to his own speech to the jury, Muir came into his own. His address has gone down in history and has been admired by lawyers and radicals alike. It was a veritable tour de force that lasted some three hours, despite the hostility of the court and the pressure that he was under. If Muir only returned to publicly defend himself in court, he certainly rose to the occasion and utilised his rhetorical skills to passionately argue the cause that he believed in. Despite being certain that he would be convicted he bravely stood his ground and prepared to accept his fate, before finally concluding:

> This is now perhaps the last time that I shall address my country … of crimes, most foul and horrible that I have been accused. Of attempting to rear the standard of civil war, and to plunge this land in blood, and to cover this land with desolation. At every step, as the evidence of the Crown advanced, my innocency has brightened … What then has been my crime? Having dared to be, according to the measure of my feeble abilities, a strenuous and active advocate for an equal representation of the people – in the House of the People … It is a good cause. It shall prevail. It shall finally triumph.[2]

Muir went on bravely to add:

I am careless and indifferent to my fate. I can look danger and I can look death in the face, for I am shielded in the consciousness of my own rectitude. I may be condemned to ascend the scaffold. Nothing can destroy my inward peace of mind, arising from the remembrance of having discharged my duty.

When his speech ended there was applause and the stamping of feet, such was its impact on all who were in the courtroom. However, this only seemed to harden the heart of Lord Braxfield. After Muir's address it was then up to the judge to give the charge to the jury, which are directions on points of law. Lord Henry Cockburn, a leading legal commentator, later described how it was an abuse to say that this was a judicial charge. Instead it was an incitement if not a demand to convict made by the judge, even if the jury was already in agreement. Braxfield stated:

I leave it for you to judge, whether it was perfectly innocent or not in Mr Muir, at such a time, to go about among ignorant country people, and among the lower classes of people making them leave off their work, and inducing them to believe that a reform was absolutely necessary to preserve their safety and their liberty, which, had it not been for him, they would never have suspected to have been in danger.

The judge's prejudice was obvious, but he also made it clear that he was protecting the position of the establishment and the interests of the landowning elite, by adding:

A Government in every country should be just like a corporation: and, in this country, it is made up of the landed interest, which alone has a right to be represented. As for the rabble, who have nothing but personal property, what hold has the nation on them? What security for the payment of their taxes? They may pack up all their property on their backs, and leave the country in the twinkling of an eye. But landed property cannot be removed.

The judge went on to accuse Muir of 'poisoning the minds of the common people and preparing them for rebellion', before finally concluding, 'I leave it with you and have no doubt of your returning such a verdict as will do you honour.'

By then it was well into the early hours of 31 August, as the courts in Scotland at that time normally sought to conclude business in one day. However, given the lateness of the hour and the importance of the case, Braxfield adjourned until later that same day. Therefore, it was early afternoon on 31 August that the court reconvened and Muir returned to learn what his fate would be.

With the courtroom packed with Muir's friends and supporters, the jury and the judges filed in. Muir impassively sat in the dock as the jury was asked for their verdict and the foreman unsurprisingly stated that they had found him guilty. The judge thanked them, and once again demonstrated his complete disdain for judicial impartiality by saying that 'the court highly approves of the verdict you have given' after previously whispering to a juror who passed by him and imploring him to convict 'ane o' thae damned scoundrels'.

The conviction had been expected by all, no doubt even Muir. What was still in doubt was the sentence. Muir's reference to the scaffold in his speech was hyperbole and a prison sentence was the likely punishment, but the length of imprisonment remained in question. Radicals convicted in earlier cases had received terms that varied from three to nine months. However, statements from the bench had been growing ever more threatening since these earlier sentences and Muir was the figurehead who was in the sights of the establishment. A heavier sentence was expected but few anticipated the severity of what followed.

A brief discussion took place between the judges and it was clear that Muir's sentence was going to be harsh. It was also evident that it was not a punishment for his actions but for his ideas. Braxfield commented that the 'indecent applause which was given the prisoner last night convinced me that a spirit of discontent still lurks in the minds of the people and it would be dangerous to allow him to remain in this country'. Braxfield then venomously pronounced that Muir's punishment was to be transported for fourteen years.

Muir was led from the court back to the Tolbooth where he remained pending transfer to hulks in London and then onwards by prison ship to his exile in Australia. Whilst conviction and punishment had been expected no one, and probably not even Muir himself, had anticipated how severe the ruling would be. Given the severity of the sentence, it is harsh to accuse Muir of thinking of himself as a martyr. Doubtless, Muir was willing to endure punishment in support of the cause he passionately believed in, but he must have believed that voluntary exile would have been a better option.

Despite their political persuasions even the jury were aghast when the verdict was announced. They considered sending a petition to the court to ask for leniency but decided against it, when one juror received an anonymous death threat. Legal and establishment figures were also shocked by the harshness of the judgment and the flagrant abuse of judicial process. The Earl of Lauderdale, an advocate and a leading Whig member of the House of Lords, raised the case with the Home Secretary, arguing that the sentence was unlawful. Such was his prestige that it was referred to the Lord Justice Clerk for consideration. But, the request to review the judgment imposed by Braxfield himself was swiftly rejected.

Passions were running high and anger as well as sadness swept throughout the ranks of the radicals. But the crackdown was underway and the authorities allowed the accused no respite nor did they show them mercy. Muir was soon to be joined in custody by another of his compatriots, as less than a fortnight after the verdict, the Reverend Thomas Fyshe Palmer appeared for trial.

Palmer had been arrested on 2 August just as Muir was returning to Scotland. Charged with sedition, he was released on bail and appeared for trial at the High Court in Perth on 12 September. This time it was not Lord Braxfield but Lord Abercromby and Lord Eskgrove who were presiding, the latter having also sat in the Muir case. Judicial partiality and prejudice were once again displayed throughout the hearing.

The Unitarian minister was charged with sedition. In June he had attended a meeting of an organisation known as the Friends of Liberty in Dundee. George Mealmaker was also at the gathering and had brought with him an address that he had drafted. Given his sympathies and his education, Palmer helped to amend it. If anything, it appears that he toned the text down so that it became an opposition to taxation for war and a call for universal suffrage. Although it was hardly revolutionary, it still expressed dangerous sentiments in the eyes of the establishment. The address was sent to the printers the following month and this appears to have been Palmer's only involvement with the document. However, this act provided the pretext for his arrest, but undoubtedly the real reason was the leading role he played in the Dundee reform movement.

The venue for the case was Perth rather than Edinburgh and Palmer was represented by an advocate. A challenge was made by Palmer's team that questioned the relevancy of the charge, but emulating the partisanship of Lord Braxfield, Lord Eskgrove responded:

> I do for one hold that the liberty of this country is doubtless closely connected with the right to petition the legislature. But if any man shall think it proper to call meetings and collect together mechanics, and those whose education and circumstances do not entitle or qualify them to judge matters of legislation, people ignorant altogether of the very grievances which they are told they are loaded with, the case is exceedingly different.

The evidence against Palmer was not only patchy, but Mealmaker even testified that he was the author of the document. This information was accepted without challenge but simply pushed aside, with Palmer's minor contributions viewed as seditious in themselves. Palmer delivered his own account with less passion than Muir but with equal sincerity, which confirmed both his gentle nature and his belief in non-violence. He stated that his cause was 'common justice, benevolence and humanity' and added that:

> These considerations induced me to connect myself with the Society of the Friends of Liberty. I thought that parliamentary Reform, was intimately connected with human happiness – with the establishment and security of the British Empire. With this view, as God is my witness, I joined the society of weavers and mechanics, as your Lordships call them; and to gain such ends, had I any connection with this handbill. The test of the society, and their endeavours, so far as I have known them, have all been confined to this one point – Parliamentary Reform.

When it came to the charge to the handpicked jury the judges were unmoved by Palmer's plea for clemency and continued in the manner in which they had commenced. They reminded the jury that the handbill had been printed with the political backdrop of the French Revolution, Paine having poisoned the minds of the supposed lower classes, and implied that Palmer was actively involved in sowing discontent. In summing up, Lord Abercromby firmly told the jury about their responsibilities:

> Gentlemen, you have been told that reform is a fair and proper object. It may be so. The right of universal suffrage is a right which the subjects of this country never enjoyed, and were they to enjoy it they would not long enjoy either liberty or a free constitution. You will therefore consider whether telling the people that they have a just right to what would unquestionably be tantamount to a total

subversion of this constitution, is such a writing as any person is entitled to compose, to print and so to publish.

This sounded more like a demand of the jury than a reprise of the evidence. Again, the proceedings dragged on and it was late in the day when the court adjourned. But it was no surprise when the following morning the jury unanimously returned a guilty verdict. Despite his meek manner and his clerical vocation there was to be no mercy for Palmer. His education and employment were seemingly considered to be aggravating factors by the bench. Doubtless, the judges harboured contempt for this man from a good social background who was not just associating with, but actively supporting, the 'lower orders'. This became evident during sentencing when the following statement was given: 'A man of liberal education, of his station, appearance, knowledge, talents, had poisoned the minds of the lower orders by encouraging working men to believe that they had the right of universal suffrage.'[3] For this crime, their Lordships had no hesitation in imposing a sentence of seven years' transportation.

Despite the loss of two leading stalwarts and the harshness of the sentences that had been handed down, morale amongst the radicals appears to have remained remarkably high. Some fled and others, particularly those who had come from the burgh and reform movements, had long since drifted away. But many persisted and seem to have remained committed to the cause, although some must have had a sense of foreboding.

Radical activity had continued since Muir had first departed for England and then France, although a few societies had wilted under the growing pressure. In the early months of the year in Edinburgh, the Abbeyhill Society burned its books and the Lawnmarket Society suspended its meetings. However, in other places the outbreak of war seemed to spur on radical sentiment. Public petitions were circulating at the time and both society members and indeed government spies confirmed that these were being eagerly signed by those who belonged to the societies as well as ordinary members of the public. The west of Scotland seems to have been particularly active as the public opposition to the war with France created a receptive audience.

Therefore it was the increasingly determined and committed delegates who met again on 30 April 1793. The discussions that took place lasted until 3 May and were again held in Edinburgh. This became known as the Second National Convention although it had neither the sense of importance nor the level of attendance of the launch event. Attendee numbers were down in comparison to the First National Convention, although given what was going on in the background that is perfectly understandable. The pressures from the authorities and loyalist associations had been mounting and fears were rising following the outbreak of war. There is also no doubt that there had been a drop-off in the membership numbers in societies in the early months of the year.

But some of this decline appears to have been geographically focused, with the collapse greatest in Edinburgh where membership was more diverse and the power of the state greater. It affected other areas too, for example, there were reports from the Lothians of the corrosive influence of church and landowners. However, in other areas, such as the west and the weaving villages, the effect seemed marginal or non-existent. These areas were clearly insulated from the growing levels of pressure and protected by the solidarity of the community.

It doubtless reflected the changes that were taking place within the membership of the societies as they became more working class. For example, in Perth there were more societies but fewer delegates and this would have been the case in other areas. Those who were less wealthy and more beholden to work commitments were limited in their ability to attend society meetings but were nonetheless active locally. Finally, whether as a result of the reduction of initial pressures or following the growing anxiety about the war, radical society membership stabilised and even increased in many areas. Accordingly, 116 delegates from some twenty-eight towns and villages met for the

Second National Convention, which was once again held in Edinburgh, and although some societies had dropped out, many others managed to attend. For example, there were no representatives from Stirling this time, although there were some from Selkirk (a list of delegates is included in Appendix A).

There were few who attended that had been at the First National Convention and the social make-up was vastly different. Gone were the Edinburgh advocates, who were replaced by working-class representatives. This seemed to change the direction of the discussions and the moderates began to struggle to stop a rising radical tone. A motion was put forward calling for the convention to demand 'their rights as men and as Britons'.[4] This was ultimately withdrawn but provided an interesting reference to a pan-British solution and also an emphasis on the rights of men. This was therefore viewed as a move from simple parliamentary reform to much wider demands, as detailed in Paine's writings. Likewise, motions against the war were postponed, with delegates being prevailed upon to simply concentrate on parliamentary reform.

Parliamentary activities were ongoing and a petition to Parliament for reform was debated in May 1793. Despite the substantial numbers who had signed the document, the move was comfortably defeated by the Tory majority. Of Scotland's representatives, just thirteen MPs supported it. This parliamentary defeat of liberal Whigs attempting to achieve some progress seems to have been the catalyst for a change in the reform movement south of the border. With the wider political atmosphere growing ever-more hostile because of war with France and concern increasing about radicalism, many moderate reformers in England gave up campaigning and some even gave the cause up entirely. In some ways this mirrored what had been happening in Scotland, with the burgh and county reform supporters drifting away.

Muir and Fyshe Palmer's convictions did not lead to a collapse of the movement, although it must have had an effect on overall numbers, with societies feeling a variety of pressures. Perhaps it was simply anger that spurred them on at the injustice meted out to colleagues. Alternatively, it may have been a belief in the justness of their cause, which as Muir had said would ultimately triumph. Revolution in France was not subsiding and discontent in Scotland was growing. Some might have thought that it was simply a matter of time before the old order crumbled and the new world was born.

Whilst many enjoyed relative obscurity and safety in their weaving communities, defiance was still widespread. Even in Edinburgh, just days after Muir's conviction and the week before Palmer's trial, the Canongate Friends of the People held a meeting which was attended by over 200 people. The attendees declared full support for their colleague and resolved that:

> So far from fainting in the day of evil … they would immediately proceed to renovate their various societies before the sitting down of Parliament, on purpose to make-up their minds about another application for redress of grievances and restoration of rights; that, with the same purpose, they would also immediately proceed to cultivate a more intimate correspondence with all the societies of Parliamentary reform in the Kingdom.

The battle cry of the radicals declared that they would continue the struggle and that they did. The threats against prominent radicals persisted; Skirving had been charged by the authorities but not yet brought to trial. But this did not stop him from supporting Palmer, as he had Muir at his trial. Indeed, ever since Muir had first departed for France Skirving began to rise to the fore. As he already had a pivotal position in the leadership and was an educated man his rise to prominence was perhaps understandable, but he also rose to the occasion in an attempt to rally the radicals. His growing influence undoubtedly helped to push the societies in a more radical direction.

Attending the court in Perth for Palmer's trial, he arranged for a shorthand writer to take notes. When these were transcribed, they were quickly published in pamphlet form and distributed far and wide through the reform societies. Although there may have been fear amongst many, there was still determination amongst most to continue the fight.

Anger in radical circles went far beyond the Scottish borders. The London Corresponding Society and other reform groups in England publicly professed their admiration and support for Muir and Palmer. Even amongst moderate Whig circles there was outrage at the manner in which these individuals were convicted. Although the pressure from loyalist groups was far greater in England, the courts were much more impartial and fair. There was no replication of the injustices delivered north of the border. Indeed, there appears to have been widespread incredulity at the extent of the partisanship of the Scottish judiciary. Unsuccessful attempts were even made to challenge the judgments in Parliament, although this was not made by the Scottish Tory MPs. Charles Fox, the leader of the Whig opposition, even stated, 'God help the people who have such judges' in Parliament.[5]

When news reached France, the events were mentioned at the National Convention where the old enmity with England resurfaced. The Scottish radicals were lauded for defending the principles of the French Revolution and for 'meriting the honour of being persecuted by the British Government'.[6] The news of the trials even travelled across the Atlantic to the United States where sympathies very much lay with the Scottish radicals and reformers, particularly given the fact that the Americans had already been through their revolution. Muir was acknowledged as a martyr in the United States, and his speech from the dock quickly found him fame; in due course he benefited from this sympathy through the provision of American assistance.

With reform organisations becoming more radical on both sides of the border, it was only natural that they would open up communication and seek to forge alliances. Lines of correspondence had been opened up and the links were already established both following the establishment of the Friends of the People and subsequently as a result of Muir's endeavours in the January when he had visited England before travelling on to France. But this collaboration would only develop over time. However, given the concerns over the Scottish links to the United Irishmen this was a dangerous alliance for the radicals and it posed huge risks.

The Friends of the People in Scotland sought to increase the cooperation with other organisations, including the London Corresponding Society and other more radical constitutional groups. Skirving, seemingly without prior approval, entered into correspondence with other organisations and began alluding to the organisation of a gathering of delegates from across the country. The idea of cross-border cooperation seems to have been initiated by Skirving although he undoubtedly would have had the support of close allies. Wider cooperation was something that had long been supported and advocated by radicals in Ireland. Their networks and contacts were more extensive but their agenda was different in many ways. Muir was obviously close to the United Irishmen, and this perhaps reflected or even helped in the formation of his nationalist views, whilst Skirving seemed to be more focused on the pan-British reform of Parliament.

However, due to the fact that the radical faction was in the ascendency of the Scottish reform societies, Skirving's overtures were privately rejected by the London Friends of the People, who believed that such beliefs were improper, which reflected how they were controlled by moderate if not aristocratic forces. Other more radical societies south of the border reacted not just favourably, but with excitement to growing discontent in Scotland. As a result, invitations for a formal gathering were sent out to many and accepted by the LCS and other societies in London and Sheffield.

With radicals on the rise on both sides of the border, Skirving would soon be joined in Edinburgh by Maurice Margarot and Joseph Gerrald. A British Convention was about to take place, but this would also seal their fate.

CHAPTER 8

THE BRITISH CONVENTION MEETS AND THE OTHER MARTYRS STAND TRIAL

With the determination of the dedicated radicals in Scotland matched by a willingness of organisations in England to collaborate, another convention was organised for 29 October 1793. Held at the Masons' Lodge, Blackfriars Wynd, in Edinburgh, the event was attended by 160 delegates, though the majority of these were from Edinburgh and Glasgow. The fraternal delegates from England had not arrived by the time the convention adjourned four days later and the same applied to the Society of United Irishmen who had also been invited. Their lack of attendance appears to have been the fault of Skirving, who despite his undoubted enthusiasm for the cause, was not so capable when it came to his administrative duties. The parties were given less than one week's notice, which was inadequate to make travel arrangements, let alone secure the organisational approval that would have been required for those residing in Ireland and England.

But the convention proceeded despite the absence of English and Irish fraternal delegates. The Scottish representatives spent a lot of time discussing formalities and dealing with bureaucracy. The gathering also provided an opportunity to exchange information about what was happening in individual areas of the country, as well as the chance to meet and mingle with kindred spirits. Despite all of the travails leading up to it, the meeting was far less cautious than the previous convention, which indicated that there was either an increased sense of confidence or a disregard for the possible consequences amongst the attendees.

The delegates arranged to send letters of support to Muir and Palmer and opened an assistance fund for them. They also reaffirmed their call for universal suffrage and annual parliaments. A discussion about the war also took place and a petition against it was agreed to be sent to the crown but more radical action was also discussed. The convention then adjourned until the following April.

Government spies were monitoring the situation and the authorities were concerned, despite there being little more said or done than what was already known. Reports circulated at the time confirmed that almost all of the societies that had been established the year before were still in existence. Moreover, the support for such groups was deep-rooted and was being sustained by events on the continent, where the revolutionaries were still making progress. The broader strength of the reform societies rather than the convention itself was what really concerned the establishment.

There had been concern about Muir's continued presence in the Tolbooth and the authorities considered moving him to London, although this had not yet been carried out. Anxiety amongst government leaders was rising and this was exacerbated by events a few days later when the delegates from Ireland and England finally arrived for the convention. From this point on, both public and private discussions became far more radical and were of greater concern.

Delegates from England reached Edinburgh on 6 November, including Maurice Margarot and Joseph Gerrald. Others attending included Charles Sinclair, originally from Edinburgh but then the secretary of another London reform organisation, and Mathew Brown from a Sheffield society. They were fêted on their arrival; the Scots were delighted to have allies from elsewhere, which served to boost their morale and heightened the significance of the gathering. Although the convention had adjourned a few days before, a further meeting was hastily called for 19 November. This supplanted the earlier convention and as a result of its increased importance, it was formally referred to as the British Convention.

Made welcome by their hosts, the English delegates agreed to stay on for the coming event. Whilst they waited, they made use of their time, and their celebrity status, to satisfy the hunger amongst the Scottish groups to hear about the situation in England. This eagerness to hear news of the events in England was not just felt in the Edinburgh societies with which they were staying, but in other groups both near and far. Margarot inaugurated a society in Broughton, and Gerrald spoke to a reform meeting in Penicuik. But the authorities were more concerned about Margarot travelling to Paisley in January, where his visit was either the cause of, or coincided with, a large open-air meeting. As a result of this event, three local men who were believed to be ringleaders were arrested.

By this point the United Irishmen had also arrived, getting there a few days before their English counterparts. Hamilton Rowan, who had been a signatory to the address that resulted in Muir's conviction and had met with him in Dublin, was joined by William Drennan and Simon Butler, who was the society president. Their attendance was soon noticed by the authorities, who had no doubt been tracking their movements since they left Ireland. As a result, Hamilton Rowan was detained. When he was questioned by the Sheriff he denied that he was attending the convention and indeed departed on the 8 November, well before the event took place.

Whether his departure was planned or a consequence of his interrogation is not known. However, what is clear is that he networked extensively whilst in Scotland and even went to meet Muir in the Tolbooth. Perhaps he felt guilt for having persuaded him to return to the country or maybe he simply wanted to inform him about the group's planned activities. But certainly, Rowan encouraged radicalism amongst the Scots. The evening before his departure he dined with Scottish delegates and regaled them about the situation in Ireland. His colleague Simon Butler explained what was happening in Ireland, where he had just been released after serving a six-month prison sentence. The situation in Ireland and the planned actions that the United Irishmen discussed lit a spark amongst many Scottish radicals and these comments made by Butler and his colleagues would later resurface at the convention.

The presence of the Society of United Irishmen unnerved the authorities and the fears about discontent and disturbances grew. This resulted in Muir being shackled before he was finally placed on an excise yacht in the Forth and dispatched to the Thames. The authorities intended to allow the convention to proceed but would watch it carefully. There had been correspondence going back and forth between Robert and Henry Dundas about the best way to react to the events and the necessary security precautions, which demonstrated the growing concerns amongst the ranks of the establishment.

And so, the British Convention took place in Edinburgh on 19 November 1793. The presence of the English reformers further energised the Scots and with the radicals now firmly in control of proceedings, the event was always going to be more controversial than previous conventions. The English delegates brought ideas for how the event should be organised, including preparations for an emergency convention as a backstop to any break-up of proceedings, as well as the allocation of work through French-style divisions. Such developments alarmed the authorities.

At prior meetings and in discussions at the convention, the English delegates waxed lyrical about the strength of the cause south of the border, although some of the suggestions made about the numbers of supporters were clearly fanciful. At the dinner hosted by Hamilton

Rowan before the Irishman departed, Margarot boasted that whole towns in England were dedicated to the reform movement and that the Sheffield area alone had 50,000 members. He even suggested that a joint meeting of the Scots and English could gather 600,000 to 700,000 attendees. Regardless of whether this was fanciful or not, it had the effect of further steeling the resolve of the Scots.

The mood on that first day was therefore buoyant, if not jubilant. The delegates continued to address one another as 'citizen' and other French revolutionary terms, mannerisms and procedures were adopted, despite war with France having broken out. The formal title for the meeting was changed to 'the British Convention of the Delegates of the Friends of the People associated to obtain Universal Suffrage and Annual Parliaments'. Revolutionary anthems were sung and the dating system for the event even copied the one used across the English Channel and it was thus described as the 'first year of the British Convention'. At the end of the proceedings, those assembled then joined hands to celebrate what was described as an important 'epoch in the history of their country'.[1] This statement again confirms that the intention of the societies in Scotland at this time was political reform in London, rather than any revocation of the Treaty of Union.

The convention also partly reflected the lack of progress that had been made by the Scottish reform societies. With the war against France raging on and the growing pressure surrounding the earlier conventions, doubts had been raised by some individuals about the direction of the movement; one delegate even proposed winding up the group. Progress was not being made and working with England seemed to be an opportunity to regroup and drive on. Equally, it also suited those who wished to pursue a more radical agenda.

Compounding all of these factors was the worsening economic situation. In itself, the war was costly, but it also interfered with the practice of trade. Standards of living were falling and deprivation and unemployment were rising. The church and other charitable organisations were struggling and towns and communities were required to look for other ways to provide relief for the destitute. For example, Glasgow and Paisley had to establish their own relief schemes that were funded by wealthier citizens.

As ever in Scotland, enlistment and emigration offered an alternative life for many. It was estimated that in 1793, 5,000 men joined the army from Glasgow alone, driven by the pressures of war and poverty. In addition, the removal of the population from the land was not simply happening in the north with the arrival of sheep and the departure of people. In October 1793 two ships sailed out of the Clyde 'full of emigrants consisting of Manufacturers Bleachers & two persons have been sent from America on purpose to entice them'.[2] With a variety of skills being sought in the New World, many others set sail across the Atlantic.

For those who remained in Scotland economic pressures continued to mount, alongside political pressures. Wages continued to decrease and some individuals who chose not to emigrate had to return to the rural areas from whence they had come. This reduced the strength of the reform societies and sapped the will of the remaining members. It has also been suggested that early radicalism was a symbol of relative economic prosperity and the fact that many members were from the affluent classes serves to support this. But, as 1793 drew to a close, the middle-ranking members were leaving the reform movement as a result of political pressures, whilst some working-class members were leaving as a result of economic pressures. The result was that those who remained were mainly working class and held much more radical beliefs.

The British Convention was thus a more radical gathering than those that had come before. This was partly caused by the injection of enthusiasm from the delegates who attended from England and Ireland, but was also as a result of the attendance of the more militant Scottish working-class reformers. 'Their sense of injustice was more profound, their language more uncompromising' and this was made evident in the debates that took place.[3] Discussions on the lack of availability of education for the children of the poor and other similar class-based grievances were raised. George Mealmaker made a passionate plea that an address to the people be prepared to set out the group's grievances. The more radical mood was also shared by the delegates who visited Muir and Palmer at the Tolbooth, displaying solidarity and a refusal to be bowed by authority.

The coming together of English and Scottish societies with the United Irishmen in the background had already alarmed the authorities, but the actions that were agreed after a discussion on events in Ireland was a much greater cause for concern. Simon Butler recounted that the Convention Act had been passed by the Irish Parliament in April, which was the equivalent of the suspension of *habeas corpus*, which required that a detained person was brought before a judge or court. This was obviously an attack on the radical movement and resulted in a reaction by the United Irishmen. The group was preparing to defend itself if attacked and had arranged for a secret committee to operate if this occurred.

At the British Convention there were fears amongst Scottish and English radicals that similar actions would be taken by the authorities against them. Accordingly, it was agreed that a secret committee be established, which would act as an emergency convention in the event of a similar bill being proposed in Britain or other events happening, such as the suspension of *habeas corpus* or military intervention. Although this precautionary measure might have been suggested by the visiting Irish delegation, it was supported by Joseph Gerrald, who suggested that the Convention Act had been 'passed in Ireland to feel the pulse of the people in Britain, that our rulers might know if it beat high with indignation, or if the blood run coldly in our veins'.[4] This rallying call was unanimously supported and on the final day of the gathering reference was even made that if the current convention was broken up, then delegates should reassemble at an agreed spot. The resolve of the radicals was hardening.

Pan-British cooperation was also to be increased, building upon the exchange of correspondence and the attendance of fraternal delegates. As with the initial decision to refer to the meeting as the British Convention, discussion also took place about forging cross-border links and Margarot even suggested that there should be a general union between the two groups. This was something that had also been raised in individual Scottish societies before the convention, which indicated that it was not simply inspired by the visitors. This collaboration appears to have been unanimously agreed upon, although given the practicalities involved with logistics and communications, it would likely have meant that the societies and the national groups would have remained distinct.

A motion in support of the Society of United Irishmen was also unanimously passed and a solemn holding of hands took place. It would appear that the distinct position of Ireland as a sovereign nation was accepted and, although the Irish were fighting for similar rights as those sought in Scotland and England, the group's nationalist political direction was acknowledged. However, although separate organisations existed in Scotland, reform was still being sought on a pan-Britain basis. This again served as evidence that aside from a few individuals, the Treaty of Union was not being challenged.

In any event the authorities had had enough. In addition to the convention itself, the meeting had attracted widespread publicity in the newspapers. Growing radicalism in Scotland was bad enough, but wider cooperation with English reformers and especially the United Irishmen was extremely worrying. The format that the British Convention adopted compounded all of this. Britain was now at war with revolutionary France but 'it invited the charge not only that it wished to introduce French – and therefore republican – principles of government, but that it was thereby representing itself as a legislative, not as a petitioning body'.[5]

As far as the authorities were concerned a line had been crossed and the British Convention had to be immediately shut down and the leading members arrested. As a result, early on 5 December Skirving, Margarot and Gerrald were all detained along with a few others. The two English delegates were arrested early in the morning at the room that they were sharing in the Black Bull Inn. Later that evening the Lord Provost accompanied by some thirty constables moved in to disperse the convention.

Despite that crackdown, the delegates seem to have been remarkably committed, reassembling the following evening where they were joined by Margarot and Gerrald, who had been released on bail. That meeting was again broken up by the authorities and as the Sheriff and his officers approached Gerrald exclaimed: 'Behold, the funeral torches of Liberty.'[6] His words would prove to be prophetic for him and his colleagues.

These events brought an end to the British Convention, but for some individuals much worse was to follow. Skirving, Margarot and Gerrald were all indicted on charges of sedition. Others were also prosecuted, whilst some chose to flee, for example, Alexander Scott who had taken over as editor of the *Edinburgh Gazetteer* opted to escape. As a justification he subsequently wrote:

> If my cause be good and if I am conscious of my innocence, why did I not stand trial? MEN OF SCOTLAND, hear my answer – The goodness of my cause has itself been my offence; for, to knaves and hirelings, what is so offensive as Virtue and Truth? And that innocence is not a shield is evidence, since men, supported by integrity and enabled by talents to defend those principles which they spoke, and which I only printed, have fallen victims to a brutal and ignorant Bench, and a corrupt, trembling, and packed Jury.[7]

Scott had already judged that he would not receive a fair trial and therefore decided to flee. It has been suggested that another individual who was indicted might have become a government spy as his case was subsequently dropped, although it may have simply been that the other figures who were detained were a higher priority for the authorities. Why those that remained chose not to flee is not known. Maybe they intended to defend the cause like Muir, maybe they were higher profile and were being watched closely by the authorities or maybe they simply felt that they could not bear to be parted from their friends and family and decided to stay put.

Whatever reason they had for remaining, they did not have to wait long for their trials. William Skirving was first up on 6 January 1794. He chose to represent himself but the fact that he did not have a lawyer was not the reason why he was convicted, even if he did not handle the case especially well. Some historical interpretations of his trial in particular, as well as some of his fellow martyrs more generally, have focused on the legal failings of the defence. It certainly seems that in procedural and conduct terms this might be correct and the defendants would have benefited from better counsel. But whether this would have made any difference to their fates is a different question.

Such interpretations all appear to assess the trials through the prism of commentators at the time from a legal rather than a political perspective. Some of the criticism is also based either on interpretations from, or comparisons with, the English legal system. However, the English courts were far fairer and good legal counsel could and did make a difference. Thomas Hardy of the LCS was prosecuted in late spring 1794 when a further clampdown swept across Britain and Ireland but he was acquitted after trial. Other English reformers were likewise either not charged, or at least given a fair trial.

There were many reasons for this discrepancy between legal practice across the border. Leading reformers in England were often part of the Whig opposition and formed part of the establishment itself; the legal profession and courts were bigger and more influential in England

and thus less susceptible to political direction; and the elite were likely to have felt less threatened as there was a greater sense of loyalism present across the country.

All of these factors and more combined to produce a judiciary in Scotland that was prejudiced and did the bidding of an establishment that was deeply fearful of change and particularly radical change. In reality it was also the unique social and economic make-up of Scotland that dictated how the judiciary operated. The power of the small elite of landowners was even greater in Scotland and the country was under the hegemony of a few individuals, such as the Dundas family, whose vested interests were very much threatened by change and they therefore reacted accordingly. This was their fiefdom and they defended it viciously, as other such potentates have done around the world over the centuries.

The court's position had already been made clear by the Lord President Ilay Campbell the year before. Campbell's post was the most senior judicial position and even ranked above Braxfield. He demonstrated that for all the vituperative and spiteful asides made by individual judges, judicial prejudice in Scotland was institutional. In January 1793 when the Lord Provost and magistrates were visiting the court, Campbell informed them that:

Those who associate in meetings to devise impracticable and unnecessary plans of reformations, sometimes from good design, and oftener from bad, affect to disdain the pernicious tenets which have been imported to use from another country [i.e. France]. They tell us, they have no view to disturb the peace of society, or to encourage licentiousness. Many of them, it is believed, speak sincerely when they use this language; but perhaps they are not aware that their actions have precisely that effect, whatever their intentions may be; for they have brought men together for the purpose of instilling prejudice into their minds, and making them believe that they feel grievances which do not exist. The consequence of this is obvious. They have not duly considered how dangerous it is to tamper with the minds and passions of uninformed men; and how impossible to say to a mob; 'this far you go, and no further.'[8]

This prejudice was displayed in the trials that followed where Braxfield in particular gave full vent to it, with the support of his colleagues. The trials of Muir and Palmer had resulted in debates in Parliament where MPs sympathetic to modest reform had raised concerns and even suggested that their sentences be postponed pending an inquiry. However, the ministers were quick to defend the judiciary even if they were privately scathing about Braxfield's behaviour. Robert Dundas in particular would broker no deviation from the agreed line and it is clear that court and government were publicly in agreement. The perversity of the situation was encapsulated in the charade where the legal proponent of the prejudice ended up being the political defendant of it. Dundas's uncle likewise staunchly defended the interests of the state. Henry Dundas was visited by leading liberal Whigs who were concerned about the nature of the trials of Muir and Palmer, some of whom had visited the inmates in their prison hulks on the Thames. Whatever assurances Dundas gave to them about seeking to ensure due process, he was privately encouraging repression.

Accordingly, these proceedings were not fair trials according to natural justice. Instead they were highly political show trials and, irrespective of what legal tactics had been implemented or arguments deployed, the conviction of the defendants and the imposition of a severe sentence was always going to follow. Legal technicalities concerning the law of sedition were irrelevant in light of the wider political atmosphere. The idea that Braxfield and his cohort were going to be persuaded by the legal submissions of learned counsel is absurd. Those appearing in the dock were doomed and they knew it. It was for this reason that the defendants sought to treat the proceedings as political trials.

In today's court system the defendants may have chosen to refuse to recognise the jurisdiction of the court or sought to highlight how the system is corrupt. But we live in different times. These individuals saw their trials as providing a platform from which they could articulate their cause and have it reported to a wider audience. So instead many of them chose to face trial; some relied on legal counsel and others chose not to have a lawyer, but they all challenged the judicial system that was judging them.

When Skirving appeared for trial he came up against a stony-faced bench under the direction of Lord Braxfield and a jury composed of members of loyalist associations. Skirving objected to the jury and the response from the bench was condemnatory. Lord Eskgrove, who was sitting along with Braxfield, remarked:

> This gentleman's objection is, that his jury ought to consist of the convention of the Friends of the People; that every person wishing to support government is incapable of passing upon his assize. And by making this objection, this panel is avowing that it was their purpose to overturn the government.

This is a telling example of the establishment's fear of the mobilisation of the uneducated, articulated through their legal representatives. Having apparently already decided upon Skirving's guilt, the court turned to hear some evidence to justify their decision. The evidence that was laid out, as with the other political trials before and after, was weak but was more than sufficient to ensure his conviction. Skirving declined to give evidence in his own defence and various individuals have criticised him for this. But what purpose would this have served? The court had already made up its mind and his fate had already been sealed. Although he did not give evidence, Skirving still sought to use the court as a platform for promoting his views. In his final plea to the bench, he stated:

Conscious of innocence, my Lords, and that I am not guilty of the crimes laid to my charge, this sentence can only affect me as the sentence of man. It is long since I laid aside the fear of man as my rule. I know that what has been done these two days will be rejudged. That is my comfort, and all my hope.

His appeal fell on deaf ears and when the court returned the following day to pronounce the verdict, he was condemned to transportation for fourteen years.

The following week, on 13 January 1794, it was Margarot's turn in the dock and by all accounts the prejudice that he experienced was even worse. The evidence indicated that Margarot was known as being an educated and clever individual and as a result was regarded as being more dangerous than his fellow prisoners. However, the fact that Margarot objected in open court to the bias of the bench at the outset of proceedings would have also further enraged the court.

The tensions in the courtroom and the community had been rising and this must have fed through to the judges who lived in what was still the small city of Edinburgh. Sympathy for the accused radicals had been growing and support for the accused had been publicly voiced. Margarot was escorted from the Black Bull Inn in the Grassmarket to the court by friends and radicals who were carrying a tree of liberty shaped like the letter 'M' and inscribed with 'Liberty, Virtue, Reason, Justice and Truth'.

Amidst rising tensions the Lord Provost and Sheriff Substitute led a group of sailors and constables armed with bludgeons to attack the group escorting Margarot to the court. Ostensibly, the authorities were seeking to quell any disorder that could arise as a result of the proceedings. However, in reality this was an orchestrated attack by the state upon an unarmed crowd in an attempt to intimidate and disperse the radical supporters who had gathered to show solidarity with Margarot.

Margarot was uninjured in the fracas but was removed by constables and taken bodily to the High Court for his trial. His ordeal had begun and the tone of how things were to unfold had been made clear. He began his defence by challenging the right of the court to try him and stated that Braxfield had already prejudged him through statements the judge had made at a dinner party. The judge had allegedly stated that the members of the British Convention deserved to be whipped and transported and added that 'the mob would be the better for the spilling of a little blood'.[9] Despite the outrageous nature of this statement, which Braxfield appeared not to deny, the motion was swiftly repelled and the trial continued.

The evidence led by the prosecution was once again insufficient and mostly based on political opposition to reform. The argument was made that calls for franchise were sufficient to justify a sedition charge, despite there being no mention of revolution or even a call to arms. As with Skirving's refusal to give evidence in his own defence, some commentators – primarily those from legal backgrounds – have criticised Margarot for his opening remarks, viewing them as incendiary and thereby sealing his fate. Indeed, the court did in fact comment that his speech to the jury was seditious in and of itself, regardless of the charges of which he was accused.

However, this argument assumes that an alternative verdict was possible or that a severe sentence was ever in doubt. As with Muir, Margarot must have known what his fate would be, but was determined to state his case. In his closing oration, which was less eloquent than Muir's remarks, but delivered in an equally forceful manner, Margarot highlighted the prejudice he and his co-defendants had faced and stated: 'Because we are poor it is sedition in us, but when your county meetings are held, it is no longer sedition, but is a thing that is authorized.'

Margarot then exclaimed that Britain was under the iron heel of a despotic government, which was levying massive taxes on the poor, sympathised with the rich and was making war. In a criticism of mass unemployment and poverty he added: 'It has been a decided plan of those in power, to plunder the poor to give to the rich.'[10]

At this point in British history class politics had not yet been developed, but Margarot most certainly was an early exponent of what was to come. His conviction was always certain but his fiery denunciation of the system provided further justification for the court. Again, a sentence of fourteen years' transportation was handed down.

Gerrald's trial did not take place until March but the outcome was to be the same. Conducted over several days in the middle of the month the crown case was again feeble, but more than adequate to secure his conviction. Gerrald did seek the services of an advocate but due to his ill health he struggled to obtain one. Many advocates would have wished to avoid tarnishing their reputation by representing political radicals, but the one who was ultimately appointed by the court declined for different reasons. Malcolm Laing was an able advocate and a committed reformer. He stated that the reason that he did not want to represent Gerrald was that he would not be granted a fair trial. It appears as if Braxfield relished the opportunity to force the honest lawyer to take on the case.

Being legally represented made not one whit of difference in Gerrald's proceedings. An objection was made about a member of the jury who had openly stated that he would condemn any member of the British Convention. Despite the allegations being unchallenged, the representations were rejected and the trial proceeded. Similarly to the other trials, Gerrald's advocate did not lead evidence in his defence. The prosecution made reference to everything, from events in France to those in the USA. Gerrald's counsel countered with valid legal and constitutional points, and even made reference to the suffering of Christ, but all in vain.

Gerrald also made a speech to the jury, which was just as passionate as his co-defendants, but was delivered in a different style.

Ill health and a quiet disposition meant that he eschewed much of the flamboyance or fiery rhetoric of others but did not shirk from defending his cause or beliefs, and argued trenchantly: 'I glory in being the advocate of a cause, with which is complicated truth, justice and freedom, which I know must and will ultimately triumph.' The jury had already decided on Gerrald's fate and a guilty verdict was returned in less than half an hour. A sentence of fourteen years' transportation followed.

Despite the intimidation techniques and even the violence perpetrated against them, sympathy for the radicals had persisted. The poet Thomas Campbell, who was then just sixteen years old, had walked from Glasgow to witness Gerrald's trial. As the defence closed its case, he remarked to someone sitting next to him that the accused was a great man and his neighbour concurred. The stranger then added, 'he is not only a great man himself, but he makes every other man feel great who listens to him'.[11] As with all of the other trials, the courtroom was packed and it is likely that many of the other attendees agreed with this sentiment. However, sympathy was one thing and practical support was another.

English radical societies condemned what had happened to their Scottish colleagues and sought to show solidarity. But there was little that they could do other than visit the condemned who were already being held in hulks on the Thames and offer their commiserations. The printing of pamphlets and the denunciation of the Scottish judiciary continued but it had little effect. However, support for the martyrs had spread far further than just across Britain and Ireland. In America the cases added to the interest and anger already caused by the plight of Muir. Meanwhile, in France more practical steps were taken and the government even ordered the navy to try and intercept the prison ships when they were bound for Botany Bay, but this amounted to nothing. The challenge of locating the ships, never mind engaging in a confrontation with their naval convoys, made this suggestion impracticable, but that it was considered indicates the esteem with which the Scottish radicals were held.

In early May 1794 the prison ship *Surprize* cast off and set sail for Botany Bay carrying Muir, Palmer, Skirving and Margarot along with other ordinary convicts. Gerrald joined them on a later ship. The voyages would take months but all individuals would arrive safely and a new chapter would open for them on the far-off shores of Australia.

As the radicals licked their wounds the establishment congratulated themselves. In loyalist clubs in England, toasts were made to Robert Dundas and the Scottish judiciary. Henry Dundas sent his nephew a congratulatory note from King George III praising the proceedings. This note highlighted the futility of the convicted in seeking petitions from the crown. Although the Glorious Revolution had made the monarch subject to Parliament, he nonetheless supported the crushing of radicalism.

As spring 1794 arrived further repression would be unleashed and some radicals began to review their philosophy and tactics and consider the direction of the reform movement. Thomas Muir had become more nationalist in his convictions, which was doubtless driven by his relationship with the United Irishmen, and this hardening belief would resurface, just as Muir would in years to come.

Others began to consider whether constitutionalism could ever be successful, given the use of oppression by the authorities. Physical force radicalism was soon to come onto the agenda. Before his transportation, Margarot had written to Thomas Hardy of the LCS from prison in January 1794, stating that armed associations had been established by the rich and asking 'wherefore should the poor not do the same?' He continued: 'Will you stretch forth your necks, like lambs, to the butcher's knife, and, like lambs, content yourselves with bleating?'[12]

In February the otherwise meek-mannered Gerrald had gone even further at a Friends of the People meeting in Edinburgh and suggested that the movement should have an assassination squad as a preliminary to revolution. Gerrald reportedly stated: 'Give me only six whom I can confide in, with daggers apiece and the business is done. Two here, three in London and one in Dublin! Nothing is easier than access to the Chambers of the Aristocrats.'[13] He then gave vent to his loathing of the ruling class and denounced the harm they had caused to the poor. However, those who were listening seemed to advocate delaying taking action rather than demurring from them, which was another sign that the membership was beginning to change, even in Edinburgh.

A further British Convention was proposed as some English radicals also began to review their strategy and countenance revolution rather than constitutionalism. This time the Scots were to attend the event in England as delegates. However, as with the initial establishment of the Friends of the People, some involved in the organisation of the convention appeared to hold back those who wanted to pursue rebellion rather than reform. The Sheffield Constitutional Society wrote to the London Friends of the People early in the year lamenting what might happen in Scotland if the oppression continued, obviously conscious of the potential backlash. The LCS meanwhile seemed intent on trying to hold the constitutional line against calls for greater radicalism. All the time meetings were taking place across the country and the discussions included not just closer cooperation with England but a change in tactics.

The movement was transforming. Although it may have been reduced in numbers, it was moving from being reformist to more revolutionary in nature, and as a result the members began to congregate under secret organisations rather than public societies. At the same time some members were starting to plan armed insurrection.

CHAPTER 9

A CHANGE IN TACTICS AND THE PIKE PLOT

In Scotland the legal onslaught and the severe sentences imposed on political reformers were having an effect. Societies across the land noticed a decline in membership as the fear of arrest spread. Whilst there may have been widespread sympathy for the radical cause, this would have been weighed against the practicalities of daily life. People feared being transported or imprisoned. Threats to business and trade likewise created an atmosphere of fear and intimidation.

In Edinburgh where there had once been twenty societies it was now difficult to find one. In Stirling public meetings stopped and only private gatherings were taking place. This situation was replicated across the country in smaller communities where the prosecution of local radicals had also taken place, albeit with less publicity and with less severe sentences than the trials of the martyrs. However, such cases were still intimidatory enough to dissuade many from joining the cause and meant that people were more cautious about their actions.

But the radical movement was far from defeated. Discontent began to simmer, especially in those areas in the west where the authorities had less influence and less information. There the 'seditious spirit' was said to be being rekindled and Thomas the Rhymer's prophecy regarding 1794 looked as if it might come true:

A mild winter, a cold spring
A bloody summer, and no King[1]

Rumblings and even occasional outbreaks of trouble started to spread, including in Edinburgh despite the collapse of the reform societies in the city. A play called *The Royal Martyr*, which was shown in April 1794 and compared Charles II and Louis XVI, incited heckles from the audience and cries of 'Ça ira' and 'The Sow's Tail to Geordie'. Fist-fights even broke out in the gallery. Both in public and away from the watchful eye of the authorities, many individuals were still prepared to stand up and even promote the radical cause.

In early January 1794 the Sheriff Clerk of Perthshire wrote the following note, which quoted a handbill that had appeared in the area:

> Shall we be free or shall we be Slaves. They call you Rebellious and seditious because you will only be taxed by your own representatives – make good your chains by your courage or seal the loss with all your blood. There is no more time to deliberate – when the Oppressors hard Labours necessitating in forging chains for you – silence would be a crime and inaction a disgrace. The preservation of the rights of Britons is your supreme law. To arms. To arms.[2]

Handbills that were reported as being distributed in Glasgow called on the people 'to take up arms in defence of their liberties'. In Hamilton one appeared which urged the public to 'remember their Friends in Edinburgh' and advocated 'the guillotine as a suitable punishment for Geordy Rex, Pitt, Dundas and Burke', as well as calling for 'a bloody summer and no king'.[3] In Perth again, April 1794 saw graffiti appear on a bridge, which stated: 'Britain must be a republic, liberty and equality.'[4] There were also reports of growing radical discontent in Montrose and Ayrshire.

At this time it was also becoming evident that many of the reform societies were changing their tactics and moving away from constitutionalism to confrontation, and this sentiment also appeared to be spreading. Government spies reported that troops in the west were being suborned and a supposed plot to attack the guards in Glasgow had been mentioned.[5] Likewise, information from the north suggested that workmen who were returning home from the west – likely as a result of the economic climate – had been radicalised and were causing disaffection amongst members of the public.[6]

Reports about radicals in Dundee and elsewhere who were planning for rebellion must have been even more concerning for the authorities. George Mealmaker was described by a government spy as a 'daring and dangerous fellow' and seems to have been at the forefront of the resurgence of radicalism. Reports reached the authorities of plans by the radicals to 'try their strength' and of individuals 'commissioning pistols from Sheffield with daggers or bayonets concealed in them, which upon touching a spring started out'. The following week a report from Edinburgh confirmed the rumours about pistols being manufactured in Sheffield.[7] In Perth, a man called Walter Miller was charged with commissioning guns and bayonets from Birmingham with other individuals planning to distribute them throughout the county. Paisley was also described as being 'in great readiness' for revolt. In East Lothian there were rumours of a rising that was due to take place on the King's birthday in June and other groups already appeared to have armed themselves, as reports were received of men drilling and marching with guns in woods near Auchterarder.

Just as the government was fearful of a French invasion, some radicals were delighted by the prospect, although they were perhaps deluded about how likely it was. Talks of invasion abounded, although at this stage at least none seemed to have been planned. However, this was further evidence that sympathy and support for revolutionary France remained strong amongst many parts of Scottish society. In Edinburgh the Friends of the People were reported as telling soldiers who were serving in fencible regiments being sent south to England that they did not need to go. Fencible corps had been established some two years earlier and although they were military units they were not required to serve outside of Scotland. Similar calls were made in Perthshire to local fencible regiments that were about to be dispatched south and it appears that a mutiny almost broke out. Details were coming in from Glasgow and elsewhere of further attempts of radicals encouraging soldiers to mutiny or desert.

Some of this information was passed on to the government by spies and other events and activities were often just assumed to be taking place. There was obvious concern amongst the establishment about the actions being taken. The building of garrisons that had commenced the year before continued apace. In one report made by a government spy, it was described how the radicals in Glasgow saw the construction of barracks across the country as being a ruse, which was designed to oppress the masses rather than as part of a confrontation with the French; and in this they were right.

Other actions were also taken to monitor discontent and impose order. The offices of Lord Lieutenant and Sheriffs Principal were formally created. Both are now well known, with the former being largely ceremonial and the latter a key component of the judicial structure in Scotland. The posts are also prestigious and the Lord Lieutenant is part of wider relations with the monarchy. However, the establishment of these offices was far less benign, as they were intended to defend the country from invasion by France and also to deal with revolution from within.

The office of Lord Lieutenant had already been established in England and those selected for the posts in Scotland were drawn from the privileged elite as was the case south of the border, for example the Duke of Atholl filled the post in Perthshire and the Duke of Buccleuch took up the office in Midlothian. Instructions to the new appointees put special emphasis on what was euphemistically described as dealing with 'internal tranquillity'. Their duties included organising volunteer companies and ensuring the loyalty of those who enlisted. In addition to providing military recruitment for the forces fighting abroad, volunteer regiments were also being sought to provide security at home. Such developments demonstrate how it was becoming ever more evident that the authorities were worried about attempts at insurrection and were preparing accordingly.

Deputy Lieutenants were also appointed and were selected on the basis of their commitment to the establishment; it was their task to monitor the loyalty of people in their area. They were also responsible for drawing up lists of those who could be recruited to their cause and, just as importantly, those that should be watched.

Whilst the country was at war with France, it was also preparing for conflict within. From the top down and all across the land preparations were being made to deal with any uprisings. And the fears of the authorities were proved to be accurate, because just as Gerrald's trial was ending in March 1794, the Pike Plot was uncovered, which was to send shockwaves through the establishment.

The Pike Plot, as with many insurrectionist or terrorist plans before and since, was discovered as much by accident as by design. The search of a house in Edinburgh's Old Town for pamphlets and radical writing uncovered twelve pike heads and other threatening material, which outlined plans to incite rebellion, suborn troops and even to capture Edinburgh Castle by force of arms. The search also revealed a web of intrigue consisting of spies, double agents and double-cross. Some historians have interpreted the plot as the work of one man, Robert Watt, who ironically, at one stage, had been a government agent and reported directly to Robert Dundas on the activities of the Friends of the People.[8] Whether through a political conversion or as a result of his pique at the inadequate reward offered by the government for his services, he turned full circle and became the lead planner of insurrection.

However, although Watt was pivotal in the inception and planning of the plot, it is also clear that the scheme went far wider than what he had organised with his accomplice David Downie, who was also tried for treason. It is evident both from the trial itself and through Watt's deathbed confession that many more individuals were involved. When Watt was brought to trial in late August 1794, he was tried for treason under the English legal procedure of oyer and terminer. The procedure was introduced under the Treason Act 1708 by Queen Anne and allowed for treason trials; in Scotland such trials were subject to the supervision of the Lord President rather than the Lord Justice Clerk. The Scottish court system largely gave the Lord Justice Clerk primacy in criminal matters, whilst the Lord President was in overall charge, but specifically dealt with civil matters. Suggestions that an English procedure was used to ensure the conviction of Watt and Downie are wrong. The reason that this procedure was followed was in order to avoid the cases being dealt with by Braxfield, whose extreme and obvious partisanship had caused widespread concern and disdain, even amongst the establishment.

In a letter that Robert Dundas wrote to his uncle in June 1794, he stated:

> I would prefer a commission were it only for this reason, that the President or Chief Baron would, in that way, fall to preside in place of the violent and intemperate gentleman who sits in the Justiciary, and whose present state of health and spirits is such as to afford no chance of his being more soberly inclined in his demeanour than he was last winter.[9]

When Watt was convicted in September 1794 it was not as a result of questionable legal processes used but as a consequence of the weight of evidence against him. Although the trial may not have met modern human rights requirements, it most certainly was fairer than previous proceedings and the conviction was certainly legally justified. The evidence proved that an insurrection had been planned and equally showed how the scheming had turned out to be much more than the musings of a deluded individual. The charges levelled against Watt included plotting the overthrow of the government, insurrection and rebellion, the planned taking of Edinburgh Castle by force of arms, the seizure of banks and excise buildings and the suborning of troops. These charges also highlight the wider evolution in the actions and aims of the radicals. Some of those who had pushed for constitutional change were now moving to become a more revolutionary underground organisation.

Watt had flipped from being a government spy to a committed radical and had even attended the British Convention in November 1793. When the convention was forcibly dispersed, Watt had been pivotal in seeking to have the remaining members reconvene and in maintaining the organisation and the pressure for change. About 100 individuals continued to meet in Simon Square in Edinburgh and Watt became a key figure in the group. They sought to pull together the remnants of the reform societies that remained in Edinburgh and establish a secret committee.

Initially their efforts involved communicating with the LCS in London and disseminating their calls for another British Convention to other radical groups in Scotland. Whilst such activity was dangerous given the wider political climate, this was innocuous when compared with what then seems to have been suggested by Watt. His extreme ideas were most certainly his own and some other individual members did indeed decide to withdraw their support at this juncture, doubtless fearful of the consequences. But some others not only stayed but also supported his scheme.

Watt's plans for armed rebellion seemed to have a currency outside Scotland, but more importantly found favour with many within the country. His deathbed confession referred to planned actions in Dublin and London, as well as Edinburgh where 4,000 or 5,000 men were to assemble. Watt alleged that the simultaneous uprising had already been prepared and simply required 'a visit to England and Ireland by intelligent and confidential persons', to confirm details.[10] Evidence presented at the trial detailed how delegates had been sent to Stirling, Campsie, St Ninians, Glasgow, Paisley and other places, where they made pleas for support in an armed struggle. However, it appears as if there was only sympathy for the cause, rather than an actual willingness to join the fight, and the response from Stirling confirmed that, whilst there was widespread support, 'the courage of the community wasn't great'. Rumours about a French invasion also proliferated although there was little basis for these reports, which seem to be predicated on hope rather than reality.

As the plans for pikes to be made and troops to be lured from the castle and then either overpowered or suborned began to be fleshed out, further emissaries were sent to Falkirk, Queensferry and Kirkintilloch. In the event of the soldiers remaining in the castle then the radicals planned to starve them into submission, which indicated that there was a significant number of rebels who were available to seal them in and repel other soldiers who might come to their rescue. However, Watt's actions went beyond the discussion of mere plans and into actual preparations for insurrection. The weapons discovered in the random search of his house were apparently part of a wider commission of pike and spearheads from blacksmiths.

James Kennedy, who was a Paisley radical and the assistant secretary to the British Convention, fled to London after the Pike Plot was discovered. He had close links to Archibald Hastie and William Mitchell who had been leading radical activists in the Paisley area. The former had been detained after meetings had been held and daggers and bayonets had been mentioned in reports. It is believed that he may be the exiled Scottish radical who, according to a spy report, attended an LCS meeting in June 1794 and claimed: 'The Scotch to be in great force, and resolved in obtaining a reform and redress of their grievances, that would long ago have proceeded to violent measures, but had been induced to wait from favourable reports they had heard of the London Corresponding Society.'[11]

David Downie who had been arrested along with Watt was also tried in September 1794. He was treasurer of the society, which was formed after the convention was dispersed and his involvement appears to have been much more peripheral. During his trial his counsel sought to focus the blame on Watt and it also appears as if he was used as a witness in the cases involving Margarot, Gerrald and others.

There is no suggestion though that Downie was a spy, and evidence during his trial confirmed his involvement in aspects of the plot. Reference was made to Watt being advised that 4,000 pikes were wanted in Perth and that Edinburgh Castle was to be taken. Documents had also been given out in Midlothian, which called on soldiers to stay home. Downie justified his actions by arguing that there was a belief that the Goldsmiths' Hall Association men were beginning to arm themselves and that the radicals felt that they needed to be similarly prepared. However, the bulk of the blame was laid on Watt.

Downie's counsel made a plea for clemency and for whatever reason this was accepted by the jury. After returning a guilty verdict, they recommended to the judge that a pardon be granted. Somewhat surprisingly, this was granted by the Lord President who was again the senior judge. This was not well received by Robert Dundas – which again confirms that Downie was not a spy – who complained in a letter to his uncle, whilst admitting that there was little that could be done. Ironically, it is highly unlikely that Lord Braxfield, who had been prevented from presiding over the case, would have shown any clemency, but the deed was done.

Conversely, there was no mercy shown to Robert Watt. He was publicly executed on 15 October 1794, firstly being hanged at the Tolbooth in Edinburgh before being decapitated for good measure. As with later radicals, the executioner held up Watt's head and stated, 'This is the head of a traitor'. This was done to demonstrate the ruthlessness with which further attempts at insurrection would be put down. Pamphlets referring to the radical plot were printed by the government and distributed widely; it also gained extensive coverage in the newspapers. All this publicity drove home the message that there was an underlying threat from radicals within the country, but also that rebellion would not be tolerated by the state.

What the organisers of the Pike Plot were striving for beyond political reform was never really stated in court, beyond general calls for change. However, the movement was undoubtedly seeking universal franchise as was sought by the Friends of the People. As before, these were calls for change in London. There was no suggestion that Watt and his colleagues were seeking a restoration of the Scottish Parliament. The enemy was the land-owning aristocracy and the route to reform was through the British Parliament.

The evidence provided at court and the reaction by the authorities confirmed that the planned insurrection was greater than the deluded thoughts of one man. The deathbed confession was written willingly by Watt without coercion, and formed a moral statement as he sought absolution before facing the executioner. In his statement Watt confirmed that his activities were part of a much bigger plot that involved many more people.

What is not known is the extent of the cooperation between the various groups across Britain. This was not discussed by Watt and the government's spies were frequently unable to penetrate many of the areas made up of close-knit communities. But it is hard to see how all of these events across the land and into neighbouring countries could have been carried out without some level of cooperation, if not coordination. The organisational structure may have been rudimentary but there must have been some communication system in place given the information that was being exchanged.

Moreover, the crackdown that followed across England and Ireland confirmed that the authorities believed there was some pan-British collusion. Military searches and heightened security that followed in Scotland proved that the emissaries who carried the message encouraging revolt across central Scotland must have been more than a mere handful of individuals and that they in turn discussed it with many more. Whilst perhaps more members of the movement sympathised with the cause rather than participated – as in Stirling – none appear to have been willing to advise the authorities and adopted a code of silence. As shown by the request from Perth and elsewhere for weapons, many of those who heard about the plans were clearly willing to join in the insurrection.

Although Tom Johnston was perhaps gilding the lily when he wrote 'that there was scarcely a blacksmith's shop in the country not busily engaged in the forging of pikes', he was undoubtedly correct when he suggested that 'many hundreds of weavers in Paisley had purchased arms'.[12] Authorities in Renfrewshire received reports in May about the presence of 'daggers, bayonets and other lethal weapons' and of 'considerable numbers of people assembling in military array' within the town.[13] As a result, assemblies both there and in neighbouring villages were prohibited and arrests were made. This in turn led to a large meeting in the High Church in Paisley where resolutions were passed to try and liberate those who had been detained. Searches were also conducted by the military in Neilston and Barrhead. Arrests were made for the making of seditious toasts but no weapons appear to have been discovered. However, troops remained stationed in Paisley, which indicated the level of alarm that remained.

Despite such developments, the rebellious events should not be overplayed. The Pike Plot had not made it much beyond the planning stage with ongoing discussions and preparation through the ordering of pikes. Searches for weapons took place after the plot was uncovered across the country and they uncovered little. Although this could be down to weapons existing and simply being well hidden rather than non-existent, it indicates that a limited amount of weapons were actually in circulation. This was not a revolution.

Although the plot was limited in what it achieved, it demonstrated the level of discontent that existed in radical circles. Moreover, as Elizabeth McFarland has noted, it also highlighted two important developments. Firstly, it showed that there was growing cooperation between radicals across Britain and Ireland. Or put more crudely: 'The swine of England, the rabble of Scotland and the wretches of Ireland', as the popular toast went, had become common characters in radical calculations.[14] Secondly, it marked the transition of radical but constitutional societies into revolutionary and secret organisations. This was partly occurring as a result of the dispersal of the British Convention, but the reaction of the authorities thereafter necessitated and ensured the escalation of the radical cause.

News of the plot in March 1794 and the suggestion of a possible widescale insurrection in London and Dublin, as well as in Edinburgh, confirmed the worst fears held by the establishment. Not only was Britain at war with revolutionary France, but it faced the threat of revolution from within. This development brought a quick, merciless and coordinated response across both Britain and Ireland.

In England and Scotland, *habeas corpus* and its equivalent were suspended on 23 May with minimal discussion and immediate effect. In the south multiple radicals were arrested and their clubs closed, dispersed or intimidated. This included Thomas Hardy of the LCS, although he was subsequently acquitted after trial. In areas beyond London and in groups with less powerful and influential members, reform organisations faced repression on an even greater scale.

The crackdown crossed the sea to Ireland where Hamilton Rowan was arrested in January 1795 for sedition and was subsequently jailed for two years. These more lenient sentences served to emphasise the severity with which the Scottish bench dealt with political radicals. On 24 May 1795 the Dublin Society of United Irishmen were finally disbanded and their papers seized. Thomas Emmet, who was to be involved in the 1798 rebellion, saw this as a body blow for the organisation as it was then forced to regroup and wait.

In Scotland, unrest continued throughout the year with reports of trouble in Breadalbane and the use of troops in Glasgow in December 1794. And in this way 1794 ended with the British Convention dispersed and the Friends of the People scattered to the wind. But the new year heralded a new stage, for the authorities had simply forced the radicals underground and turned them into revolutionary organisations.

CHAPTER 10

GEORGE MEALMAKER AND THE SOCIETY OF THE UNITED SCOTSMEN

The repression that was unleashed following the Pike Plot pushed the cause of reform back considerably. Intimidation was not only provided through loyalist associations and threats by landowners and the well to do, but was openly practised by the state. The harassment of radicals worsened. Tradesmen with radical sympathies had their credit stopped by the banks and workmen with questionable loyalty to the state were summarily dismissed from their employment. Some of this had occurred before, but after the Pike Plot the attacks were more severe and more venomous.

As Henry Meikle stated: 'Combinations or strikes were put down with a ruthless hand, and philanthropic work was regarded with distrust.'[1] Many middle-class reformers also began to feel the pressure, with calls made to boycott lectures from academics with radical views and Whig-supporting lawyers finding that their work was drying up. As there were no juries in civil cases it was believed that judges would not find in favour of any litigant represented by a radical lawyer, which was incentive enough for many to distance themselves. Things were more extreme for some individuals: for example, Henry Erskine, who was a Whig and radical-supporting lawyer, was forced out of his position as Dean of the Faculty of Advocates in 1795 and other members were pressurised into making pledges of loyalty.

The collapse of the radical societies accelerated as many members distanced themselves from their past associations. This was evidenced by a heartfelt letter from George Mealmaker to London reformists in September 1795:

> The late arbitrary proceedings of the enemies of liberty operated in so terrifying a manner on the Scots Patriots in general, that for a time their spirits sunk beneath the standard of mediocrity, in conse-quence of which their efforts became languid and the sacred flame which had been kindled in their breasts almost extinguished.[2]

But it was not only pressure from without that the reform societies faced, but also demoralisation from within.

Whether driven by the concern about rebellion or through a desire to appear to be loyal to the state, recruitment into the recently estab-lished volunteer forces surged. It has been suggested 'that by July 1796 forty-one districts in Scotland had either a regiment or a company'.[3] This certainly appeared to have had little to do with the warding off of a French invasion. In many forces, such as that based in Edinburgh,

> nothing was said of serving against a foreign foe; but the members formally reprobated the doctrine of universal suffrage and Jacobin political principles, disapproved of the Friends of the People and the British Convention, and obliged themselves to prevent such societies being formed and such meetings being held in the future.[4]

However, not all volunteers were driven by the zeal to crush revolu-tionary intent. Some were coerced into signing up by landowners or employers. Even Rabbie Burns enlisted in the Royal Dumfries Vol-unteers, which was ostensibly an attempt to demonstrate his loyalty and to avoid being dismissed from his government post, given his previous public support for the radical cause. The increase in volunteer recruitment was arguably more reflective of state pressure rather than public-spiritedness, although it most definitely had the effect of further dispiriting radical supporters.

But whilst the strength of the radical cause was visibly diminished, public discontent remained. The economic situation was deteriorating as the war with France continued and the cost of living increased. Some of this was a direct result of the conflict, but this was also compounded by a series of bad harvests that saw prices rise significantly. Such was the destitution that one in eight were on relief or in receipt of public assistance in Edinburgh in 1795. Despite government efforts to mitigate hardship, riots broke out in Dundee and elsewhere across the country. Unlike some past disturbances these incidents seem to have had no political motivation and were simply outbreaks of rage and desperation. The problems and destitution existed across the country and were only mitigated by war work, which boosted wages in some sectors in the west where disturbances would have otherwise been expected.

Although the economy slightly revived in 1796, it again started to struggle in early 1797, as British war fortunes faltered. Napoleon's armies were defeating Britain's continental allies in Austria and Prussia and even the Royal Navy, which had for so long been regarded as the ultimate barrier from foreign forces, was facing challenges. In the winter of 1796 a French invasion fleet appeared off Bantry Bay in Ireland, only to be dispersed by bad weather. Meanwhile, in England mutinies broke out in several fleets as the sailors grew restless. Financial panic was only averted following government intervention but the economy remained weak, and poverty, especially amongst weavers and other tradesmen, increased.

Throughout this period, the government was therefore apprehensive as discontent manifested itself in England, as well as in Scotland.

Whilst north of the border open political opposition had been all but silenced, in England it had been muted, but pro-reform groups still operated, as a result of the more liberal legal system. The Whig opposition were pushing an agenda for peace, both in Parliament and in the press. Calls for reform and an end to the war were made by organisations such as the London Corresponding Society, which had been re-established after the clampdown of spring 1794. A huge crowd attended a rally organised by the resurgent LCS in autumn 1795 and a few days later a crowd attacked the King's carriage, whilst shouting for 'Bread' 'Peace' and 'No Pitt'.

Despite the fact that the number of radical societies had dissipated in Scotland, calls for radical reform continued to reverberate. In February 1795 George Mealmaker gave a sermon at the dissenting church he attended and later had it published. It showed how strongly the fire for reform still burned and provided an insight into the radical position of many secessionist congregations. Based on biblical teachings, it 'promised God's damnation to royalty, aristocrats, ministers of the state and Romish priests'. The sermon discussed how 'a kingdom of truth and righteousness' would be established that would require

> great convulsions and consequently great calamities would neces-
> sarily occur; but mankind should not despair, for at that very hour
> the Divine Will was being realised in France and the peroration
> concluded; As God is visiting the earth, I think it will not be long
> before His Appearance will make His Enemies here tremble also,
> and wander in a wilderness where there is no road; and as that will
> be a time of war, trouble, and great judgement you ought seriously
> to prepare for it.[5]

As the number and scale of rallies and demonstrations seemed to be increasing across the land, the government again chose to introduce repressive legislation. This time the Treason Act 1795 was invoked (sometimes known as the Treasonable and Seditious Practices Act), in addition to the Seditious Meetings Act 1795. The former widened the definition of treason to include spoken and written words. The latter prohibited political assemblies unless the authorities had been notified and approved of the gathering in advance and also gave local magistrates powers to disperse such meetings.

Despite the clampdown, the legislation caused huge concern and provoked outrage on both sides of the border. Henry Dundas sought to have councils and other official bodies provide their public backing for the new laws but this was offset by public petitions, which were created in opposition to the new bills. In Glasgow, 10,000 individuals signed the petition, 8,000 signed in Edinburgh and even 2,500 signed in Paisley. Despite public resistance, the legislation was pushed through Parliament by the Tories, who were more fearful of the growing discontent than they were concerned about public disapproval with the laws.

The age of repression had formally dawned and advocates of reform were driven underground. The radical movement was reduced in size and number and took on a more clandestine nature and insurrectionary approach. With the Friends of the People to all intents and purposes dissolved, the Society of the United Scotsmen was set to take its place. Before this point there were links that existed between the two organisations. In May 1794 Henry Dundas wrote to the Lord Privy Seal to inform him about the discovery of the Pike Plot, enclosing a leaflet that had been printed in Dundee, which called on the militia to resist being sent overseas. He stated that its origin was 'traced home to certain Persons some of whom are in Custody … the principal and most active members of the British Convention'.[6]

However, although the United Scotsmen had roots that stretched back to the Friends of the People, it seems that as soon as the group came into being, an early rift developed within its ranks. Many of the adherents to the older societies drifted away from the group as they were uncomfortable with its radical undercurrents, which mirrored what happened with members of the Friends of the People and Robert Watt in the prelude to the Pike Plot. Although there was no known link between Watt and the United Scotsmen, the parting of the insurrectionists and constitutionalists within the groups unfolded in a similar way.

From 1795 it was the United Scotsmen that rose to prominence and the foremost members amongst them was George Mealmaker. This was a natural development as Mealmaker had been a prominent figure in the Friends of the People, as both a secretary of the Dundee Society and a delegate to the British Convention. But it was within the United Scotsmen that he made his name and the cause for which he paid the price of martyrdom. His leadership also reflected the change in the social make-up of the new radical group, as it moved from being led by those who were wealthier and more educated to being rooted in and led by the artisan and weaving communities. Reports from the government's spies soon began to confirm both Mealmaker's leading role in the rising radical tide, as well as the individual threat that he posed.

Publicly available information about the organisation is limited as a result of its clandestine nature, but the group was modelled on the Society of United Irishmen, from which it had taken its name, and operated through a cell structure, in a similar way to modern revolutionary groups. The society was also based in communities that were close-knit where loyalty was given or could be demanded, and where spies could not penetrate. The society prospered in Fife, Angus and Perthshire and throughout the west, in the small weaving communities around Paisley, in Renfrewshire and Ayrshire where it seems to have originated.

The Society of the United Scotsmen appears to have come into existence as the radical mood moved towards physical confrontation or at least a willingness to resist; whether the group initiated or reacted to this shift is not known. The first evidence that this transition had occurred was the Pike Plot, but a more physical approach seems to have been fully embraced by 1795. Peter Berresford Ellis and Seumas Mac A' Ghobhainn have suggested that the United Scotsmen were formed in Glasgow on 13 November 1793.[7] Unfortunately the authors provided no citation of any authority for this date and neither is any additional information about the formation of the society supplied. Tom Johnston mentioned that a Society of United Scotsmen had been formed in Glasgow in 1793 but described it as being a literary society, which would therefore mean that it was constitutional. It is possible that this is the same organisation, as was reported in the *Glasgow Advertiser*.[8] Perhaps, the group changed over future years but it is more likely that radicals just took inspiration and the name from the Irish organisation, rather than its far less prominent Scottish counterpart. Neither historians nor government records seem to pinpoint the circumstances that surrounded the founding of the society, which is understandable given its secretive nature. However, the group was not specifically mentioned in the trial of Watt or Downie, which were perhaps the first manifestations of a shift in the structure and tactics of the reformists, aside from Dundas's letter that referenced the seditious leaflet detailed above.

What is clear is that with the discovery of the Pike Plot and the execution of Watt, radical underground groups were beginning to reassemble. In July 1796 Alexander Leslie, who was an Edinburgh bookseller, wrote to the London Corresponding Society seeking to become their representative in Scotland. In his letter he advised that he had 'agents' all over Scotland; although no specific reference was made to the United Scotsmen, it is evident that multiple links had been forged and both cross-border and internal communications within Scotland were ongoing between radicals.

By 1795 the society had been mentioned by one of the founders of the United Irishmen, Wolfe Tone, just as the larger and more powerful

Irish organisation sought to forge alliances. Over this period many members of the United Irishmen had also been fleeing to Scotland, as repression and danger was increasing in their homeland. Such was the concern of the authorities that at one stage security at Portpatrick was significantly increased. The Irish members who did move to Scotland brought with them not just their radical convictions but ideas from the structure and organisation of their society. A letter from an Irish loyalist to the *Glasgow Courier* in early 1797 warned about impending danger:

> Let me tell you, while your neighbour's house is on fire, to take care of your own. A vast number of United Irishmen have fled into your country. Some of the highest Up men in Belfast have … taken homes. They have several Societies established as far back as February last (1797) and therefore the magistrates of Scotland ought to be on their guard against them. They will out the peasantry up in the Western Counties particularly, before you know what you are doing; they go abroad under the pretence of seeking work, service and selling linens, remnants and such like and their lure among them, I understand is very fascinating, and has been for some time.[9]

There were certainly close links between the two organisations but they remained entirely separate and vastly different in many ways. The far greater number of members and more severe repression in Ireland provided far more fertile soil for the society. There were also differences between the two countries brought about by religion in particular but also other social and economic variances. All of this meant that whilst the formal written constitutions of the organisations were almost identical, with 'North Britain' inserted instead of 'Ireland', the terrain on which the groups operated remained vastly different.

However, it is clear that not only did agents from the United Irishmen operate in Scotland in an attempt to discover information and forge alliances, but Irish émigrés significantly bolstered the new Scottish radical cause. This applied not just in the west and southwest where many individuals settled, but across the country; the government explained much of the rise of radicalism in such areas as being a result of Irish immigration. In Thornliebank, then on the outskirts of Glasgow, membership was described in a government report as being 'of the lowest order, and mostly Irishmen'.[10] Meanwhile in Ayrshire, Theophilus McAllister, an Irishman who had been working in Irvine and Kilwinning since his arrival in February 1796, was considered by the authorities to be a typical United Scotsmen activist. The influx and influence of Irish emigrants extended well beyond radical circles as many Irish citizens relocated in search of work and other opportunities and this included to such radical hotbeds as Perth and its surrounding villages. Although not all of the new Irish population sided with the radical faction, the evidence suggests that they certainly increased membership numbers and the activity of the newer and more radical Scottish societies.

Most Irish emigrants appear to have come from the north of Ireland and were overwhelmingly Protestant. This shared religious doctrine, as well as the membership of Masonic groups, helps explain the close affinity of both the people and the organisations. At this point the phrase 'planting Irish potatoes' seems to have entered the radical vocabulary, as a euphemism for physical force opposition to the authorities. To be engaged in this act was perceived as a willingness to confront the authorities militarily rather than just through protest.

The new organisation sought to forge links not only with their Irish mentors but with groups in England and, more importantly, many travelled the country to spread the cause. Agents and activists criss-crossed Scotland to sign up individuals and administer the oath of membership as the organisation sought to expand; and in this Mealmaker again became prominent. Amongst the authorities there were concerns following information that 'a French emissary was touring radical groupings in

Scotland, and lecturing'.[11] As with the incitement to revolution made by the United Scotsmen and the United Irishmen, the suggestion of French invasion plans were concerning to say the least.

In addition to his involvement in the Palmer prosecution in 1793, Mealmaker himself was arrested in May 1794 after the discovery of the Pike Plot where, as outlined earlier in Henry Dundas's letter, he had been referred to as one of the principal activists then in custody who had links to the British Convention. The week before Dundas sent this letter there was a significant clampdown across Britain and Ireland with numerous arrests made following the suspension of *habeas corpus*. Having attended the British Convention and in his role as secretary of the Dundee Friends of Liberty, it was understandable that Mealmaker would be caught up in the government clampdown. His house was raided and his personal papers were impounded; he and a friend fled to Arbroath but they were soon picked up by the authorities.

The two were taken to Edinburgh in June 1795 and were brought before magistrates for judicial examination, which consisted of a court appearance before any trial and allowed for questioning by the prosecution. Mealmaker denied any knowledge of plans either for armed rebellion or of the leaflet, which called on the militia to refuse to serve. He did admit to providing training in boxing and fencing but stated that it was solely for recreation and enjoyment. No specific questions were asked about the United Scotsmen and no prosecution followed; he was released from custody shortly thereafter.

However, Mealmaker was most definitely a leading light in the organisation and seems to have been the promoter of its constitution and rules. As early as December 1793 and before his arrest in the wake of the Pike Plot, an informant described him as a 'daring and dangerous fellow' but that whilst he had been going throughout the northeast propagating the radical cause, 'talk was he currently had no arms'.[12] Despite this intelligence the authorities did not obtain a conviction but were doubtless keeping a watchful eye over him.

As with others, Mealmaker was coming to believe that physical force was necessary. In the summer of 1796 the constitution of the United Scotsmen was formally adopted with Irish delegates putting forward their model which was adapted; and Mealmaker appears to have been pivotal in this process.

Such was his profile that even before the constitution was agreed he was named in a popular radical song that was doing the rounds in the mid-1790s. This highlights his influence within wider radical circles and within the organisation itself. Its first verse was:

> Fy, let us a' to the meetin'
> For many braw lads will be there,
> Explaining the wrongs o' Great Britain
> And pointing them out to a hair...
> An' there will be George Mealmaker,
> An twa three lads mair from the north,
> An there will be Hastie the baker,
> An' Callender's son of Craigforth.[13]

From this point onwards government informant reports referencing the clandestine group increased, even though specific information on their activities was limited. Subsequent information that came to light in future trials confirmed that the United Scotsmen expanded rapidly after April 1797, as the spirit of resistance was inculcated in many radical groups. As a member stated when later interrogated about his activities: 'Democrats were informed that much blood had been shed ... there was a new kind of reform coming into the Country the object of which was to impress upon minds of the people a belief in the badness of the time.'[14] Activists and agents took this message around the country. William Craig from Irvine was sent to establish groups in St Ninians, Stirling and Kincardine in April and May of 1797 and members from Dundee took the message into Tayside and

Fife. Important committees, in some cases regional in scope, were known to have gathered in Dundee and Kilmarnock and it is believed that the national committee met in Glasgow.

Divisions formed in some areas between those who had signed up to the Society of the United Scotsmen and those who refused to get involved. In Perth, despite its history as a hotbed of radicalism, many if not most in the democratic societies declined to join the new group. In this area the principal advocate for the United Scotsmen was the Irish émigré James Craigdallie. Other areas were similarly divided, for example, William Sands who had been arrested with Mealmaker in 1793 refused to join and condemned his former compatriot for joining the society; he even subsequently became a prosecution witness against Mealmaker.

Mealmaker's exact role or title in the group is unknown and, as with so much of the history surrounding the United Scotsmen, his position can only be speculated upon. He was certainly the leading figure in Tayside, if not beyond. More importantly, though, was the fact that he was regarded as the ringleader by the authorities. A memorandum from Robert Dundas to Henry Dundas dated 13 January 1798 and sent immediately after Mealmaker's trial and conviction, advised that he was the ringleader and that the organisation had been modelled on the United Irishmen.[15]

Berresford Ellis and Mac A' Gobhainn named Angus Cameron as the leader of the organisation but did not provide either a citation or any evidence to back up this claim. Cameron was certainly a leading organiser, undoubtedly in Perthshire, and probably far beyond. He came to prominence during the Militia Act riots which would follow. But there is little evidence about his involvement in the leadership of the United Scotsmen and Mealmaker is more often designated as being the lynchpin of the society.

By autumn 1797 the popularity of the organisation appears to have reached its peak; at a national meeting in Edinburgh in September it was stated that membership had reached 9,653.[16] The membership was highly concentrated in weaving areas in Fife, Tayside and in the west. A report from a government informant in December 1797 described how in Perth 'seventeen citizens were united' and another seventeen were 'supposed to be united'.[17] Other reports suggested that there were hundreds of dedicated supporters in some smaller villages such as Auchtermuchty and Strathmiglo. These differences in the level of support in such areas could be linked to how radical involvement was uncommon in some communities, whereas in other close-knit areas involvement in radicalism was the norm. This is similar to the spirit and solidarity that would develop in mining villages in future generations.

Many who joined or sympathised with the cause had only a vague idea of the precise details about the societies and simply broadly accepted the 'French principles and French laws'.[18] However, they must have understood the risks involved in being part of a clandestine society; upon joining 'initiates were told that they joined a movement linked to others in Ireland and England, with leaders in London, Glasgow, Edinburgh, Belfast and Dublin'.[19]

The authorities were also aware that clandestine societies were being established and as a result introduced the Unlawful Oaths Act in July 1797, which made it a criminal offence to take or administer unlawful oaths. Information about the existence of such societies had been increasing, which explains why new legislation was brought in rather than using existing laws on treason or sedition.

There were suggestions from some who had been detained and questioned that by 1796 and 1797 military preparations were also being made in some areas:

United men in the north of Glasgow were reported to be arming and exercising, acting on instructions that 'It was proper for them to go into the Militia or Volunteers in order to exercise.' There were also reports of attempts to suborn soldiers and volunteers in various parts of Scotland from Renfrew to Perth.[20]

Plans were made by some groups to attack and disarm local volunteer regiments, whilst schemes to undermine others from within were organised. Precise details are limited but they no doubt caused alarm amongst the authorities. For example, the Earl of Fife was certain that his regiment had been infiltrated and a member of the Stirling Volunteers was reported as proposing a toast to 'a speedy landing to the French'.

Such operations were not restricted to Scotland either. Another report from a government informant in 1797 suggested that gunpowder was being sent to Ireland.[21] This confirmed the involvement of agents from the United Irishmen, as well as suggestions of Scots having gone across to Ulster. At this time attempts to create a relay system of messengers to allow for information to go back and forth across the North Channel was broken up by government agents. There also appears to have been links developing with organisations in northwest England, with Cumberland and Westmorland receiving visits from United Scotsmen and communications with existing radical groups in London continuing throughout this period.

The authorities were no doubt becoming increasingly alarmed during this turbulent period as numerous risings and insurrections continued to break out across the country, and George Mealmaker was viewed as being pivotal in these events. When Mealmaker was first arrested on 13 November 1797, the *Glasgow Courier* report the following day read:

The trial of George Mealmaker, weaver, in Dundee for sedition has timeously and fortuitously for the country exposed a deep conspiracy to overturn the British Constitution in Church and State and to establish in its room a Republican Government. To accomplish this the object of their antics, all were to be cut off who would dare to oppose their measures.

The following month, before the case had even come to trial in Scotland, the same paper was carrying reports of stories circulating in London about the case:

> Some accounts have been received from Scotland, stating that a deep-laid plot had been discovered of a very extensive and dangerous tendency. Happily, the discovery has prevented every danger and several of the ringleaders have been effectively secured. As the public will soon have accurate particulars, we shall merely state at present that several young men who were entered at Edinburgh University were discovered to have been sent over by the United Irishmen for the worst of purposes.

However, whilst Mealmaker accepted the allegation that he was a member of a clandestine organisation, he denied that he or the group itself were pursuing armed insurrection. He proclaimed that the United Scotsmen were simply an organisation seeking universal franchise, which basically operated as an extension of the Friends of the People, albeit in a more clandestine form. Of course this may have been simply an attempt to mitigate his involvement in the cause and limit the severity of his sentence.

The evidence produced at Mealmaker's trial provided limited information and details about any attempts at insurrection, aside from remarks he made which alluded to wider unspecified threats. The prosecution decided to concentrate on the clandestine nature of the organisation. This indicated that the authorities considered that there was a much deeper plot that Mealmaker was involved in beyond the charges that he actually faced but in order to secure a conviction, the court proceeded with membership of a subversive organisation.

The indictment served on Mealmaker, which once again was brought in the name of the Lord Advocate Robert Dundas, listed charges of sedition and the administration of oaths. He was accused of

> In 1797 in Fife, Forfar and Perth having formed 'The Society of the United Scotsmen' whose object and purpose was reform and the obtaining of annual Parliaments and universal suffrage, to create in the minds of the people a spirit of disaffection and disloyalty to the King and the Established Government, and ultimately to excite and stir them up to acts of violence and opposition to the laws and constitution of this country.

The charge explained how this was done through the formation of linked small societies and then described the structure within the group. It also detailed that an oath was taken as part of the initiation upon joining the group and that secret codes were used between members. Mealmaker was described as being a leading figure and having administered the oaths across various communities in Tayside, as well as attending meetings and being a national committee member. He was also allegedly responsible for writing the 'Resolution and Constitution of the Society of the United Scotsmen'. Finally, the charges detailed how Mealmaker had distributed seditious pamphlets, and in particular his paper entitled *The Moral and Political Catechism of Man*.

As is still the case in Scotland, the court document served on Mealmaker, as well as referring to the charge, provided other information that was to be used in court against him. This included the Resolution and Constitution of the Society of the United Scotsmen of which he was accused of being the instigator in addition to defining the purpose and structure of the organisation (these documents are included in Appendix B).

There is little in the documents that would be viewed as controversial today, let alone confrontational, but this was not the case in the late 1790s. Violence was eschewed within the precise wording of the documents, but it was the sentiments behind the words that worried the authorities, and this would have been interpreted as being a threat to the established social order. The authorities believed that such a challenge was being planned even though they lacked any such proof. Therefore, Mealmaker's charges and trial must be seen in the context of other disturbances taking place, which will be analysed in further detail in the following chapter.

Whatever doubts there may have been over the charges laid, a conviction was never in doubt. The jury was comprised of bankers, merchants and lawyers, all of whom were loyally supportive of the authorities and resolutely opposed to reform. Twenty-nine witnesses were cited for the case which commenced at the High Court of Justiciary in Edinburgh on 10 January 1798.

Mealmaker was represented by legal counsel. This could be explained by the fact that he was less familiar with the court system than the other radicals, who either had legal training, as was the case with Muir, or an understanding of the system, as with Skirving and Margarot. Mealmaker was obviously very intelligent and highly literate given his writing endeavours, but he may have just felt that representing himself in court was beyond his abilities. In addition, although he was both a major driver and organiser of the United Scotsmen, he was not one of the society's leading orators.

At the outset Mealmaker's advocate objected to the relevancy of the case laid against him. He stated that many individuals, including leading members of the establishment, held similarly radical views and that therefore they could not be viewed as being seditious. However, whatever logic and reason there was in this argument was swiftly rebutted by the crown, with the prosecutor stating that 'the plan was more dangerous and alarming than any ever brought. It was a plan for the overturning of the Government.'[22] This claim provides further evidence that the authorities believed that Mealmaker was involved in more extensive revolutionary schemes than those that he had been explicitly accused of. It goes without saying that the court firmly rejected the preliminary argument made by the defence.

The first witness called was a weaver from Newburgh named John Aitken, who testified that he had joined the society the year before, had been formally admitted as a member and that he personally knew Mealmaker. Under continued questioning, Aitken described how society delegates paid a fee and used secret signs and passwords to identify one another. This coded identification system apparently consisted of an individual joining their hands together and coupling their fingers, and then whilst keeping their hands joined, turning their palms outwards. In response the other member would put one of their hands on the back of the other and couple their fingers. Aitken also explained how the verbal code consisted of one member stating 'I have light' and the other responding 'I hate light'.

Aitken claimed that the societies kept in touch by sending deputations to visit each other and he also indicated the strength of the group in his own area by confirming that there were four in Cupar, and also clubs in Leslie, Ceres and Auchtermuchty. All of these were small weaving communities but this showed the strength of the movement and the high number of people involved; he also added that members were expected to try and recruit as many new supporters as possible.

Aitken recounted how he had been sent to Mealmaker's house for information about parliamentary reform and had been given his book *The Moral and Political Catechism of Man*. Apparently, Mealmaker was away when he arrived but he was directed by his wife to a nearby pub where a United Scotsmen meeting was taking place. When Aitken arrived at the gathering, the people present identified themselves as coming from across the area, including Brechin, Kirriemuir, Coupar Angus and Dundee, and that this was a regional gathering with arrangements made for a further meeting in Brechin some three or four weeks later. Under pressure from the court, Aitken added that it was

Mealmaker who was selected by the group to go as a delegate to the national committee.

Evidence was given by Aitken and others about discussions on parliamentary reform and the existence of similar societies across the country, including radical groups in England. The group in Cupar was described as being formed after a society had been established in Dundee, as initially members had travelled there until eventually the amount of supporters had increased sufficiently to form an independent association. Those who joined the movement from the west had also had contact with William Sands, who, as mentioned earlier, had been arrested with Mealmaker earlier in 1793. The court also heard about how the societies had expanded, with progress having been made in the highlands and even amongst members of the gentry.

Further witnesses described similar discussions and meetings and claimed that Mealmaker's publication had been widely distributed with pamphlets taken to Dundee. Others gave evidence that pamphlets had come north from Edinburgh and a printer from Edinburgh even testified to having published Mealmaker's book. Despite objections by Mealmaker's counsel, a government informant called Robert Bell was also allowed to give evidence. He stated that he had obtained pamphlets from the accused, which were kept hidden away from his home presumably because it was subject to being both watched and searched. However, not all of the witnesses that were called agreed to cooperate with the proceedings. David Douglas, a wright from Cupar, was called to give evidence but after prevaricating in the stand he was jailed, which highlighted the level of pressure that the authorities were exerting on witnesses.

Perhaps the most serious allegation was made by Walter Brown, a bleacher from Cupar, who indicated that he had been disturbed by comments that he had heard at a meeting, which described how houses would be burned down and that any soldiers would not be able to intervene in time. Brown seemingly contacted the authorities but he continued to attend the meetings. Although he was not accused by Mealmaker's counsel of being a spy, Brown certainly seems to have been working for the authorities. He also testified that he had been told about a planned uprising that would take place simultaneously in Scotland and England, with troop numbers and the level of support for the rising being discussed. Finally, after the giving of evidence had continued into a second day, the officers involved testified to the events leading up to Mealmaker's arrest and the prosecution closed its case at 9 p.m. on 11 January 1798.

Mealmaker's counsel declined to call any witnesses in his defence and the speeches to the jury then proceeded, with the Lord Advocate going first. He began by apologising for the lateness of the hour but emphasised that the 'magnitude of the offence and the consequences for the British Empire required it'. Comparing Mealmaker with the previous martyrs, the Lord Advocate pointed out how just four years had passed since the earlier convictions and suggested that through the British Convention and the French Convention another societal challenge had been made, led by Mealmaker. He acknowledged that it was Mealmaker rather than Palmer who had been the author of the seditious document for which the latter had been transported, although there was no hint of an apology or a proposal for clemency for Palmer.

For his recent actions, the Lord Advocate accused Mealmaker of inciting violence and referenced events in Ireland, despite the fact that almost no evidence was provided during the trial which proved this link between the two societies. Instead this accusation was purely based on innuendo and circumstantial evidence to paint a picture of a revolutionary leader. More sinister and damaging was the accusation that Mealmaker had stated that any magistrates who dared resist would have their throats cut, though again no witness appeared to provide any evidence for him having made this threat.

In his summing up the Lord Advocate once again contrasted the supposed liberality of the British Constitution 'where every man has the right to investigate the measures of government and may find fault with any Minister', with the threat of revolution from abroad, which was apparently 'not the fair open and manly manner which has hitherto distinguished Britain'. All this was said without any shame or sense of irony, despite how the radical trials had been conducted and the repressive regime that had been unleashed.

As the Lord Advocate concluded, the real reason that Mealmaker was guilty – as was the case with the other convicted radicals – was because he was a ringleader who posed a threat to the good order of the state. In reality this was the establishment's position and as a result the Lord Advocate asked the jury to impose 'such a punishment as may deter others from making similar daring attempts to overturn the happy constitution of this country, which has hitherto remained the admiration and wonder of surrounding nations.'[23]

The speech by Mealmaker's counsel was largely legalistic with multiple references to the greater tolerance for reform that existed in England. But whilst that system may have worked for Thomas Hardy and other English radicals, it carried no weight north of the border. By the time the speeches to the jury had finished it was 3.30 a.m. and the court adjourned to return at 2 p.m. later that day on 12 January 1798.

However, little time was afforded Mealmaker for rest or reflection. When the case reconvened, the jury were quickly addressed by the judges, with Lord Eskgrove taking the lead, and almost as quickly returning a unanimously guilty verdict. The court was as unsympathetic as it had been in previous cases. As with all his fellow martyrs, other than Palmer, Mealmaker was sentenced to fourteen years' penal transportation.

Although he had not given evidence in his own defence, Mealmaker addressed the court after his sentence was handed down and his statement was reported in the *Caledonian Mercury*. He delivered his speech with less eloquence than Muir and less ferocity than Margarot, but it was a heartfelt address, if somewhat subdued, although this was perfectly understandable given the sentence that had just been imposed upon him.

Mealmaker stated that:

He thought his sentence hard, considering it had only been proved against him that he had published his Catechism, which he solemnly declared was merely intended as simple or abstract political propositions and with no view to ignite the country. However, he saw that he was to be another victim to the pursuit of a Parliamentary Reform; but he could easily submit and go to that distant country where others had gone before him. He did not fear it. His wife and children would still be provided for, as they had been before, and the young Mealmakers would be fed by that God who feeds the ravens. As to the Court, he had nothing to say: but he thought the jury had acted very hastily, for if he was rightly informed, they had taken less than a half an hour to consider the whole of his case. They would know best whether their consciences said they had done him justice, but there was a day coming when they would be brought before a jury, where there was no partial government, and where the secrets of the heart were known – he begged to take leave of them all.

And so, Mealmaker was sent to join the other martyrs in Botany Bay. There is no doubt that he was involved in radical politics and in the organisation of a secret and subversive society and this was sufficient to ensure his conviction in those febrile times. Whilst such actions might have been acceptable in England, as the acquittal of Thomas Hardy and others confirmed, Scotland was another legal jurisdiction and had an entirely different political atmosphere. Conviction was therefore almost certainly assured, once Mealmaker was arrested. Although his was by far the harshest sentence imposed on those convicted at that time, again he was not alone as further arrests and sentences quickly followed over the proceeding months. Indeed, Robert Dundas was anxious to have Mealmaker's sentence carried out forthwith to send a message to the public about the consequences of confronting the state. Mass arrests also took place across the country, especially in what were viewed as hotbed areas for sedition 'with Glasgow, Cupar and Ayrshire targeted'.[24] This mirrored actions that were simultaneously taken in England and Ireland as the authorities moved swiftly to crush potential rebellion.

Even before Mealmaker had been arrested, other radicals had been identified and proceedings were being prepared through what was called 'criminal letters'. Basically, such letters outlined the charges an individual was facing, but they also contained the authority for them to be detained. In September 1797 James Craigdallie, the Irish weaver from Perth, who had been pivotal in moving the Scottish societies in a more radical direction, was accused of sedition, being a United Scotsman and of forming clubs and threatening violence. At another trial in 1798 Robert Sands, who was also from Perth, ascribed the growth of the organisation to 'incendiaries from the west', which highlighted the radical evangelism that had spread as Irishmen and others moved about the country.[25]

After Mealmaker's trial and in the wake of the Militia Act riots, many other individuals were speedily rounded up and appeared before the courts. They included some of the leading lights in the Society of the United Scotsmen and supporters in the community, even if their precise roles were obscured by the secrecy of the organisation.

Alexander Leslie, the bookseller from Edinburgh mentioned earlier, came before the court in March 1798, charged with sedition. Despite the fact that the timing and nature of his arrest was similar to members of the United Scotsmen, he was not accused of being a member of the group. His alleged crime was the distribution of literature, including Thomas Paine's *Rights of Man* and *The Age of Reason*, as well as other Jacobin and radical writings. He fled whilst on bail, but his trial highlights the fears that the authorities held about the existence of a wider network and links with radical groups elsewhere in Britain and Ireland.

Born in Jedburgh, Leslie had moved to Edinburgh as an apprentice shoemaker before opening a bookshop in the capital's Southside in March 1796. The shop became a well-known haunt for radicals and democrats, and Leslie also published pamphlets, including some written by himself. As well as providing this publishing service for the local community, he forged links with other booksellers and radicals around Scotland and in London; as a result of travelling around the country he obviously forged an extensive list of contacts. His marriage to a weaver's daughter from Glasgow further embedded him in radical communities.

The authorities did not target Leslie just because he had extensive contacts around the country and within the London reform societies. His role in bookselling and publishing must have also been a considerable concern. The sharing of books, newspapers and pamphlets and reading clubs were a core part of the dissemination of the radical cause, especially in the weaving communities where literacy and education were venerated and books were shared amongst many given how expensive they were. In addition to clamping down on radical societies, the authorities wished to restrict the supply and distribution of information.

Although Leslie was neither charged nor proven to be a United Scotsman, he was certainly at least a sympathiser for the cause. In a letter to a fellow radical he expressed his strident views and referred to 'these cursed Brigands and Ruffians, for they are a race of Monsters that ought to be exterminate the Earth, Kings & Priests have in all ages been a Curse in making Ruinous & Bloody War'.[26] Incriminating documents relating to oath-taking societies were found at Leslie's premises and he was found to be in possession of a letter from a reformist in Dunfermline from November 1797, which stated:

Fife seems to yield a pretty good crop of Pattatoes this season but not good in this corner as might have been expected. The soil of this corner seems to produce the Royal Blood kind best, the new kind you know fore kings from what I hear this sort of crop has not been very luxuriant around Edinburgh.[27]

Euphemistic it may have been with its allusion to planting potatoes, but this letter must have sent alarm bells ringing for the authorities.

Similarly, Leslie's contacts in London would have raised concerns. Despite the influx of members from Ireland and the imitation of the group's name and constitution, many if not most in the United Scotsmen would have sought out allies in London rather than Ireland. This again demonstrates that although the society operated entirely separately from sister organisations south of the border, much was still predicated on British-wide constitutional change, as opposed to the restoration of an independent Scotland. Other documents found in Leslie's possession included pamphlets from the British Union Society, which had broken away from the LCS and was far more extreme, if not openly insurrectionist. It is unknown whether there were any formal links beyond the incriminating documents mentioned above, but with the knowledge that the LCS had dispatched agents north, stopping any cross-border cooperation would have been viewed as essential by the authorities.

Yet more radicals were soon to face trial. Archibald Gray, a warehouse keeper from Irvine, was likewise accused of sedition and of being a United Scotsman operating in the Ayr and Renfrewshire areas. He was charged with distributing anti-government leaflets, promoting disloyalty and threatening acts of violence. As with Mealmaker, he appears to have had a relatively senior role in the society. For example, he travelled across Scotland promoting the cause and encouraging the formation of groups.

David Clouston from Glasgow and John Johnston, a weaver from Pollokshaws, were charged with sedition and accused of being members of the United Scotsmen. Subsequently, in September 1799, John Kennedy faced charges at the High Court in Ayr of sedition with reference to being a United Scotsman. He failed to appear and was outlawed. His Ayrshire comrade Archibald Gray also decided to flee rather than face certain conviction. Rather than heading abroad, he decided to hide amongst the weavers in Strathaven where his presence remained undetected for several years.

Later David Black, a weaver from Banff, and James Paterson, a weaver from Pittencrieff, were accused of being United Scotsmen and of administering oaths in Dunfermline. They also allegedly attempted to suborn soldiers, and celebrated the rebellion that had broken out in Ireland in 1798, which had largely been driven by the United Irishmen. Black fled and was outlawed, but Paterson stood trial and was unsurprisingly convicted by a jury that was packed with members of the landed gentry. He was sentenced to transportation for five years. Other convictions took place elsewhere in the country, many of which did not receive the same profile or attention as the cases mentioned here. Some proceedings were dropped or dismissed, including those against Theophilus McAllister, the Irish weaver who failed to appear for trial on charges of sedition. The Lord Advocate explained that McAllister had enlisted in the army and on that basis a warrant would not be sought. Similarly, the case against the co-accused William Neilson, a weaver from Kilwinning, was deserted, which meant that the prosecution was abandoned.

All of these cases confirm the wide influence that the Society of the United Scotsmen had across the country, from west to east. As with the Pike Plot it is easy to overestimate the numbers involved and the extent of support across the country. Whilst it bore the same name, the United Scotsmen never reached the same size nor exerted the same influence as its Irish counterpart. However, it is clear that the numbers involved in the group were far from insignificant and their impact was huge in many communities. Given the pressures the movement faced and the secrecy with which it was required to operate, the group was far from an insignificant organisation, which explains why the government was so fearful of it. What is of more interest is what actions the Society of the United Scotsmen actually sought to do.

Any evidence of planned insurrection or violence was almost totally absent from Mealmaker's trial, despite what the Lord Advocate suggested in his speech to the jury. Reference was made to what was at best hearsay evidence about threats to burn houses and perpetrate violence. Despite this, 'the weight of sworn and documentary evidence was sufficient to make absurd the prisoner's defence that he was merely a member of a reading circle which bought and studied works of political, historical and religious interest'.[28]

Perhaps Mealmaker's activism was best described as 'the right of resistance' rather than 'militant revolutionism'. This was a philosophical position adopted by many utopian thinkers at the time and provided justification for the confrontation of the authorities acting harshly, as opposed to planning insurrection. Although the evidence at Mealmaker's trial was limited, it gave credence to the government's suspicions that rebellion, and not resistance, was being coordinated. And this is a consideration that must be borne in mind when looking at the riots and disturbances that occurred as the crackdown on the United Scotsmen commenced.

CHAPTER 11

THE MILITIA ACT RIOTS

By the late 1790s the war with revolutionary France was draining all available military resources and recruitment was beginning to dry up, with even the additional numbers provided by the volunteer regiments proving inadequate. Further recruits were therefore required and conscription was to be introduced. This was something that had never before applied in Scotland, although conscription had been used in England as far back as 1759.

Popular sentiment north of the border was distinctly hostile to the concept of conscription, more so than south of the border, which belied the image that seems to have arisen over later years of the Scottish as proud champions of their military heritage and renowned regiments. Many individuals enlisted for service as the empire began to expand but most who signed up were driven by poverty and circumstance. The military also proved to be unpopular in many Scottish communities following the actions of soldiers during bread riots and other civil disturbances. The forces were also especially disliked in towns where they had been billeted and in areas that had become garrison towns as fortifications were laid. Disorder amongst off-duty soldiers, often fuelled by drink, hardly endeared them further to the local community and activities, including press ganging, compounded the distrust and open dislike that many Scottish people felt towards the military.

There had been discussion in Scotland regarding conscription earlier in the eighteenth century when it was brought in elsewhere in Britain but the government had decided against introducing it north of the border. During the American Revolution it was considered again but was once more rejected, due to the lack of public support for it and a view 'that it would be rather dangerous to put arms in the hands of the fanatics in the west of Scotland'.[1] This was obviously a major concern for the authorities and it carried more weight than the need for extra forces.

In December 1792 Henry Dundas once again considered introducing the measure as war with France loomed, but once more decided against it for similar reasons to those listed above. A note from the Lord Provost of Glasgow confirmed the same fears that existed before and stated: 'The idea of a militia is giving serious uneasiness to many people in this town and its neighbourhood, and I am fully convinced that it would be highly improper to trust arms in the hands of the lower classes of people here and in Paisley.'[2]

However, by 1797 the initiation of conscription could be delayed no longer. Fears of a French invasion were very real given the appearance of the French fleet and soldiers off Bantry Bay on the southwest coast of Ireland in December 1796, and it was believed that similar plans existed for Scotland. The appearance of French privateers off Scottish coasts served to exacerbate concerns about an external attack. Both the recruitment of volunteer regiments and the garrison building that had commenced in the preceding years only seemed to offer reassurances about discontent from within.

And so, in March 1797 Henry Dundas wrote a lengthy epistle on the subject to his nephew the Lord Advocate. In it he confirmed the role of the volunteer regiments in both repelling any potential foreign invasion, but primarily ensuring internal tranquillity. However, he questioned their suitability for the former role particularly in the coastal areas and stressed that he believed a more professional military unit was required. The new militia were to be limited in number, but would be charged with the specific task of protecting ports, especially the Firth of Forth and locations further up the east coast, with a similar force deployed on the Firth of Clyde.

As a consequence, enrolment in volunteer regiments was suspended, except in coastal areas, and in June, the Militia Act was enacted. Under the Act, 6,000 men were to be called up selected from lists made up by schoolmasters across the country. The lists included all able-bodied men between the ages of nineteen and twenty-three in every parish. Married men with more than two children were exempt, as were articled clerks, apprentices and all volunteers. These names were then to be posted on the local parish church door and there was to be a meeting of the Deputy Lieutenants in the district where representations could be made before the list was finalised. The ballot would take place shortly thereafter.

Despite the limited number of men listed and the fact that it had already been invoked in England, the conscription drive was, as had been anticipated, much more controversial in Scotland. Anger was caused by multiple aspects of the process, for example the age range used included many of the most economically active men in the community. As substitutes could also be paid, this meant that the conscription burden would fall on the poor, who were unable to find funds to avoid being enlisted. Hostility also seems to have existed more widely, and simply as a reaction to the general principle of conscription. Opposition to the Act came not just from within radical ranks or from the working class, but across a far wider spectrum of society, including the middle classes. Much of this anger was expressed against the army as an institution with some petitions describing the 'abhorrence of the military life'.[3] Once again this contradicts the idea of a people willing to serve in the military for their country.

The strength of the opposition to enrolment was recognised immediately. In May 1797, Robert Dundas wrote to the Home Secretary, the Duke of Portland, who had succeeded Henry Dundas after he had moved to the War Office. Dundas warned that due to the level of discontent and the late implementation of the measure, the troops recruited could not be relied on for that summer. However, the extent of the hostility was to prove even greater than the authorities could ever have imagined.

Tension had been simmering during the summer, largely as a result of economic discontent and general unease about the war. However, when steps were taken to enforce the Militia Act, trouble erupted. Much of it took place over a few days in late August 1797, as school-teachers, church ministers and Deputy Lieutenants attempted to carry out the preparatory steps for recruitment. Some people took part in peaceful protests, by sharing petitions and organising meetings to register opposition and through other non-violent actions. But other actions went far beyond this; there was major rioting in many parts and even open rebellion in some.

Kenneth Logue, who is the foremost authority on this period of unrest, has described how there were forty major disturbances across the country, whilst others historians have claimed there were even more. E. W. McFarland has written of 'riots ranged over seventy counties from New Galloway to Strathtay'. Tom Johnston has mentioned riots in Kirkintilloch, Strathaven, Galston, Dalry as well as in Aberdeenshire, Perthshire and the Borders.

The best summary is probably that by Bob Harris, who wrote that:

Although they began as early as the end of July, protests properly began in Berwickshire, Stirlingshire and Abernethy and several other parishes in Perthshire in mid-August. Few counties or areas in the lowlands were completely unaffected, although in several counties unrest was particularly serious – East Lothian, Ayrshire, Dunbartonshire, Fife and the south-western countries of Dumfriesshire and Galloway. At the end of August, parts of highland Perthshire rose in opposition to the Act in what the Duke of Atholl described at the time as a 'kind of phrenzy', while upper Deeside in Aberdeenshire was the scene of the final spasm of unrest in mid-September.[4]

Although the issue quickly came to a head, tensions had been gradually rising throughout the process as the authorities and those responsible for the bureaucratic arrangements behind the conscription drive laid the groundwork. Deputy Lieutenants had a central role in the selection process but as discontent increased, Lord Lieutenants had to step in as the establishment sought to shore up support for the plans. Rumours had been spreading across several parts of the country that those enlisted would be sent to the East or West Indies or to other distant countries. At this time, such places were perceived to be disease-ridden and dangerous and a few years later some highland regiments even mutinied over duty in such countries. Partly to dispel such rumours but also no doubt to promote the acceptance of the measures, the Duke of Hamilton paid for a handbill to be displayed across his Lieutenancy, which emphasised the supposed limited nature of the enlistment drive. In Midlothian the Lord Lieutenant, the Duke of Buccleuch, did the same and paid for an advert in the local and national papers, which followed the government line.

As is evident from the riotous and disorderly occurrence that has taken place in some of the neighbouring counties to the Militia Act – misrepresentations used to mislead the people and to prejudice them against a measure which, but a few months before, was loudly demanded by the whole nation, the Lord Lieutenant thinks it proper to do all in his power to counteract the efforts of the seditious and to explain the true meaning of the Militia Act. When the Act is properly explained he's satisfied that the people themselves will see through the designs of those who have attempted to deceive them and who would excite them to resist an Act which gives to this country a force, which has always been the pride of England,

and is justly considered by all ranks there as their best and most constitutional defence.

The duke went on to emphasise the limited number of men and the age ranges that would be involved, as well as the exemptions that applied.

Further attempts to paint an image emphasising the reasonableness of the proposals were made; it was pointed out that whilst the Scots could not be made to serve in England, the opposite applied. But such was the discontent that troops and militia had to be brought north from England to suppress the growing disorder. The Cinque Ports Cavalry arrived in Berwickshire before the end of August. The Pembrokeshire Regiment and Windsor Fencibles soon joined them along with other army units, as well as militias, including those from Shropshire and Cheshire. These units had to be dispatched north because at this time so many Scottish regiments were serving abroad and there were no doubt concerns about the reliability of remaining Scottish troops in any event.

The government was obviously worried, as demonstrated by the transportation of soldiers from England, and their fears were confirmed by reports that were being received from around the country. Government records attested to the mounting level of alarm during August and September 1797 and communications to Dundas also confirmed this. A note from the Duke of Montrose that requested support from the military for the enforcement of the Militia Act arrived in early September and another note from the Duke of Atholl suggested that the rising in Perthshire had in fact become treasonous and seemed to go well beyond straightforward opposition to the Militia Act.[5] A further report from the Duke of Atholl about the situation in Perthshire stated that it was 'clear that they had lost control, and there was almost panic'.

There were also alarming reports from Aberdeenshire and the Sheriff wrote about his concerns for the events that were unfolding there. As a result, Robert Dundas confirmed that there were serious concerns about discontent in Aberdeenshire, Banff, Elgin and Nairnshire. However, it was not just the rioting that concerned the government as reports were also emerging of potential mutinies in Balfron in Stirlingshire and elsewhere in the county.[6] Such events indicated that, as in highland Perthshire, the disturbances were about more than just agitation against the Militia Act.

However, just as events had rapidly escalated, things calmed down equally quickly. By the time winter took hold in 1797, the authorities were satisfied that the threat from the protests had abated. Lord Adam Gordon, the Commander-in-Chief in Scotland, believed that peace had been restored and began to stand down the military reinforcements that had been brought in. Much of this belief seems predicated on the swift and brutal response that was meted out by the state, not only through the visible military power on display, but in the suppression of instances of unrest.[7]

For after the Militia Act was passed by Parliament on 19 July 1797 it was not long before trouble started breaking out. Before the month was out, a farmer in Campsie went up to the session clerk and tore out the pages of the parish register that listed his sons to prevent them from being balloted. A few weeks later reports stated that the young men of Strathaven were meeting to discuss their reactions to the new law. Trouble soon began to be recorded in Berwickshire by Lord Home, with Deputy Lieutenants being assaulted in Eccles and being forced by an angry mob to resign from office and leave the village. Further trouble was anticipated in nearby Lauder.

Whilst initially the authorities were not too concerned by the rumblings of public discontent, things grew serious when it became evident that this was not just a localised concern and that the group was growing. Lord Adam Gordon reported to the Home Secretary on 23 August about:

> The very disorderly and very turbulent State in which many parts of Scotland are actually in at the present – and many more have the appearance of being in before many days ... If this bad spirit shall become general and spread to different parts of Scotland – all the forces I can command will be inadequate to force a compliance, and more force must be had.[8]

His request was quickly met and 3,000 soldiers were sent north.

The commander's concerns appear to have been particularly prescient as reports began to filter in from across the country of disturbances on a small but increasing scale. The first outbreak of violence occurred in the small Berwickshire village of Eccles on 17 August where the Deputy Lieutenant was chased away. On 21 August as the Deputy Lieutenant and other members of the gentry gathered to discuss the conscription procedure in Selkirk, several hundred men and women marched through the town and threatened vengeance against any individual who might put their names on an enrolment list. One of the deputies was attacked and others were forced to flee. The following day a large crowd armed with weapons gathered in Jedburgh to oppose the Act. They wanted to confront the Deputy Lieutenant and the major from a Yeomanry Cavalry regiment who were supervising the enlistment process. After being confronted by the cavalry, the protesters fought back before attacking the Deputy Lieutenant. Several individuals were arrested and the rest of the group were forcibly dispersed. On the same day in New Galloway, a crowd stormed the local courthouse where a meeting about the implementation of the Act was taking place; they destroyed the paperwork and threatened the officials and judges that were in attendance. The report that was sent to the authorities in Edinburgh about this disturbance mentioned that it had all the hallmarks of being planned.

It was not just in the south of the country but far beyond that trouble started to break out. In Stirlingshire local meetings held to implement the enrolment legislation saw schoolmasters obstructed and church lists that had been pinned up torn down. But the violence escalated and the outhouses to the Minister of Campsie's manse were burned down, the schoolmaster in Kilsyth was threatened and the planned deputies' meeting in Balfron had to be abandoned.

The authorities were most concerned that the trouble might move beyond more rural parts and into industrial areas, and this soon happened when trouble flared in West Lothian. Threats had been made in Kirkliston and the Earl of Hopetoun had requested military aid, fearing that the Yeomanry would be inadequate to suppress the unrest. Members of the Yeomanry were indeed threatened and some had their homes and farms attacked; as a result the county was then left to the military. On 24 August a large crowd of approximately 2,000 individuals gathered on Bathgate Muir in opposition to the Act. The crowd came not just from the town itself but from neighbouring villages, including Livingston, Torphichen and Whitburn. They demanded that the lists of names be handed over and that the Deputy Lieutenants sign agreements to take no further action in implementation of the Act. A judge was waylaid and the two Deputy Lieutenants were threatened, as a committee to oppose the Act was established.

In Cambusnethan, near Wishaw, a crowd demanded the list from the schoolmaster before proceeding to the Deputy Lieutenant's house where they made it clear that they would oppose the list, suggesting that all Scotland was doing likewise. A few days later on 28 August a crowd gathered in Carstairs and forced the schoolmaster to surrender the session book before surrounding the house of the Deputy Lieutenant and requiring him to sign an agreement to take no further action. He then wrote to the Duke of Hamilton, who was the Lord Lieutenant for Lanarkshire, seeking military assistance and asking for someone else to take over in his place. In Lanark the following day the

Provost was forced to sign a declaration that stated that he would take no further action on the militia enlistment.

Such was the strength of the opposition across Lanarkshire that the Duke of Hamilton halted efforts to impose the legislation in the county; he wrote to the Home Secretary and explained how the middle and lower ranks across the entire country were vehemently opposed to it. However, this appeal fell on deaf ears in London and he was directed to impose the Act regardless, which he subsequently did. Following this, virulent opposition remained in the county for a considerable time, with further disturbances being reported in Strathaven, Kirkintilloch and in the parishes around Glasgow.

Further west in Dunbartonshire disturbances were also breaking out. On 25 August the schoolmaster's house at New Kilpatrick was raided and the parish list was seized. A large and threatening crowd then forced a meeting to be abandoned. The Deputy Lieutenants had fled by this stage, but later returned with cavalry reinforcements and the crowd was dispersed and arrests made. It was suggested that many of those who had gathered had been Irish or from outside of the area. On the same day groups from Kirkintilloch and Cumbernauld numbering several thousand assembled at Condorrat Toll, and again many members of the Irish community were reportedly involved.

But it was not just in the central belt of Scotland that challenges were faced; on 25 August disruption also began in the southwest. In Kirkpatrick-Fleming in Dumfriesshire a meeting was disrupted, parish lists were taken and the Deputy Lieutenants were forced to take oaths to cease their actions. Seditious speeches were made, which were the prelude for widespread disorder across the region and in particular in Dumfries itself, but also in the neighbouring villages of Dunscore, Holyrood and Caerlaverock. Such was the extent of the unrest that the Provost of Dumfries reported that he thought it impossible to implement the Act as schoolmasters and other officials were fearful of their lives; and thus, by 27 August all meetings in Dumfries and many in Galloway had been abandoned.

There was a riot in the village of Dunscore on 28 August and three days later a unit of the Lancaster Fencible Cavalry had difficulty in dispersing a crowd at Boreland of Dryfe. Along the Solway coast in Wigtown a crowd broke up a meeting at the courthouse, even though there was a military presence nearby. This indicated that the crowds had been rash in organising the gathering or that they were keen to confront the soldiers.

Up the coast in Ayrshire, disturbances began on 26 August when a large crowd marched from Beith to Dalry to disrupt a militia meeting being held there. On their arrival they planted a tree of liberty and posted guards on roads into the town. The Deputy Lieutenants and the Earl of Eglinton who were there to conduct the meeting were forced to make a quick escape. Elsewhere in the county, populations in Galston, Newmilns and Stewarton were said to be disaffected though there were no actual disturbances, other than a tree of liberty being planted at Galston where a militia meeting was planned. The attempt to hold the meeting saw the Deputy Lieutenants surrounded by an angry crowd and told in no uncertain terms that the Act had been firmly rejected by the people of Ayrshire and across the land. A few days later disturbances were reported in Ochiltree and in New Cumnock, where the local schoolmaster was assaulted.

In Fife and Kinross there was a meeting in Falkland of representatives from parishes across the counties on 21 August to express opposition to the Act and to organise petitioning the King. Whilst it was initially peaceful, trouble soon broke out in Leuchars and then on 28 August the parish list in Auchtermuchty was seized. Two days later in Markinch the list was also taken and the Deputy Lieutenants were coerced into signing declarations that the Act would not be enforced. A mob went to the house of another Deputy Lieutenant at Balgonie and attacked him.

The following day 200 people assembled in Pathhead and took the parish list from the schoolmaster before making their way along the sands to Abbotshall, where others had also congregated. The groups joined up with yet another crowd from Linktown, then made their way to the Deputy Lieutenant's house but dispersed when they heard that a military contingent was on its way.

Discontent continued with a follow-up gathering to the Falkland meeting taking place in early September, which was attended by delegates from across Fife and beyond. The attitude of the authorities was also hardening. Supported by the Sheriff and a detachment of cavalry, the Lord Lieutenant confronted the gathering. The stand-off passed off peacefully but the Sheriff subsequently wrote to the Lord Advocate and warned him about the coordinated and planned opposition that was being orchestrated across the country.

Meanwhile, north of the Tay the situation became even more worrying for the authorities. Early in August the schoolmasters in Monifieth and Newtyle were forced by angry crowds to surrender the parish conscription lists. Then on 24 August two Deputy Lieutenants and the Sheriff Substitute for Forfarshire were intercepted on Barry Links by a group of young men and women, forced to hand over the lists and made to sign pledges not to take any further action. On 28 August the schoolmaster at Alyth was forced to surrender his lists when a crowd approached him; they then marched to nearby Rattray, where they ordered the teacher to tear up the enrolment list. These actions seem to have had widespread local support, as the following day large crowds marched from both communities with church bells ringing in Blairgowrie where they forced the abandonment of a militia meeting. That same day meetings in Crieff and Madderty were held up in opposition to the Act, although both ended peacefully.

Wider public opinion seemed much more militant throughout Perthshire generally, with the Lord Lieutenant, the Duke of Atholl, reporting to Edinburgh that many schoolmasters were worried and that those in the Carse of Gowrie would rather resign than risk implementing the legislation. Similarly, in Perth some constables even refused to enforce the Act in fear of reprisals. Meanwhile, some people from highland Perthshire had been amongst the crowd at Blairgowrie and disturbances soon started to move even further north. In this highland part of the county conscription was viewed as an 'alien force not in keeping with local tradition'.[9]

On 30 August a crowd gathered in Grandtully and forced the schoolmaster from Dull to hand over the parish lists, before marching him to Aberfeldy where he was held until he signed an undertaking promising that he would take no further part in enlistment. Although these may have been rural areas, the dissension began to spread like wildfire. By 2 September crowds, including one led by a piper, were marching to the homes of officials in Balnakeilly and Faskally demanding that statements that they would take no further action be signed. The situation worsened the following day when the parish list was torn from the church door in Weem as it was being posted, the schoolmaster in Foss was visited by a crowd and general expressions of discontent bubbled over across Strathtay. Even the most senior establishment representative in the area, the Duke of Atholl, was confronted with a mob descending on his house in Blair Atholl, and forcing him to sign an undertaking. This not only demonstrated the willingness of the people to confront authority, but also exposed supposed clan deference as being non-existent.

However, this was only the prelude to the much more coordinated action that would be the largest of the disturbances across the country. The gathering was led by Angus Cameron, a wright who lived in Weem but was originally from Lochaber and who worked in Aberfeldy constructing a factory and houses. He was staying there with James Menzies and his mother and was already well known as a 'democrat'. As mentioned earlier, it was suggested by Berresford Ellis and Mac A' Gobhainn that he was the leader of the Society of the

United Scotsmen. Although there is little evidence to support this claim, he certainly was a leading organiser in the movement as the events demonstrated. The disturbance was instigated mainly by Cameron and his co-accused and landlord James Menzies, both of whom were United Scotsmen. However, although there is no doubt of the involvement of this pair and that other members of the organisation may have been involved, it does appear that most of the individuals who joined in the rebellion at Weem were simply local people who were opposed to the Militia Act.

From all across Strathtay crowds were congregating as passions against the Militia Act rose. By Monday 4 September a large crowd from numerous villages had come together at Weem where they fell under the direction of Cameron and Menzies. The manse was surrounded and the minister was forced to join them as they marched to the house of a Deputy Lieutenant called Sir John Menzies. At Castle Menzies demands were made for the usual undertaking to be signed not just by the deputy but also by other notable figures who had been taken from their houses and brought along by the group. By then the crowd numbered over 1,000.

Protesters continued arriving from all across the district and by mid-afternoon the crowd had grown to several thousand, with many armed with bludgeons. Although the mob had initially remained outside the gates of the house, this did not last for long. The gates were forced open and the crowd spilled in, rushing to the door of the grand house, shouting threats to the Deputy Lieutenant and forcing him to sign the agreement. The Deputy Lieutenant's son refused to sign and was dragged from the house and beaten. Thereafter, the group withdrew and Cameron addressed them from a pillar at the entrance to the grounds. As well as emphasising the justness of their case and urging them to stay true to their beliefs, he had them raise their right hands and take an oath to be true to each other and united in opposition to the Militia Act. It may not have been a formal induction into the ranks of the United Scotsmen but it was similar to it in many ways.

Thereafter, with Cameron riding up front on horseback, the crowd proceeded to the homes of other dignitaries and deputies in villages, menacing them and forcing them to sign the undertaking. By evening the numbers had continued to swell, although Cameron had broken off to meet a group coming towards them from the Atholl area. After returning with them, they joined up with the existing crowd and Cameron once again exhorted them to continue their efforts. Many spent the night outdoors where the atmosphere seemed more akin to a celebration with singing and dancing taking place. The following morning the crowd – by now numbering several thousand – marched to the homes of other gentry and ministers nearby, forcing them to sign the same undertaking, whilst threatening and harassing others. Once he heard what was going on, the Duke of Atholl martialled loyal tenants to help defend him and the crowd veered away. As the horde swept across the area over a number of days, protesters appear to have come and gone and the numbers in the crowd fluctuated, no doubt many having to deal with their land and business.

Then on Sunday 10 September in Kenmore, Angus Cameron addressed people gathered in the kirkyard. He addressed them in Gaelic and told them that there was a meeting organised near Fortingall the following day where 15,000 to 16,000 people from all across Strathtay would be gathering to demand the repeal of the Act. He then headed to Kinloch Rannoch where he delivered the same message, exhorting crowds to go to Fortingall the following day. Cameron's enthusiasm for action apparently extended far beyond opposing the legislation. He made reference to a petition to the King that could attract a million signatures and he also spoke about breaking open the armouries in grand houses.

However, despite Cameron's best efforts the turnout was limited. Perhaps people had tired of the demonstrations or simply they had to get back to their homes and land. Maybe his desire for rebellion was too far beyond their wish for an abandonment of the Act. But for whatever reason this marked the end of the disturbance and people began to drift away, doubtless disheartened by the low number of people that attended and the fact that the reality failed to live up to Cameron's rhetoric.

The indications that the crowd was wavering and weakening were also the signal for the militia to intervene. A section of the Windsor Foresters Regiment had been stationed near Blair Atholl for several days; whether through discretion or fear they had refrained from taking any action, but were ready to pounce. That may also have been a factor in the diminishing support for the rebellion, as the community would have heard about the arrival of trained soldiers. In addition, the Lancashire Dragoons and the Scottish fencible and volunteer regiments had also been mobilised, the latter of whom had been given a bonus for extra duty.

Soldiers seized Cameron and Menzies from their beds at home in Weem several days later and marched them off to jail in Perth. However, a group of 400 or 500 supporters – some of whom were armed – pursued the military detail as far as Dunkeld. Shots were fired and attempts were repeatedly made by the crowd to free the two men. However, the discipline and strength of the soldiers meant that they managed to repel the mob and continue south with their prisoners.

North Perthshire was quiet thereafter, though a sombre and sullen mood was reported in the area. Grievance and anger remained even if outright opposition had ceased. But disturbances still continued in other parts of the country. Aberdeenshire was to see the final flourish of Militia Act disturbances. On 6 September the Earl of Aboyne reported that the area was in such a ferment that he was unsure whether to continue trying to impose the legislation and feared confrontations if planned meetings proceeded. His fears were echoed a few days later by the Sheriff Deputy of Aberdeenshire, although he believed that the trouble would be restricted to Aboyne and some coastal parishes.

As it was, on 16 September crowds descended on Aboyne from all across the county where they tore up lists, insulted ministers and schoolteachers and confronted a Deputy Lieutenant. Three days later a similar event was reported near Ballater where crowds from four or five parishes gathered to confront the authorities. Reports received in Edinburgh also suggested that individuals were going from Aberdeenshire into neighbouring Inverness-shire seeking to stoke up discontent.

Just as they had materialised without notice, the Militia Act riots ended without any specific acknowledgment. The disturbances simply stopped occurring despite the fact that discontent and anger lingered. By early October 1797 Robert Dundas reported to London that the troubles were over. Lord Adam Gordon, the Commander-in-Chief in Scotland, started to allow the English troops that had been brought north to head back south as he was confident in his ability to maintain order. The killings in Tranent (covered in Chapter 12) and arrests elsewhere were widely reported in the press and no doubt served as a warning for many. In the same month a report from Perth stated that the city had been 'completely subdued by terror' although democratic sympathies still lingered.[10] Radicalism may have been suppressed, but it was most certainly not dead.

In addition, as had occurred previously a softer response was also used and this was received well. More advertisements and notifications were issued by landowners and the wealthy, and pardons for misdemeanours were offered. In some areas funds were even set up by the gentry to pay for substitutes. This quickly had an effect and in Beith, which was once a hotbed of dissent, it was reported by the Earl of Eglinton that former rioters were now anxious to pledge their loyalty.

But, for some, their tribulations were just beginning as those who were arrested faced trial for their actions and, as with past radicals, there was to be limited justice and little mercy. Eighty individuals faced charges, which ranged from mobbing and rioting through to sedition.

Twenty-three followed the path of many others and absconded, heading south or abroad, and were outlawed. Nineteen were acquitted and for fourteen of the protesters, their cases did not proceed. Twenty-one were convicted and eight were sentenced to be transported. As ever, the trials were quickly organised with most taking place in October 1797, and a handful the following spring.

First up at the High Court in Edinburgh were those charged with the riot at Eccles in Berwickshire on 17 August: Robert Little, a blacksmith from Haddington, Elizabeth Wilson and Christopher Kerr from Eccles, Peter Glasgow from Whiteback and James Richardson from Crooklaw. One of the accused failed to appear and disappeared rather than risk appearing before the court. In hindsight this was wise as the other four, including Elizabeth Wilson, came before Lord Braxfield, who continued in the manner in which he was accustomed.

Although the jury found the defendants guilty, they submitted a note requesting that leniency be shown, as they believed that the accused had simply been misled. This may have been evidence of wider political involvement in the case or alternatively it could be that the jurors felt sympathy for the defendants. Whatever the reason for this request, it did not matter to Lord Braxfield, who described the actions as akin to high treason and that the acts 'had a tendency to break the bonds of society, and to effect the dissolution of the state'.

His comments confirmed that it was the threat to the established order rather than the specific actions by the protesters for which they were sentenced. The allegations amounted to chasing the Deputy Lieutenant out of Eccles, but without causing him any injury. Noting the jury's request for clemency he indicated that the instigation of the offence was irrelevant to the judgment, which was perhaps a cursory nod to suggestions of outside agitation. However, almost contemptuously acknowledging the plea, he said he would restrict the period of transportation imposed from life to fourteen years. Once again, Braxfield stunned the watching crowd with the severity of his sentencing. However, this also seems to have been counterproductive as some of the juries in later trials found the charges not proven, as they were presumably concerned about the harshness of the sentence that might follow if they were convicted. This was acknowledged by Robert Dundas in another note that he sent to London.

However, the accused continued to be brought before the courts around the country. The incidents at Markinch saw John Christie, a tenant farmer from the village, and Christopher Campbell, a weaver from Kennoway, sentenced to transportation for seven and five years respectively, with James Ramsey, also from Markinch, imprisoned for a year. Two of those involved in the Jedburgh riots were given two years' imprisonment with the other cases being found not proven. Robert Fraser from Eckford and Andrew Sprott, a weaver from Bonjedward, were held by the jury to have been active in the mob, although they were not convicted of assault. As a result, they were sentenced to two years' imprisonment.

Next up was the main event; the trial of Angus Cameron and James Menzies. Having been safely locked up in Perth despite the best endeavours of their supporters, they were then brought to stand trial in Edinburgh on charges of mobbing and rioting, although there are suggestions that the Lord Advocate considered levelling treason before rejecting this charge. After appearing at the High Court on 15 January 1798 Cameron was surprisingly granted bail, having been in custody since his detention in September 1797. When the case was next called on 17 January, Cameron failed to appear and a sentence of outlawing was passed. The Lord Advocate declined to proceed against Menzies in Cameron's absence, holding that the latter was the major party involved.

Cameron fled to Hamburg where many Scottish and Irish radicals were already resident. Remaining there for many years, he returned to Scotland only once the revolutionary years had passed. In February 1825 he applied to the court to have the sentence of outlawry revoked, stating that he had been unaware that the Lord Advocate had been intent on continuing with his prosecution and that he had been living in Glasgow for several years. He was admitted to bail but the crown declined to put him on trial and he continued to live out his days in the city.

Kenneth Logue has speculated that Cameron may have provided information to the authorities about the Society of the United Scotsmen and as a consequence of which he was allowed to flee.[11] Although there is no evidence of this from any specific source, it certainly is a compelling explanation. The decision to restrict the charges to mobbing and rioting rather than treason, the unusual granting of bail at a very critical juncture in the case and the conviction of Mealmaker just days before the trial, all lend credence to this idea.

Other radicals were not to be so fortunate, as trials for other incidents came before the court as the year unfolded. Although the case against the New Galloway rioters did not proceed to court, the one involving those at Wigtown did. However, only one of the accused appeared, the others having taken flight. Thomas Carnochan, a shoemaker from Wigtown, was charged with sedition and found guilty by a jury but they then sought clemency. The High Court – perhaps as a reaction to Lord Braxfield's earlier severe sentencing which had caused a public outcry – let him go, having argued that they were sceptical that a crime had been committed.

February 1798 saw another trial as a result of the disturbances in Fife. Robert Williamson, a shoemaker from Markinch, David Henderson, a wright from Coalton of Balgonie, James Aitken, another wright from Balgonie, John Drummond, a tailor from Dalginch, Sarah Greig from Brunton and Ann Williamson from Kennoway were all charged with mobbing and rioting and resisting the Militia Act. All were convicted, although Sarah Greig was held to have been only involved on the fringes. The men were all sentenced to one year's imprisonment and Ann Williamson and Sarah Greig received two months' and one month respectively.

Perth High Court was to be the venue for the remaining Tayside trials from the incidents at Blairgowrie and Strathtay. The first case to be called on 3 May involved the disturbances in the Strathtay area, but the two accused had already fled and were outlawed. Next up were four accused, including James Menzies who had seen his earlier prosecution deserted when he had been charged with Angus Cameron. Menzies was described as a merchant from Weem, his co-accused were John McLaggan, commonly called Duke Lennox, John Stewart alias McCulloch, a merchant in Newbigging, and James McIntosh. All four were convicted of mobbing and rioting at Castle Menzies where the Deputy Lieutenant had been intimidated and his son assaulted.

Despite the Lord Advocate's previous protestations that Cameron was the major instigator, Menzies was still sentenced to seven years' transportation. John Stewart was also due to face the journey to Botany Bay, but was subsequently released. Of the remaining accused, McLaggan was sentenced to three months' imprisonment and then banishment for five years and McIntosh was sentenced to three months' imprisonment but then bound over to keep the peace for two years.

The next day a further seven protesters faced trial as a result of the incidents in highland Perthshire. Two fled and were outlawed. The remaining five were convicted of mobbing and rioting, three were banished for five years and the other two imprisoned for a year each. Sentencing for the disturbances in Blairgowrie was similar. Nine people had been charged initially with mobbing and rioting, but the crown did not proceed with the case against three and another two fled before trial. Of the four who remained, one was acquitted by the jury and the other three were convicted and sentenced to one year's imprisonment. This largely brought the Militia Act trials to a conclusion.

Many, if not most of those convicted actually had little known involvement with the United Scotsmen and few were known to be members other than Menzies. However, the organisation itself had been rocked by this onslaught and no doubt morale had been considerably weakened. Moreover, as membership was a crime in itself, those involved would have sought to distance themselves from the group. Despite that, the organisation continued to operate throughout that period, showing its roots in some communities.

However, a further wave of arrests of United Scotsmen in the heartland areas of Glasgow and Renfrewshire in February and then April 1798 seemed to finally crush the society. There was limited reporting of these prosecutions as those involved were viewed as being of less significance or seniority than the other radicals who had preceded them. Many may have been allowed to simply leave the group and others may have enlisted to avoid imprisonment. A further reference was made to the organisation in 1801 but by then it had largely disappeared from official and public consciousness, even if democratic and radical sentiments remained.

As on later occasions, an iron fist response was followed by demonstrations of leniency. The Militia Act was implemented later that year although it was accompanied by a concerted effort by the authorities to allay public fears and strenuous efforts were made to promote it. The ongoing war with France was also beginning to have an effect as popular loyalism rose and antagonism towards the foreign enemy increased. Events in revolutionary France, with the rise of Bonapartism, also saw public sympathy for radicalism damaged. The brief history of the United Scotsmen was all but over.

This did not mean that either dissent or disturbances completely stopped, even though they dissipated substantially. Only a few years later in 1800 trouble broke out as a result of economic conditions rather than conscription. Although such unrest was localised it was still widespread across some areas, with rioting breaking out in Ayrshire, Renfrewshire and Glasgow in February and March and a few months after in Edinburgh. Later in the year Glasgow again saw disorder, as did Pollokshaws and Ayr. In some areas the military had to be brought in and in Edinburgh the volunteers were armed and deployed on the streets to keep order. Whilst the primary cause of the rioting was understandably poverty and hunger, it was conceded by the authorities that underpinning it were the same radical sentiments that had bubbled over before. Indeed, Scottish radicals appear to have latched onto these ideas and published handbills supporting action in some areas. There were also suggestions that in many of the areas worst affected it was once again Irish immigrants and the United Irishmen or at least former members who were involved in inciting discontent. This was certainly the case in Kilmarnock where many Irish immigrants had found work in nearby coal mines.

This was compounded by events in Ireland when in 1798 open rebellion broke out initiated by the United Irishmen. Some Scots would have supported their radical colleagues, as they did later in other conflicts in Ireland. As referred to in Chapter 10, there were reports of gunpowder being shipped across to Ireland and the United Irishmen were active in trying to gain support in Scotland. However, the authorities were aware of the links and steps were taken to intercept those crossing from Ireland, as well as monitoring what was happening in Scotland. Despite the endeavours of agents of the United Irishmen, there were to be no risings in Britain along with Ireland. They were on their own.

The 1798 rebellion broke out haphazardly around Dublin in the May. Ulster saw troubles the following month and there was even a landing of French troops along with Wolfe Tone later on in the year. Having managed to persuade the French of the possibilities of a successful rising, two expeditions were dispatched from France but were too late into the field and lacked the strength to defeat the British. However, the United Irishmen were joined in the uprising by the Defenders, a Catholic and primarily rural organisation. Sectarian atrocities were perpetrated by both sides as battles waged across the land leaving a legacy of bitterness that, for many, lingers to this day.

Despite early setbacks the British military machine was eventually able to restore order and as elsewhere brutally repressed those that had rebelled.

Scottish soldiers were involved in the ruthless suppression that followed, especially in Ulster where many Scottish regiments were based, and many of which behaved far worse than the English soldiers had in their own land. In Castlebar, the Fraser Fencibles 'raised a spirit of discontent and disaffection which did not before exist' and appear to have acted viciously and indiscriminately.[12] Thankfully most Scottish soldiers behaved orderly and adhered to command and discipline. However, there was an obvious disdain towards the Irish people, something that would be reflected in later conflicts. Any hopes that the United Irishmen might have held of the Scottish regiments siding with them soon evaporated.

A popular song for Scottish soldiers at the time highlighted the contempt they felt for the Irish rebels:

> Ye Croppies of Wexford, I'd have you be wise
> And not go to meddle with Mid-Lothian boys,
> For the Mid-Lothian boys, they vow and declare,
> They'll crop off your heads as well as your hair,
> Remember at Ross and at Vinegar Hill,
> How your heads flew about like chaff in a mill,
> For the Mid-Lothian boys when a croppy they see,
> They blow out his daylights or tip him cut three.[13]

As a result of the conflict many rebels from the north of Ireland sought sanctuary in Scotland. Some took part in the rebellion itself but many more fled the sectarian violence that followed in its wake, as resentment over land and religion spilled over. Initially, the authorities in Scotland took steps to try and turn refugees away but the volume was such that many simply slipped through. In addition, posing as civilians, some members of the United Irishmen also sought to avoid capture or imprisonment by crossing the North Channel.

It was not easy for those who fled regardless of whether they were radicals or refugees. Volunteers in parts of southwest Scotland were mobilised. Hundreds were arrested and fighting at one time broke out between the Ayr Volunteer Corps and an armed Irish group, who were doubtless United Irishmen on the run. Thousands of Irish citizens arrived and dispersed across the country or travelled down to England. Such was the concern of the Lord Advocate that he even considered bringing in a Repatriation Act.

Ironically, although many came bringing their radical ideas, as others had done before, a few also brought over Orangeism. The sectarian violence that had broken out caused some Ulster Protestants to reconsider their position and moved from promoting radicalism to defending their religion. Most of those who helped establish the Orange Order had not been involved with the United Irishmen but had fled as sectarian conflict broke out. It is believed that the first lodge established in Maybole may have come about from returning Scottish militia from Ayrshire and Wigtownshire who brought the concept with them. They were soon joined by Protestant settlers and by a few former United Irishmen, although as with volunteering for the armed forces in Scotland, some of that may have been part of an effort to be seen to be renouncing past loyalties. However, this also helped to sow the seeds for an extension of popular loyalism and fuel sectarianism in Scotland.

One other group of United Irishmen would also arrive in Scotland and they were prisoners. Many leading figures had been killed and Wolfe Tone had committed suicide, whilst waiting to be hanged. He had requested that he be shot by firing squad as he considered himself to be a soldier, but his request was refused by the British authorities who convicted him after a summary trial. However, others were captured and imprisoned, which for security reasons was in Scotland rather than Ireland. This included most of the senior figures in the United Irishmen as most ordinary prisoners were pressed into military service or banished abroad. Government documents show that consideration was given to various sites to hold prisoners, from the Bass Rock to Dumbarton Castle, before they finally elected on Fort George in the highlands. As the military caravan escorting the twenty prisoners wound its weary way north from Gourock where it had landed, crowds gathered to watch, though it seems more through curiosity than affection or disdain.

The clampdown on and prohibition of the United Irishmen, along with their Scottish namesakes, brought an end to this chapter in Scotland's revolutionary story. But there is one disturbance during the Militia Act period that has not been covered and which was the scene of a major atrocity; the massacre of Tranent.

CHAPTER 12

THE MASSACRE
OF TRANENT

During the Militia Act riots, a massacre took place that is sadly little known in Scotland. Although fewer individuals were slain than at Peterloo two decades later, the massacre was carried out in a far smaller community and where the casualties were proportionally greater. But despite the events in Tranent having taken place in central Scotland, the Peterloo tragedy, which took place 200 miles south in Manchester, remains more widely known. The massacre of Tranent was a military atrocity covered up by the authorities and is reminiscent of actions in the highlands after Culloden.

Events in East Lothian had mirrored those in other parts of the country, with Militia Act disturbances breaking out in late August 1797. A riot was reported in Gifford on 27 August and it was feared that more would break out in Haddington and Dunbar over the following days. As it was those meetings proceeded peacefully although a large crowd did gather in Gifford on 29 August. And it was on that day that another large protest was anticipated at a meeting to be held in Tranent, a few miles west.

Tension had been building over the preceding days with reports of crowds threatening John Cadell, a Deputy Lieutenant from Cockenzie and a local mine owner, and women and children confronting a dragoon, pelting him with stones as he rode past. People in neighbouring parishes were also being mobilised to attend the Tranent meeting, as were workers at numerous nearby collieries. On the eve of the meeting, hundreds gathered and, being led by the town drummer, marched up and down the town streets before parading through the nearby villages of Seton, Meadowmill, Cockenzie and Prestonpans, shouting, 'No Militia!' and calling on people to rally in Tranent the following day.

At a meeting in Prestonpans that evening a letter was drawn up to be submitted to the authorities, which laid out the people's grievances. The document stated their unanimous opposition to the Militia Act and demanded its repeal; they declared that they were peaceful and loyal subjects, but that they would react to any aggression against them. Though the document was signed, names were appended in a circle so that no one could be identified as a leader.

The mood both there and in Tranent was more defiant than ugly, although the schoolmaster in the latter had already fled before he could be approached for the parish list. He went to St Germain's House, the nearby home of David Anderson, a Deputy Lieutenant and later a president of the Board of Revenue in Bengal, who on hearing what was happening feared for public order and immediately sent for military assistance.

Accordingly, when the crowd gathered the following day on 29 August 1797 to protest against the Militia Act, the military were also preparing to confront them. Leading dignitaries had joined those already at St Germain's House, including John Cadell, who had been threatened the night before, and other Deputy Lieutenants. Lord Adam Gordon, the military commander in Scotland, was initially on the scene but would soon return to Edinburgh leaving others in charge. A troop of the Cinque Port Light Dragoons not long arrived from England that had been stationed in Haddington also attended, as did local volunteers and Yeomanry. The Marquis of Tweedale, East Lothian's Lord Lieutenant, had ordered the local volunteer regiments to assemble, as he saw the situation worsening. Commanding the cavalry troops was Lord Hawkesbury, later the Earl of Liverpool and a British Prime Minister, though he remained at St Germain's, whilst his soldiers went to Tranent, a decision for which he would later be criticised. Further reinforcements were still sought and a messenger was sent to Musselburgh early that morning requesting troops from the Pembrokeshire Cavalry who were stationed there. A further eighty mounted soldiers from that regiment would descend on Tranent.

The high-level involvement of senior military and civilian figures demonstrates that this was not the rogue action of badly led soldiers, but part of a general military crackdown. Culpability went to the highest ranks, either as a result of direct orders or a failure to exercise control. For meanwhile people were gathering in Tranent. As with the evening before, the mood was light-hearted yet the protesters were determined. The crowd reaffirmed that they were unwilling to serve in the militia but were intent on protesting peacefully. A drum was being pounded, as it had been the night before, which helped call more people onto the street and whipped up the tempo.

The main street was thronged – estimates vary from between 2,000 and 5,000 people being gathered in the streets – when the deputies arrived, supported by the Cinque Port Light Dragoons and local Yeomanry. Leaving their military escort at the east end of the town, as they thought it would provoke the crowd further, the deputies and their constables proceeded to John Glen's pub where a lieutenancy meeting was being held. As they made their way along the street they were jostled and threatened by the group, which at this stage primarily consisted of women and children. It seems as though the small gang were equally far from polite in their responses. The Deputy Lieutenants, especially John Cadell, were described as being caustic in their remarks and in their general attitude.

Once inside the inn, the deputies set to work but the crowd continued to press and tempers were rising. The street was now packed with men, many of whom were armed with sticks and stones, as well as women and children. The officials decided to let the crowd know how the meeting was going to be conducted and an attempt to do so was made by shouting from an upper window. Stones were then thrown by some in the mob, whilst others demanded a discussion. Bravely or perhaps rashly, Major Wright, who was in command of the Yeomanry Cavalry, ventured out. He was a local man from Ormiston but had become wealthy due to his involvement in the East India Company. Outside, a group of men encircled him in front of the premises and emphasised that the Militia Act was entirely unacceptable to them. A collier stepped forward and advised that if Wright and the Deputy Lieutenants abandoned their task, then they would be allowed to leave without injury. Major Wright summarily rejected this proposition and stepped back into the premises to proceed with the meeting.

Despite the general melee outside, an attempt was then made to compile the conscription lists, starting with some smaller villages and the nearby town of Ormiston. A few individuals ventured forward with information that might exclude them from service. Moving on to deal with the names from Prestonpans, a man stepped forward and the deputies assumed that he intended to provide information. Instead, he presented the document from Prestonpans, which had been composed by the residents in opposition to the Militia Act. This outraged the deputies; they considered arresting the man but wiser counsel prevailed and they allowed him to leave.

His removal initially seemed to hush the crowd but it was only the calm before the storm, as a volley of stones then hit the building. At that point a platoon of six or seven mounted Cinque Port Light Dragoons came down the street to try and calm the situation. They started out with their swords in their scabbards but as they stood in front of the pub door a stone was flung by a woman and their weapons were unsheathed and brandished. This only inflamed the crowd further and as the horses pranced, as they were trained, to try and move the crowd back, a further hail of stones, sticks and bottles was hurled. At this stage the Deputy Lieutenants decided to read out the Riot Act, although it was initially impossible given the tumult taking place outside.

At the same time that the situation at the pub was deteriorating, confrontation was also taking place where the troops had remained in the east end of town. There, a captain had drawn his sword when another hostile crowd had approached, only for him to be faced down by a protester carrying a large bludgeon. This too seemed to further incense the crowd. Meanwhile, back outside the inn the English soldiers were being abused and the deputies were confined inside, as attempts to set foot outside continued to be met by a hail of objects.

By this time the Pembrokeshire Cavalry had arrived to lend support. In an attempt to restore order, mounted soldiers from both regiments then tried to clear the main street by riding down it, three or four abreast. They then began patrolling up and down the road, firing their pistols in the air, which were loaded only with shot and without balls.

However, the absence of live ammunition was also noted by the crowd, who whether for that reason or simply through increasing rage continued with their actions and the situation rapidly deteriorated. Protesters began disappearing up adjacent alleys or paths to sites that were higher than the street, with some even appearing on rooftops. They then began pelting the troops with stones and even chimney stacks. Others went around to the back of the pub and threw stones at the room where the deputies had been conducting proceedings, which brought them to an abrupt halt.

Some cavalry troops were trying to form a line in front of the pub, whilst others were still riding up and down the street with their swords drawn. Order had well and truly broken down. As well as the stones pelting the pub from all directions, some men were also now trying to force their way in through the front door. A burly constable was required to muster all his strength to bar their entry, and only just succeeded in doing so. The deputies were beginning to become fearful for their own safety rather than just feeling anxious about the situation generally. Further attempts were made to read the Riot Act, but this was again simply drowned out by the jeering mob and was met with further stone throwing.

Whether the Riot Act was ever fully read out is doubtful, but it was still deemed as being in effect. However, specific authority was required from a civilian magistrate before the army was able to fire on the crowd. Overall control still rested with civil rather than military powers. With people acting in the heat of the moment and with the threat of later possible sanctions, it is understandable that discovering the truth of what actually happened that night was always going to be hard. No one admitted to providing authority to the military. There were suggestions that it was John Cadell, the Deputy Lieutenant, who had been abusing local women and who seemed most worked up at the time. It was also suggested that it was Major Wright from the Yeomanry who had asked passing cavalry troops why they were not firing. In the circumstances this seems to be a logical explanation, but who gave official authorisation will never be known. All that is known is that the firing commenced and with lethal effect.

However, there is no doubt over who gave the order to fire. Captain Finlay ordered the Pembrokeshire Cavalry to fire their pistols, which by this time had been loaded with ball as well as shot. Regardless, even this round of fire seemed to neither hit anyone, nor have any effect on the behaviour of the crowd. On both the street and up on the rooftops, trouble continued unabated. There were suggestions that the crowd realised that the pistols were largely ineffective from such a distance and that the troops would soon run out of powder. If the shots that were fired had therefore been intended as a warning, it was entirely ineffective. But the order to fire had been for real, as was soon to be shown.

Whether as a result of the failure to have the crowds disperse or as an alternative tactic in an attempt to remove them, Captain Price, the officer in charge of the Pembrokeshire Cavalry, took a troop of Cinque Port soldiers to the back of the houses on the north side of the street. There he ordered them to dismount and to use their carbines on the crowd, which were both more powerful and more accurate than pistols. This had an immediate and lethal effect as a local man, William Hunter, tumbled down from a roof, shot dead. Then, whether in rage or from pent-up frustration at the abuse they had endured, the military ran amok. What followed was cold-blooded slaughter as men, women and children were shot or cut down, throughout the town and across the surrounding countryside.

The onslaught continued for approximately thirty minutes with the troops fanning out and proceeding down the main street, as well as along roads running off it. The shooting was seemingly indiscriminate, with George Elder from Tranent killed on the street as the soldiers moved down it. William Smith, also from the town, was shot in a stairwell opposite the John Glen pub and Isabel Roger, just nineteen years old, was chased by a dragoon into a doorway in her hometown, where she too was slain. Joan Crookston from Pencaitland was found shot dead in a nearby field. She was said to have been beating a drum and leading the crowd earlier.

Whatever desire some locals may have had of confronting the troops swiftly evaporated, as trained soldiers were unleashed on innocent civilians. A massacre was underway. Five were killed in the town but seven more died as people fled and dragoons rampaged after them. The soldiers chased and hunted down people of all ages, across fields and along the roads running from Tranent. Even innocent civilians who were heading to the town, oblivious to what was going on, were injured and slain.

Just as it was uncertain who gave the initial order to fire, it was also unclear who ordered the protesters to be pursued. Afterwards, when it came to a consideration of the events there was conflicting evidence over who had given the command and what it was that soldiers were instructed to do. Much of the later evidence was provided in an attempt to deny that any specific instructions to fire were given and from the Cinque Port Light Dragoons protesting that they had sounded ceasefire on several occasions to bring their own men back as the town quietened and the crowd dispersed.

Responsibility seems to lie with the Pembrokeshire Cavalry, which was perhaps confirmed by the fact that no one from the regiment was available to give evidence when later enquiries took place. Given their direct involvement it is highly suspicious that none were called to give evidence. They also appeared to have no understanding of a bugle ceasefire call, as this was mentioned by other army witnesses, although this is rather surprising and may have been said to exculpate the Cinque Ports Cavalry. Whether they did not understand the ceasefire or simply that blood lust took over will never be known. But what is clear is that the troops raced out and killed with abandon.

Peter Ness, a sawyer from Ormiston, had gone to Tranent that day, to pick up wages owed to him by an employer. Accompanied by a colleague, John Gould, they became caught up in the crowd but denied any involvement in the riot. Whether this was true cannot be confirmed, but they certainly were not involved in any violence, as they sought to safely make their way home. Having taken shelter in a local house, Ness then decided to set off, wishing to return to work as he was afraid of being arrested.

Despite advice to remain where he was, with eye witnesses saying that the military were killing people like pheasants in a field, Ness left the safety of the house. Leaving by the backdoor he jumped a dyke and was making his away across fields towards Prestonpans, when he was spotted by a party of dragoons. Five or six of them then pursued him as he ran through a corn field until he stumbled. Even as he lay on the ground he was not safe and two dragoons rode up and shot him. Gould remained in the house and was spared, as the soldiers passed by.

The troopers then continued down the Ormiston road. Stephen Brotherstone from Pencaitland was also heading to Tranent, he was following his sons who had gone to the town earlier in the day, although they were not involved in the disorder. He was accompanied by his wife and an old man who was also walking in the direction of Tranent, but this did not prevent the ruthless behaviour of the soldiers. After sensing danger, Brotherstone took cover behind a hedge, but as the troops rode past they shot him through the bush. Even after being wounded by the shot, one soldier dismounted and struck him and the old man with his sword. The old man survived, although his face was slashed through to the bone, but Brotherstone was not so fortunate.

Despite his wife's pleas and the fact that he was evidently dying from the gunshot wound, the soldier struck him several times with his sword. Struggling to save her husband, she sought help and a local carter was eventually prevailed upon to come and take him home. Most people were so terrified by the marauding soldiers that they refused to help the wounded man until the carter agreed to help. Unfortunately it was all to no avail and Brotherstone died shortly thereafter.

Meanwhile, the troops continued with their slaughter. A carpenter called William Lawson was making his way home to Tranent with a cartload of wood. Again, there was no suggestion that he had been involved in the riot or had done anything thereafter, all of which must have been obvious to the troops given the time and direction from which he was coming. Nonetheless two soldiers stopped him and despite his pleas one shot him from close range and the other cruelly cocked his pistol several times whilst it was placed against Lawson's head. Lawson survived the assault but died later that week.[1]

William Laidlaw, a farm servant from Winton, which is a hamlet near Pencaitland on the Tranent road, was working in the fields, along with his friend and fellow worker Alexander Robertson. Seeing the cavalry in the distance and hoping to avoid them, they started making their way across adjacent fields. However, they had been spotted and were quickly run down by the mounted soldiers. Robertson begged for mercy but was struck down by the blows from troopers' swords. He was knocked unconscious and covered in blood, which probably saved his life as the mounted officers swiftly moved on. Sadly his friend was not so blessed; Laidlaw was found dead in a nearby field from sword wounds inflicted by the marauding troops.

Women were not spared from the violence in Tranent and neither were children in the fields surrounding the town. William Kemp, aged eleven, from Pencaitland and his brother, who is only named in the records as D. Kemp, who was just two years older, had slipped away to Tranent to watch the action, as young boys have done since time immemorial. Observing the unfolding events from a stairwell in the town, they decided it was time to leave as armed troopers began to clear the streets. As they were sauntering home on the Ormiston road a mile or so from Tranent they heard cavalry behind them and realised that bullets were being fired at them.

Splitting up, William fled down the Ormiston road, whilst his elder brother cut across fields towards the Pencaitland road. The younger boy was soon run down by a mounted trooper who cursed him and swiped at him with his sword. Luckily the soldier only cut off the top of a stick that the child had been playing with and was carrying in his hand. His good fortune continued as the horse galloped on and the soldier did not return. However, his older brother was not so lucky. Pursued by a dragoon, he was stabbed in the chest with a sword and then his head was almost cut in two by a further blow.

Cooperation with the soldiers' orders was also insufficient to ensure mercy. William Moffatt, a brewer's servant from Pencaitland, had not been at the riot, but was quietly working in a field near the Tranent road. One dragoon fired at him but missed and Moffatt then ran off across the field. Another trooper pursued him but his hat fell off during the chase; he then called on Moffatt to pick it up and assured him that no harm would come to him if he did. Having complied with the order and whilst walking away in the belief that he was safe, the soldier coldly shot Moffatt dead.

John Adam, a collier from Macmerry, had been working that morning and was heading for Tranent. By all accounts, he was entirely unaware of what had happened previously that day, until he was met on the road by some young people fleeing the horror. It was soon to become all too real for him.

Adam Blair, a young boy from nearby Penston, had been in Tranent to see the schoolmaster, although the teacher had departed by then and his journey was fruitless. As the riot ensued, Blair sought to make his way home and had met up with other lads trying to do the same. North of the town and hearing bullets whistling by, they ran for their lives. With the group separating, Adam Blair was hunted down by troopers who rode past with one slashing at him with his sword; he was cut on the arm and left for dead.

After recovering, Blair was making his way forlornly home when he met William Tait, a young apprentice tailor from Pencaitland who had witnessed the attack on him, but had stayed away from the troopers for safety. The two lads then linked up and came across John Adam. Persuading him to abandon his journey, all three then set off back towards Macmerry. On their way they saw some twenty troopers in the distance who had obviously got ahead of them and were then heading back towards Tranent.

After holding a brief discussion amongst themselves the soldiers then rode at the small group, firing their pistols as they galloped past. All of the trio dived or were knocked into a ditch, with Tait managing to scramble out, through a hedge and into hiding. From there he saw several soldiers return. Spotting Blair first, one soldier slashed him on the head and neck, despite the youngster's insistence that he had not been involved and his pleas for mercy. One of the soldiers who stabbed him recognised him as the youth he had struck down earlier and said 'that's the bastard whom I stabbed before'.[2] He told his colleagues not to waste any more time on him as he was now sure to die. Thankfully, although Blair was seriously wounded, he did survive and grew up to become a Church of Scotland minister, but never forgot the atrocity he had survived in Tranent.

However, John Adam was not so lucky. Having been shot as the troopers had ridden by, he begged for mercy whilst lying in the ditch. According to William Tait, who heard what happened from his cover, a soldier approached Adam and stated 'there's your mercy', before shooting him again. As he groaned in agony, yet another soldier taunted him for his cries of pain. A subsequent medical examination of Adam showed several sword wounds to his arms and body, as well as two bullet wounds.[3] Even more shamefully, there were suggestions that Adam was robbed by the troopers who had dismounted as he lay dying. With his wife in labour, he had taken two shillings from his purse earlier in the morning and had been going to Tranent to buy provisions. No money was found on him when the body was returned to the family.

Fortunately these were the only individuals killed that day, but many more were wounded; such was the cruelty and disregard for life. As described, Adam Blair and William Tait who had met up with John Adam and warned him to steer clear of the town were struck down. Blair suffered significant loss of blood and given his injuries and limited medical facilities it is miraculous that he survived. William Tait, who had managed to hide, escaped with superficial cuts and a slashed pocket. However, others suffered severe injuries.

Alexander Robertson, a farm servant from North Winton, near Pencaitland, had been working in the fields when three dragoons suddenly fell upon him. Begging for mercy he was badly cut after putting his hand up to ward off a slash at his face, before being struck down by a further blow from behind. After falling to the ground unconscious, he was left alone, presumably as it was thought he was dead. He came round and was helped home by some people who had found him, and despite sustaining deep cuts and losing a lot of blood, he recovered.

Others across the area suffered likewise as the cavalry fanned out. John Blackie, a carter, was walking along the Haddington road, about a mile and a half east of Tranent, when a party of dragoons galloped past. One fired a shot at him which grazed his ear and then others struck out with their sabres, but somehow he managed to avoid their blows as they rode on.

In a field north of that road, William Montgomery, an old man of seventy, was spreading manure on his small farm, opposite the field where John Adam had been slain. The same soldiers crossed over the highway and were set to attack the innocent old man when an officer intervened. Despite the unfolding carnage, this showed that at least a semblance of military order could still be asserted.

Other military units were far less disciplined. The cavalry party that had threatened Montgomery and killed Adam, then attacked a cottage that belonged to George Tillans.[4] Riding up, the door was opened by the farm servant's wife and the soldiers fired at her. Fortunately they hit the lintel above her head, but the shots were so close they singed her hair. After she slammed the door shut, shots were then fired through the windows and the door was broken open. She and others in the house, including children, escaped out of a back window but were captured by troopers. Her husband and two other farm workers were arrested and taken away.

Although they were taken prisoner and unharmed the household were oblivious to what they were supposed to have done. Meanwhile, others from the same cavalry detachment continued their marauding. Moving on, they reached the home of a Mr Carnegie who was away at the time, but they amused themselves by threatening his wife and pressing the tips of their swords against her breasts.

Robert Ross, a mason from Pencaitland, and John Symington, a colliery worker, were walking on the Tranent road, once again apparently oblivious to the events that had unfolded earlier that day, when about eighteen dragoons descended on them. Sworn at and threatened, Ross spotted an officer and clung to his horse's harness seeking protection. Despite grumblings from the troops the officer refused to allow his party to kill them and they both escaped unharmed.

Many other people of all ages and genders must have been assaulted or threatened, but they either chose not to complain or did not want to be identified to the authorities in later investigations. They may have been involved in the riot or may simply have decided that discretion was more sensible and remained silent; for a round-up was underway.

Back in Tranent the crowd had cleared and the deputies and their constables ventured out. John Cadell, who appeared to have still been in a frenzy, randomly grabbed a coal bearer called Janet Hood, who was coming out of a house. Kicking and punching her, he dragged her back into the pub, banging her head against the door as she struggled against him. Nicholas Outerside was then recognised as being one of the Prestonpans men who had presented the anti-militia document and he and others who were with him were pursued down the road by deputies and constables. Cornered in a backyard he was beaten, then arrested, as were his colleagues. Arrests continued as officers seemed to go from door to door in search of any individuals they thought had been involved or were hiding within.

Soldiers surrounded any suspected radicals and thirty-six were taken to Haddington where they were locked up in the Tolbooth. None of the cavalry who had been involved in the killing and maiming were reprimanded. Instead all of those who were imprisoned were civilians and most were from Tranent, having been detained in the subsequent round-up. The summary justice meted out seemed to suffice for the countryside, other than for those who were detained after escaping the assault at George Tillans's house. Most were released after a few days following questioning, although some would be required to stand trial at the High Court in Edinburgh.

The trials quickly came around and David Duncan, a collier from Penston, Alison Duncan, a servant from Elphinstone, John Nicholson, a servant from Windymains, Francis Wilson, a merchant in Tranent, Robert Mitchell, a servant also from Tranent, and Neil Reidpath, a servant from near Tranent, were charged with mobbing and rioting.[5] David Duncan, Nicholson and Wilson failed to appear and were outlawed, though Wilson later appeared claiming to have been unable to get there sooner.

The trial against Alison Duncan, Robert Mitchell and Neil Reidpath proceeded in the interim on 11 October. Duncan said she had been sent to Tranent by her employer to buy cloth. Claiming to have been on the street only to look for her father and to having then been arrested in a friend's house, she denied committing any violence or disorderly conduct. The others similarly denied their involvement.

Mitchell was identified by a Cinque Port soldier as having run up a stair and thrown a bludgeon at cavalry troops down below, but other soldiers failed to pick him out. Defence witnesses spoke to him having been elsewhere. Reidpath was identified by cavalry soldiers as having been on the fringes of the mob but only one stated that they saw him throwing stones. Other evidence from the military witnesses seemed equally contradictory and muddled. The jury found the charges not proven. This may very well have been because of the flimsy evidence laid against them, that those in the dock were only peripheral figures in the events or even that the jury was sympathetic to the accused given the atrocity that had been widely reported. It is also no doubt fortunate that Braxfield was not presiding.

Some of those who had fled appeared to accept a bit more culpability. When first detained David Duncan admitted that he had flung a stone and brandished a stick, as well as producing a sword and striking out with it. It was probably for this reason that he took off. Wilson and Nicholson though seemed to suggest that they had simply been caught up in proceedings, even if the former had flippantly suggested that his name was Henry Dundas when first detained. Thomas Cunningham from Pencaitland and James Whitelaw, a servant from Woodlands, were also charged with having instigated the events and being involved in the mobbing and rioting. But they too fled and were outlawed.

That brought the formal proceedings to an end but investigation and litigation would rumble on for some time. However, despite clear evidence of the events at Tranent being a military atrocity, no soldier, nor any member of the authorities was charged. Instead, those who printed articles about the massacre and sought to pursue justice for the victims were hounded. For early enquiries had quickly shown the soldiers to be culpable. A memorandum from the Lord Advocate, Robert Dundas, to his uncle Henry Dundas in late December 1797 stated that only seven of those killed had been actively involved in the riots.[6] Who they were or the level of their involvement was not specified, but Dundas did admit that two slain had been 'entirely innocent'. They were named as William Lawson, the carpenter making his way home, and John Adam, the collier, ambushed along with the two young men Blair and Tait. The Lord Advocate even mentioned that whilst this merited a murder charge, it could not be proven which soldier had actually shot him. Dundas then went on to question why the military had left the town and mused over whether the acts in the surrounding countryside were unlawful. Scotland's most senior law officer who was effectively in charge of the nation, admitted that command had been lost and that it appeared as if no orders had been given for the slaughter.

Despite or more likely because of what he knew, Dundas closed down attempts by others to investigate the case. It was reported in the *Glasgow Advertiser* on 26 October that Alex Ritchie, a lawyer from

Edinburgh, and William Nelson, a weaver, were speaking to victims' families about a murder charge being brought against the soldiers and about bringing a petition forward. However, this was quickly crushed by the Lord Advocate who said that they were suborning poor and illiterate people; he even attempted to have Ritchie prosecuted. Fortunately, this was held as incompetent by the court. Despite such attempts, as far as the Lord Advocate was concerned the case was closed and there would be no prosecutions for those who committed the atrocity.

A civil case was heard but it was brought by the perpetrators not the victims. Archibald Roger, the brother of Isabel Roger, who was shot in a stairwell, penned a heartfelt letter about the events, which was published in a magazine. It described his sister as one of six people shot dead on the spot and untold others killed as the cavalry pursued them through the cornfields cutting and shooting them down. He went on to state that the actions were unprovoked, with only a few stones having been flung by some boys and women before the dragoons rampaged.

John Cadell, the Deputy Lieutenant, and one of the most violent aggressors of those in Tranent that day, reacted strenuously to the letter, suing not the bereaved brother but the publisher and editor of the magazine, presumably as he was seeking damages and they had more funds. He alleged that he had been defamed as he believed that what had occurred in Tranent had been lawful and carried out in an appropriate manner. There appears to have been restrictions imposed upon what the defendants were allowed to plead regarding the events and the publisher seems to have got cold feet, citing public outcry as the reason for printing the account and suggesting that he had limited knowledge of it at the time. Eventually, after a lengthy hearing, the publisher was found guilty of libel and fined £300. Subsequently the decision was reversed on appeal to the House of Lords, but the money appears not to have been paid and the case was simply closed.

Today a statue stands on the main street in the centre of Tranent. Anyone passing through the town will notice a woman beating a drum accompanied by a small child, although the monument is not signposted and many only catch a glimpse of it as they speed past. The image immortalises Joan Crookston from Pencaitland who was gunned down in a nearby field and who had supposedly been beating a drum to mobilise support. Little else is noted alongside the memorial and those without any knowledge of the atrocity would be unable to make any connection between it and the events in 1797.

As indicated earlier, the Militia Act riots ended almost as quickly as they had begun. By the middle of September, the final flourish in Aberdeenshire had passed and at least a semblance of peace prevailed. Whether this was as a result of an inability to sustain the insurrections or as a result of the brutal military repression is not clear. The atrocity in Tranent had certainly received widespread publicity and the military presence across the country had been substantially increased. Indeed, when he heard of the disturbances, Henry Dundas immediately wrote to his nephew offering even more soldiers and calling for the leaders to be rounded up; although he did also suggest that some modifications to the Militia Act may be possible.[7]

Yet, another crackdown was underway as the arrests of members of the Society of the United Scotsmen, also referred to in Chapter 10, began that very month. James Craigdallie, the Irishman from Perth, and Archibald Gray from Irvine were both detained in September, and Mealmaker was arrested on 13 November. The trials of those involved in the disturbances in response to the Militia Act, as well as those who were accused of being United Scotsmen, were well underway and would continue for several months after the disturbances ended.

The question then arises as to whether the Militia Act riots were all simply localised and spontaneous reactions to deeply unpopular legislation, or was there some planning and coordination behind what were widespread and often significant outbreaks of disorder, albeit over a very short period of time? Kenneth Logue, the major authority on the riots, certainly considered them to have been the former and E. W. McFarland has agreed.[8] Others, particularly Mac A' Ghobhainn, were convinced that they were part of a planned uprising, though he has offered little evidence to support this idea.[9] Tom Johnston referred to the United Scotsmen and alluded to their actions, but stopped short of a direct link between the society and the Militia Act riots.[10]

Logue and many others have been meticulous in their research and analysis of contemporary documents. Whilst acknowledging the difficulties caused by the clandestine nature of the organisation and the clannishness of the communities in question, there are certainly plenty of governmental papers and in particular informant reports, as well as accurate court reports to draw from.[11] It is clear from such documents that whilst there was concern over the United Scotsmen, the Militia Act riots were most certainly not believed to have been orchestrated by them. Analysis shows that the communities were specifically concerned about the imposed conscription, even though such discontent was often underpinned by wider hostility to the authorities.

Likewise, there was little mention at the trials that those who participated in the riots were involved with the Society of the United Scotsmen, other than Angus Cameron, who had led the opposition in Strathtay. Even in the prosecution that followed the atrocity at Tranent, the civil case and the private inquiries that were made by the Lord Advocate, there was no reference made to outside agitation, let alone support being provided by the United Scotsmen. The incidents and causes were, of course, similar in many ways, but this seems to be more of a coincidence than a coordinated effort.

Although the window in which the riots occurred was short, that can perhaps be best explained as being a result of the speed with which the legislation was implemented. The timing was driven more by the demand by the authorities for recruitment rather than those planning to oppose it. The Deputy Lieutenants were operating on a timescale that resulted in a rush at the end of August. There is also little evidence that those involved in the riots sought to link up with other groups, apart from Angus Cameron rallying his followers at Strathtay. Most others were simply opposing the attempt by the Deputy Lieutenants to complete the lists for conscription in their own community, with no wider or further agenda, other than deep-rooted antagonism towards the landed gentry and their acolytes.

The round-up and trials of the United Scotsmen were also mostly predicated on their membership of a secret society and no links were made to the disturbances that had occurred around the same time. The charges included membership of a secret society and seditious activities related to this, rather than insurrection or rioting. It was evident in these trials that the government feared what these individuals might be planning, more than what they had done.

But there is still some underlying doubt that these riots were all spontaneous and that there was no prior discussion or encouragement by the United Scotsmen. There is clearly no indication of direct support aside from those United Scotsmen who crossed the country agitating and encouraging the planting of 'Irish potatoes'. However, the actions of the authorities both before and after the uprisings indicated not just a fear, but a genuine belief that armed rebellion was being planned. It was for this reason that garrisons were built, volunteer regiments enrolled and military units brought up from England, all to deal with the maintenance of internal tranquillity.

Additionally, reports of preparations being made, from the provision of military training to the acquisition of arms, demonstrate that there was more than mere talk taking place. References made by the Lord Advocate indicate that he believed the United Scotsmen to be an insurrectionist group that was either directly or indirectly involved in the disturbances. The memorandum from Henry Dundas and the speedy round-up of alleged members thereafter also confirmed such suspicions about collaboration held by the authorities. The same applies to Robert Dundas's response to his uncle that the Scottish group had copied the United Irishmen.

The truth, as they say, is probably somewhere in the middle. The United Scotsmen were almost certainly an insurrectionist organisation that had been seeking armed resistance, if not revolt. But it was a pale shadow of its Irish namesake, lacking both strength and support. Its links to Ireland gave many members hope and encouragement and Irish members of the Scottish society were also important in pushing the more radical agenda in many areas of the country.

However, the society's larger Celtic counterpart was always aware of the limitations of the group in Scotland, which was best shown in Wolfe Tone's disdain for the movement. Ironically, despite the ties with Ireland and the agents that came and went between the two countries, the political direction of the organisation remained pan-British rather than secessionist. A few individuals may have expressed nationalist sentiments, but most wanted universal franchise through Parliament in London. Still more members were driven by their hatred for the landed gentry and a desire for a more equal society.

Such individuals were limited in numbers, but were not insubstantial. They agitated and encouraged opposition to the Militia Act, certainly in the weaving areas where their strength lay. It was for this reason that George Mealmaker and others were crossing the country and agents were coming and going to Ireland. It is fair to conclude that the Militia Act both motivated and bolstered the cause of the United Scotsmen. Recruitment appeared to increase not just through their own activities but as a result of public opposition to the legislation.

Whilst many members of local level authorities believed that the Militia Act riots were organised, they could have been coordinated by other radical groups or simply by those in the communities who were most active and vocal. Although it is clear, as the Annan magistrates stated, that the unrest 'originated in a few individuals whose principles stand in opposition to the Government', as indicated earlier, there is no evidence that all of the uprisings involved United Scotsmen and indeed many, if not most, did not.[12]

There is also no evidence that any rising was actually coordinated by the United Scotsmen; perhaps at most members told communities that other areas were considering taking action and would follow or support them if they did. The United Scotsmen probably hoped to build upon such events or even to expand on them, if and when they happened. It is also likely that the group's ability to act when the opportunity arose was curtailed as a result of its ruthless suppression.

Nonetheless, the authorities had good reason to fear rebellion even if they might have overestimated the potential strength of it. A threat certainly existed with disturbances occurring across the land and with an organisation that was eager to foment them. Compounding the challenges at home was the risk of invasion from abroad. Around this time attempts were made to encourage the landing of foreign armies and the United Scotsmen were implicated in such schemes. This threat was real, as had been demonstrated just the year before at Bantry Bay in Ireland and would become apparent again the following year, when rebellion broke out across the Irish Sea. Considering what was happening abroad affords an insight into what had occurred and what was being planned in Scotland.

CHAPTER 13

FOREIGN ARMIES AND
THE DUTCH INVASION

As the French Revolution inspired many Scots, it also ignited French interest in Scotland. This was mostly for strategic reasons, although some individuals sought to carry the revolution beyond the borders of France. However, as had previously been the case, knowledge about the 'Auld Alliance' was greatest in the country least powerful and that which would benefit most from it. And so it was with the French Revolution, where the talk of launching an invasion was never as great or ever to be as imminent for the French, and inspired hope amongst some in Scotland.

French dreams of the revolution crossing the channel and breaking out in Britain were soon crushed as war broke out. However, interest in the political affairs of Britain persisted amongst many French citizens and a recognition of a distinct political landscape in Scotland existed. Coverage in newspapers and even references to the situation in debates increased, although far less than the reverse situation in Scotland where talk and passion for the French Revolution was everywhere.

As early as January 1793 Armand de Kersaint, a member of the Legislative Assembly in France stated:

The English People, like all conquerors, have long oppressed Scotland and Ireland; but it should be noted that these two nations, always restive, and secretly in revolt against the injustice of the dominating race, have acquired at different epochs concessions which have engendered the hope of ultimately regaining their entire independence.[1]

He went on to suggest that the spirit of the French Revolution was finding favour in Scotland, adding: 'Nowhere is more joy caused by your victories than in Scotland, the principal towns of which have been illuminated to celebrate them.'

His was by no means an isolated view, as French spies reported favourably on the public mood and the possibility for revolution in Scotland. Visiting Scots, including Muir, described the growing radicalism north of the border, though much was hyperbole and some simply false. A report laid before a French minister in March 1793 described 'the enthusiasm for the revolution evinced by the people in the west of Scotland, the subscription raised in Glasgow on behalf of the National Assembly, the rise of the Friends of the People, and of the counter constitutional associations'.[2] Explaining that despite the persecution the latter had endured, the report emphasised that the group still remained in existence. A further report a few months later suggested that 'though the time and the circumstances were not yet propitious, a foreign enemy would soon cause a revolution'.[3]

An invasion of mainland Britain and Ireland was therefore an early consideration for the French authorities and options began to be considered. Soon the Committee of Public Safety considered plans containing the suggestion of supporting the people of Ireland and Scotland, if they rebelled. Events in Scotland evidenced growing radical support, which provided further impetus. The British Convention held in Edinburgh in November 1793 offered further signs that the political ground was moving favourably, in Scotland at least. The event was widely reported in the French papers and was viewed as positive encouragement to consider plans further.

As a result of the signs of rebellion in the early 1790s, as mentioned earlier in Chapter 8, the French Directorate considered trying to rescue Muir and his comrades from their fate in Botany Bay. Although this plan was aborted, its consideration at such a senior level demonstrated how seriously it was taken, even if it was unlikely to have been successful as the ship sailed with a Royal Navy escort. But as the war dragged on options for invading Britain and Ireland continued to be considered, both to undermine the enemy within and break the military stalemate that had developed on the continent. The main areas of conflict remained on the high seas and continental Europe where the revolutionaries had been experiencing some success. However, the thoughts about a full invasion had never been fully abandoned and would soon resurface.

In 1796 Wolfe Tone arrived in France, as an emissary for the United Irishmen, his purpose to hold discussions with revolutionary leaders about support for a rebellion in Ireland. On the basis of his submissions, along with other available military intelligence, further consideration was given to an invasion.[4] However, Tone feared that the plans might only be part of a proposal for a far wider assault on Britain and even at this early juncture Tone expressed his doubts. He stated to a French general that whilst there might be support in Scotland, he was certain it did not exist in England. He was adamant though that nothing could be done without first setting the revolutionary ball rolling in Ireland.

Tone continued to express these concerns through until the Irish rebellion in 1798. And with good reason, as many in senior positions in revolutionary France preferred the idea of an invasion of Britain, and especially England, to a landing in Ireland, despite greater hostility in the former and larger support in the latter. Perhaps it was simply the size of the country and the opportunity it afforded for the wider expansion of the revolution? Maybe there was hope that Thomas Paine's works could prove successful in the land of his birth, no matter how naïve that may have been. Or, maybe they believed that striking strategically at the enemy's centre could lead to a quicker victory? The precise reasoning is not known but the actions taken certainly confirmed Tone's fears that England was always the preferred landing place for an invasion.

The revolutionary leaders decided to gather more information before coming to a final decision and a spy was therefore sent across the Channel to report back. Heading to London first, he was ordered to find out the level of sympathy for radicalism there. In Scotland he was to ascertain the level of support for a rising and ensure that the Scots were in communication with the United Irishmen. Thereafter similar enquiries were to be made in Ireland, before returning to France.

Citoyen Mengaud was selected for the task, and departed on his mission in 1796, not returning to France until July 1797. His report was very general in nature and Henry Meikle in *Scotland and the French Revolution* understandably wonders whether he actually ever visited Scotland, despite protestations that he had gone to both Edinburgh and Glasgow.[5] In his report Mengaud stated that: 'The Scots, he found, were more disposed to a revolution than the English, and the Irish to a still greater degree. This feeling, which had existed since the Union of England and Scotland and the conquest of Ireland, could be used to excite a civil war.' Some of what he stated was self-evident and such information was already available from reports in papers or through comments from visitors. Much, though, also appeared to be wishful thinking and was certainly not based on evidence on the ground, despite the discontent that existed and recent efforts made by the United Scotsmen. There is also no evidence that he was even in contact with the Society of the United Scotsmen or that he even specifically mentioned them upon his return.

What is more surprising is that the Mengaud venture had taken place after the unsuccessful landing of French troops in Bantry Bay in

December 1796. During the landing, General Lazare Hoche had sailed to Ireland from Brest with an invasion force, but upon finding no sign of any rising and his doubts being compounded by bad weather, he simply returned home. As with some later landings for Irish rebellions the invasion was hampered by poor communications and dogged by ill fate; during the expedition 2,000 soldiers and sailors lost their lives. Despite this failure, it appears as if Mengaud's theoretical report, which he provided upon his return in 1797, was met with enthusiasm and thoughts turned once again to a planned invasion.

However, the next assault was not going to be conducted by the French but by a client state, the Dutch Batavian Republic. The state had been established in January 1795 when revolutionary forces had overrun the old Dutch Republic and it remained in existence until early into the next century. The rebellion that established the nation had popular support, but also required French military power to deliver it. The fledgling state was therefore dominated by its larger and more powerful neighbour, and its government was beholden to it. It was therefore to the Dutch that revolutionary France looked when the next invasion was planned, and the young republic's leaders were only happy to try and prove their worth.[6]

The initial plan was for an invasion of Ireland in the summer of 1797. This followed the earlier failed effort by General Hoche, but still made sense given pledges of support from Tone and the Society of United Irishmen. The Bantry Bay debacle demonstrated a lack of coordination rather than an absence of will amongst the people. Therefore, troops were embarked but weather conditions once again hampered them, and this time they were detained for several weeks in port. By the time conditions were suitable to sail, it was agreed that it was too late in the year, the journey requiring them to go around the north of Scotland to reach their Irish landing places, presumably to avoid the British fleet located in the English Channel.

General Herman Daendels, the Dutch army commander, then

came up with a plan to land in Scotland, before re-embarking for Ireland. A note containing the plans for the Dutch invasion of Scotland can be found in the National Library of Ireland. Although it was written by Wolfe Tone in mid-August 1797, it records Daendels's thoughts, as the Irishman served on his staff at the time.

The Dutch general had interviewed two Irish radicals who had recently arrived from Ulster, via Hamburg. Asking about the possibility of an expedition to Scotland as an alternative, he was advised that they had spoken to comrades who had been in Scotland organising United Scotsmen. However, they stated that 'they could not pretend to say whether the Scottish patriots were up to such a decided part as to take arms in case of an invasion but their opinion rather was that they were not so far advanced'.[7]

Notwithstanding this negative reply, Daendels seemed undaunted and decided to proceed further. Outlining his plan to Tone a few weeks later, they formed a note that the Irishman was to take to General Hoche, who was at this time in overall command of the French forces. The plan was to land 15,000 men at Leith where there was no real military presence, meaning that Edinburgh would lie open before them. Indeed, there were limited military forces in Scotland, which helped explain why English troops were required to be dispatched north to deal with the Militia Act riots.

Having disembarked, the men were then to march across central Scotland to Glasgow. Artillery and munitions were to be carried by barge along the Forth and Clyde canal that had opened in 1790. Mirroring in some ways the geography of the Antonine Wall from Roman days, which stretched from Falkirk to Dumbarton, the waterway would also form a line of defence, if they were challenged by troops from the south. In any event, it was thought that supply lines for British forces would have been cut and communications in the south would be hampered by the invasion. Possessing the element of surprise, it was believed that the troops landing would be able to see off resistance in Scotland and it would be quite some time before adequate reinforcements could be brought north from England.

It was also hoped that Scottish radicals in the central belt would rise, as well as those in the highlands. The information and discussions seem predicated on the two sets of potential allies being distinct and separate. Presumably, the United Scotsmen and other radical allies were expected to revolt in the south and in the highlands dissident Jacobites and supressed citizens would perhaps join them.

The Scots could thereafter be left to deal with any opposition that lingered or may arrive from the south, as it was the intention of the Dutch forces to re-embark once they had marched to the Clyde. Five or six frigates which had landed them in Leith were to sail unloaded around the north coast and meet them. There troops and artillery would re-board the ships, and use other boats that would be available for the short sail to Ulster. Estimates were provided about the large number of ships available in Greenock and at other Clyde ports that were more than adequate for the task.

For Ireland was to be the ultimate destination, as not only was that where the fleet were headed, but French soldiers were also to be sent there directly. By all accounts Daendels was a very able military commander – he even served later in Napoleon's ill-fated *Grande Armée* that disastrously invaded Russia – but this plan was rather far-fetched. He was correct in his analysis of the weakness of military forces in Scotland and that the plan possessed the element of surprise. Also, the British fleet had experienced substantial mutinies that summer at Spithead and the Nore and it must have been presumed that morale would be low amongst the troops and naval ratings. Though they were ultimately resolved, the mutinies rocked the admiralty, and whilst driven by poor conditions and harsh discipline, there also appears to be evidence that members of the United Irishmen agents sought to recruit and encourage revolt amongst their compatriots.[8] This also occurred within the army.

However, the plans for disembarkation and re-embarkation, allied with the sailing of the unloaded ships around the north of Scotland, were ambitious to say the least. Tone had always been sceptical, if not scathing, about anything other than an invasion of Ireland and he was equally caustic about the scheme. Despite his concerns, he obeyed orders and took the memorandum to General Hoche. He also outlined his commander's suggestion that the army should be led by General Jacques Macdonald who was the son of a Scottish Jacobite from the Hebrides and a rising star in the revolutionary army.

On reading the memorandum and hearing about the plans, Tone's scepticism was shared by the French commander. The United Irishman noted in his journal on 13 September that Hoche apparently shook his head at the idea of a second embarkation at the mouth of the Clyde. The French commander also added that Macdonald 'was a good officer, but he knew he would not go'.[9] The plan was not rejected outright and Hoche promised to consider it, though that may simply have been out of politeness towards a senior colleague in an allied army. However, Hoche was seriously unwell and would die within days and the plans died with him. Both the Dutch government and the succeeding French military commanders rejected the idea. The planned Dutch invasion of Scotland was not to be.

However, Scotland's involvement in Dutch military affairs was not yet at an end. It was decided to proceed with one part of the original plan and to attempt an invasion of Ireland, despite it being late in the year. This decision was apparently driven by a desire by the Dutch government to display to their French allies not just their willingness to act but their naval ability. Despite being on a lesser scale than the original plan involving Scotland, it still seemed designed to show what the Dutch were prepared to do rather than what it might strategically achieve. To land in Ireland they first had to get there, and that meant the Dutch fleet would have to confront the Royal Navy fleet, then located in the North Sea.

Yet again the plans were hampered by bad weather. Admiral Jan Willem de Winter was delayed by storms before finally being able to leave the Texel. Sailing out he confronted the British fleet off Camperduin, a small Dutch town on the North Sea, on 11 October. There the Dutch navy suffered one of its biggest defeats at the hands of the British fleet, which was under the command of Admiral Adam Duncan. Not only were the Dutch routed but it was to be the only time that one of their admirals was to be captured, with de Winter forced to surrender.

The British hero was Adam Duncan. Born in 1731, he was the son of the Baron of Lundie, a one-time Provost of Dundee. Scottish he may have been, but he was far from radical. His father was a wealthy man and Duncan himself has already been mentioned in Chapter 4 for his involvement in the King's birthday riots, where he confronted those attacking the house of Henry Dundas's mother. He was firmly part of the establishment surrounding Dundas and supporting the landed gentry. Having joined the navy, he quickly rose through the ranks and was given command of the North Sea fleet in 1795.

His victory at Camperdown, as the British were to call it, was roundly celebrated by the establishment and as a result he was raised to the peerage as Viscount Duncan. The land he owned in Dundee serves as a reminder to his historic triumph and today forms part of Camperdown Park. Newspapers at the time were gushing with praise as Duncan was fêted wherever he went. Ironically, the reports about the accolades granted to him were released at the same time as reports about the Scottish radicals being imprisoned and the United Scotsmen being arrested were published.[10] It was noticeable that in the main, the celebrations for Duncan came from amongst the wealthy rather than the working people, which perhaps showed where wider public sympathies lay. But as with the monuments that were later constructed, history was being written by the victors and Adam Duncan was lauded whilst George Mealmaker was transported. And so, the situation sadly remains today with the hero of Camperdown widely known, yet the leading figure of the United Scotsmen is still largely unknown in the country of his birth.

Despite the Camperdown debacle, French revolutionary forces remained focused on defeating Britain by military invasion. An 'Armée d'Angleterre' under the command of Napoleon Bonaparte was established, with the new commander still basking in the glory of his successful campaign in Italy. This boosted the hopes not just of Wolfe Tone for a further Irish landing, but also of some exiled Scots, that Scotland might be included in a future campaign. Tone met with the French army commander on several occasions to advise him about his thoughts and to seek support for an Irish rising. Some Scots in Paris sought to stoke the flames both in their adopted land and in their homeland. Pamphlets were published for distribution amongst radicals in Scotland calling for support for an invasion and articles appeared in French papers denouncing the despotic government under which Scotland laboured. But it appears to have been sound and fury rather than tangible actions or military preparation.

However, the efforts of those exiled Scots were boosted by the arrival once more of Thomas Muir in Paris, where he was immediately received as a revolutionary hero. Already revered in France because of his courage and early support for their revolutionary cause, his reputation was burnished as a result of his tales of swashbuckling adventures in escaping from Botany Bay. Having never settled to life in the penal colony and with farming holding little interest for the radical lawyer, he soon set about plotting his escape. This finally came about when he was notified about an American vessel called the *Otter* anchored in the bay, whose Captain Ebenezer Dorr was willing to take prisoners on board. His fellow radicals declined to join him as Skirving was recovering from a bout of yellow fever and Gerrald – who had arrived shortly before – was ill with tuberculosis. Palmer was fit and able but was nursing his sick friends and decided to stay.

Captain Dorr insisted that any prisoner seeking to board had to make their way out beyond the bay to avoid any confrontation with the British military. After managing to evade his captors, Muir made his way out from the coast and joined the vessel. Departing on 18 February 1796 the ship took him across the Pacific Ocean, which was still then largely uncharted, to the shores of what is now western Canada on 22 June.[11] There as the vessel lay off Vancouver Island, the American captain was notified that a Royal Navy ship was patrolling in the area. With capture leading to his almost certain execution, Muir chose to transfer to a Spanish ship, and headed down the coast towards Monterrey in California.

However, far from finding sanctuary in California, on 12 August the Scot was imprisoned on alleged spying charges; in reality he was persecuted because he was a foreigner and the international mood was tense due to the ongoing wars. At this time, these lands were Spanish colonies and the country's relationship with Britain was fraught, despite a shared opposition to the French Revolution. Whatever hopes Muir had of being liberated and allowed to proceed to the United States soon evaporated and he was instead taken under escort to Mexico City. Arriving there on 12 October, further efforts to ensure his liberation were unsuccessful and he was then taken to Veracruz on the Atlantic. From there he was placed on a small ship that took him to Havana in Cuba.

Whilst under detention Muir was still allowed to write and was in correspondence with many, including Hamilton Rowan of the United Irishmen, who by then was exiled in Wilmington, Delaware. Muir must still have hoped that he would be released and allowed to journey to America where he could start a new life, as it was a short sail from Havana. The opportunity to pursue his legal career in a country with a democracy that he admired must have been tempting, after all he had considered this option before he returned to stand trial in Scotland. But it was not to be. Despite their mutual hatred of the French Revolution, the interest of competing empires resulted in Britain and Spain going to war. As a result, the colonial authorities decided to send him back to mainland Spain to be dealt with and any lingering hopes Muir had of freedom were dashed. On 25 March 1797 he was placed on a Spanish warship bound for Cadiz and transported once again to captivity.

A month later on 25 April, as the Spanish warship, and a sister vessel accompanying it, approached Cadiz Harbour, they came across a British fleet under Admiral John Jervis laying siege to the city. Their ships were soon sighted and the following day it became clear that the Royal Navy were going to attack. Muir sought to be put ashore as a civilian but this was not possible so he offered to fight for the Spanish. Whatever assistance he had sought to offer his captors was soon rendered useless, as he was seriously injured as cannon fusillades struck the ship. As he drifted in and out consciousness, having lost his left eye and suffering severe wounds to the side of his face, ironically it was the severity of his injuries that proved to be his salvation. Worse could have followed as British sailors boarded the stricken Spanish vessel and enquired after him, with some even reported to have been Scots. However, as he was badly disfigured he was not spotted and after a Spanish sailor suggested that he had been killed, the British sailors quickly moved on from the foundering vessel. It has also been suggested that Muir was actually treated by a Scottish Royal Navy doctor, who had been a school friend of his and recognised him, but failed to notify his superiors. In any event, however the lack of identification came about, Muir was thereafter taken ashore along with other Spanish dead and wounded. There he was placed in the care of the nuns running a local hospital.

His recuperation then began, which soon led to his release. His injuries were serious, requiring him to wear a mask covering the left side of his face for the rest of his life. It is that image which has been immortalised in busts of him ever since. But, in Cadiz he soon recovered and began communicating and was mobile once again, with his other faculties undamaged. Contacting the French consul, shortly thereafter, his fame was instantly recognised by the authorities in revolutionary France, even if it had not been by royalist Spain. Angry representations were speedily made by the resident French diplomat, as well as by Parisian authorities, and shortly after he was released to the care of the French. American intelligence reports mentioned in the *Caledonian Mercury* in December 1797, referred to representations having been made by the French who described Muir as 'a good man, condemned only for his political beliefs'. Once he had sufficiently recovered the French authorities arranged for Muir to leave Spain.

By September 1797, as the Militia Act riots were coming to an end and the round-up of the members of the United Scotsmen was beginning, Thomas Muir arrived in Bordeaux where he was treated as a revolutionary hero. Celebrated at a banquet in his honour, he was toasted by the 500 guests as 'The Brave Scottish Advocate of Liberty, now the Adopted Citizen of France', with an even larger crowd outside the venue cheering his appearance on a balcony.[12]

From Bordeaux it was on to Paris. By now portraits of '*Le célèbre* Thomas Muir' were being displayed and articles were appearing in newspapers. *Le Moniteur Universel* carried a piece that stated:

> He arrives in France at the very moment when the Grande nation is menacing England and is taking steps to realise the project which he had conceived. Let this apostle of philanthropy come among us, let him find in his new fatherland friends and brothers, and may our victorious cohorts call him back to the country which gave him birth there to establish liberty ... It would be impolitic as well as inhuman to leave in oblivion and expose to penury those illustrious strangers to whom we offer a place of refuge.[13]

Muir was equally grateful and gushing in his response to his hosts. The

Caledonian Mercury again referred to intelligence reports and an apparent letter by the Scot to the French revolutionary leaders in which he stated:

> Two days have elapsed since I arrived at Paris, very weak and very indisposed. Permit me to pour out all the dutiful and grateful effusions of my heart. To you I owe my life, but there are considerations of infinitely greater importance, which must strike my mind with an irresistible pulse.

For Muir was eager to build upon the evident sympathy, not only held for him but for all radicals in Scotland, and intended to pursue that agenda. However, he would not have known much about what was happening in Scotland at this time. In many ways his knowledge of Scotland was stuck in a time warp, from the time that he had been arrested and his ultimate transportation. Several years had elapsed since then and the country's political landscape had altered dramatically. The change in make-up of the radical groups had passed him by, along with the arrival of new organisations with an even more revolutionary edge. However, these were factors that would have appealed to Muir and he may well have sensed that there were opportunities from the limited information he had received. Despite the fact that he may have been in tune with the new chord that was being struck, he was out of touch with those who were seeking to play it.

More problematic, perhaps, was Muir's understanding of what was actually happening on the ground. Some of those who communicated with him were either deluded or hopelessly optimistic in their assessment of the situation in Scotland. Suggestions that reached him about the level of support that existed back home were often fantastical. One source was Robert Watson, a Scot who had gone to London before moving on to Paris. Although he had been involved in the London Corresponding Society, he appears to have given himself an unmerited level of prominence and suggested substantial support for a rising without any evidence to back this claim up. It seems as though Watson was merely delusional rather than acting as an agent provocateur. He had been acquitted after trial in London and was sincere in his revolutionary commitment, even if he lacked understanding. Other visitors to Muir from his homeland were sometimes more realistic and circumspect. But perhaps he heard what he wanted to hear and persisted with the notion that there was substantial support for rebellion in Scotland.

The reality was vastly different. Garrison building, the enlistment of volunteers and the detention of opponents and suppression of movements had all increased. There had also been a growth in popular loyalism and a discernible loss of sympathy towards France, as wartime solidarity and war weariness set in. So, whilst Muir was keen to re-join the fray albeit from afar, he was not best placed to advise nor were his arguments founded on any solid evidence.

Muir was provided with a pension by the revolutionary authority that allowed him to live reasonably comfortably. His injuries restricted him from military service but his enthusiasm was undiminished and he was eager to serve his new adopted country. Setting to with a will, he used his pen to argue and lobby in support of the radical cause, both in his new homeland and his old. Seeking to unite the two campaigns, he endeavoured to obtain French support for a further invasion despite the failure of the Dutch efforts. He even prepared documents for the Foreign Ministry, which argued that whilst there was no evidence of support amongst the working people in England, this was most certainly not the case in Scotland. In Scotland, he argued there was both a deeper history and a different political context. His sentiments were by now overtly nationalistic, touching on everything from the Enlightenment to the Treaty of Union. His advocacy of universal franchise for all in Britain had been replaced by the desire for a Scottish Republic: 'Scotland was asking liberty, justice, and vengeance, from the French Republic.'[14]

This was considerably different from what the Friends of the People had argued for and at variance with even what most in the United Scotsmen were calling for. In another document Muir argued that Scotland had been inspired by the French Revolution and had held a convention in 1792 'but its members had been without arms, without money, without means of defence'.[15] He differentiated this convention from the subsequent British Convention, which he disparaged, rather shamefully perhaps given its outcome and the transportation of fellow martyrs that happened as a direct result. No doubt he did this to emphasise the need to support a distinctive Scottish revolution, as this certainly appears to be inconsistent with his views at the time.

In this way he was no different from Wolfe Tone who was seeking a particular Irish response, but the United Irishman had both greater knowledge of the situation on the ground and a sense of realism as to the strength of support that existed. Some of Muir's comments seem fanciful and draw heavily from newspaper reports of the Militia Act riots. Suggestions of highlanders rallying to the cause seem to have partly been predicated on reports of highland regiments refusing to fire on United Irishmen. In fact, as mentioned earlier, Scottish troops were to play a major and shameful role in the crushing of the Irish rebellion. Other individuals, including the Dutch, had also assumed that the north of Scotland could rise in support of a central belt-based rebellion. But again, this assessment was made on little evidence other than a sense of hope and the history of Jacobite rebellions. Similarly, Muir's estimation of support for a rising in the lowlands where he suggested that 100,000 could rally to the cause was wildly optimistic. Given the limited numbers in the Militia Act disturbances and the size of the United Scotsmen this figure is incredible.

Muir suggested to the revolutionary leadership that:

The Republic should send officers, munitions of war, and money; a proclamation should be issued allowing freedom of worship and the right of every class to choose its own pastors; and the French troops should be warned to conduct themselves circumspectly. A provisional government could then be set up and an independent republic finally established.[16]

This may have reflected the hopes of some in the Society of the United Scotsmen, but it was far from the views held by many others. Those who supported physical force were a small minority and many sought the franchise on a pan-British basis. This is probably why Muir's relationship with Wolfe Tone was fraught to say the least, as the Irishman sought to have support channelled into Ireland rather than Scotland or even Britain. It again seems a case of Muir's hopes outweighing the reality on the ground.

Notwithstanding this situation, Muir had some success; in January 1798 the British government received an intelligence communique, which suggested that it was the intention of the French to establish separate republics in England, Scotland and Ireland. The document even narrated that those who were to form the 'Scotch directory' included Muir and Angus Cameron.[17] However, it was not to be. Not only at this point had Angus Cameron been arrested – though he was soon to flee – but more importantly French military tactics and plans had been changed. Napoleon Bonaparte was now in charge and he had different ideas.

Alongside his hopes for revolution in Scotland, Thomas Muir himself would soon be dead. With his influence receding as the French Revolution entered yet another stage, he became a marginal figure in Paris. This was mostly as a result of changes taking place within the revolutionary leadership, but also no doubt through a growing desperation for revolution in his own country that saw him alienate potential allies. His stridency, along with his friendship with the quixotic Irishman James Napper Tandy, alienated him from Wolfe Tone. This must further have reduced his credibility in Paris. Partly in a state of despair and certainly with his health worsening, he moved to Chantilly just outside the French capital. However, he was not to survive long there, and passed away in his bed on 26 January 1799 aged just thirty-three.

Buried in his adopted land, Muir has remained a beacon for Scottish radicals ever since. But buried with him were also the chances of French or foreign support for an invasion of Scotland. A few other Scottish exiles remained in Paris but none had either the desire for revolution that Muir had possessed or more importantly the influence that he had once had. Scottish radicals were once more on their own. A period of relative calm was now to descend despite the pressures of war and poverty. But a legacy of radicalism remained.

CHAPTER 14

A LEGACY REMAINS AND THE FATE OF THE OTHER MARTYRS

The dawn of the new century marked the demise not only of the Society of the United Scotsmen but also the end of 'the direct influence of the French Revolution on Scotland'.[1] France would move from a republic to an empire under Napoleon, and lose its role as the inspiration for radicalism. Though the effects of the momentous event lingered in part, the huge upsurge of support that had washed over Scotland had receded. Popular loyalism had grown, public perception of the revolution had changed and war with Britain compounded this.

Henry Cockburn, the Whig lawyer, who had previously described the effect of the revolution as soaking everything in that one event, was now painting a vastly different picture. He recorded in his memoirs that:

> Napoleon's obvious progress towards military despotism opened the eyes of those who used to see nothing but liberty in the French Revolution; and the threat of invasion, while it combined all parties in the defence of the country, raised the confidence of the people in those who trusted them with arms, and gave them the pleasure of playing at soldiers. Instead of Jacobinism, Invasion became the word.[2]

This changed the political landscape for radicals. Widescale arrest and imprisonment, as well as the suppression of the United Scotsmen, saw the radical cause dramatically reduced in numbers. Those who remained had to be circumspect, if not silent. With the public mood swinging against them, as well as official action likely to be taken, it is unsurprising that many radicals simply gave up the cause. Some kept their heads down and awaited a change in political fortunes, others chose the path of emigration. Many took off for the United States of America, where the democracy they sought was openly practised, and where dissenting ministers and others had gone before them.

As well as the loss of support for the revolution, the external threat to the country ignited hostility. The fear of invasion was genuine. Amongst many working people, sympathy for the revolution was supplanted by fear and anger towards France. As Cockburn stated, the rise of Bonaparte had made the revolution a threat not just to the establishment but the entire country. Far from being socially liberating, France was beginning to be viewed as expansionist and threatening.

Consequently, popular loyalism enjoyed a resurgence. Joining the volunteers changed from being something that had been disdained to something that was actively supported. The organisation became viewed as 'a patriotic rather than political organisation'.[3] This was partly driven by a sentiment to support the country in its time of need, although it was also the case that enlisting in the volunteers excused service in the militia, and this was considered the less onerous option by many working people.

Army recruitment also increased substantially, bringing with it a solidarity with those serving in Ireland or against France. As in most countries and through most conflicts, people stand by their kith and kin. However, enlistment was still based more on economic factors and was driven by the desire to escape poverty, rather than any supposedly indigenous martial spirit, perhaps aside from amongst the wealthier sections of society and 'the officer class'. Amongst this group in society, supposed leadership traditions were maintained and ambitious young men believed they could make their mark, whilst embarking on a military adventure.

The war also badly affected the economy. The draining of exchequer funds for the army and navy was compounded by the damage to trade. Not only was demand at home down as incomes plunged, but restrictions on trade, whether imposed by the government or as a result of war, strangled the lifeblood of business. The start of the century brought economic depression and many of the most radical areas in Scotland suffered considerably. As would oft-times be repeated amongst future generations, economic depression and emigration worked to dissipate radical spirt rather than ignite revolution. The weaving and cotton industries were especially badly hit; 2,000 looms were said to have been set aside in April 1801 in the Glasgow and Paisley areas alone, which led to poverty and destitution. It was estimated that 'over 3,000 weavers had enlisted in the army' from the same area, since the previous November.[4] This theme was replicated all across the land, and served to drain the radical cause of all its energy.

Although disturbances had continued since the crushing of the Militia Act riots, they were localised and far less serious than before. Driven largely by social and economic conditions, rather than any underlying political activism, such activities appear to have been less prevalent in Scotland than they were south of the border. This perhaps reflected the social and economic divergences rather than the political differences between the two countries. By this time England was far more urbanised and the Industrial Revolution had moved at a far greater pace in the south. The transformation of large parts of the west of Scotland, with its huge population growth and extensive industrial development, had not yet commenced.

The reaction of the authorities to the social and economic problems was also different to the responses made towards a political threat. With political discontent an iron fist had been used, even if softer actions often followed thereafter. Whereas, with non-military social and economic grievances, a far more swift and more socially aware response was forthcoming. Some of this was strategic and delivered by government direction.

As with future social and economic crises, a loosening of control and the offering of reward for critical sectors was practised. No doubt such steps were taken to defuse tensions and forestall any possible dissent. Colliers were emancipated in 1799, which ended the bondage and indeed slavery that many had endured. Stipends for schoolmasters were also increased in 1803. Action was even taken by the government to enter directly into economic affairs, despite supposed political aversion by the Tories to market intervention. However, the political demands of alleviating distress and protecting employment required action and intervention through the acquisition of food supplies and the regulation of trade.

Many of the wealthy and landed gentry also sought to provide relief for distressed communities. Public kitchens were opened across the country to mitigate hardship. 'In Glasgow in July 1800, there were nine public kitchens in operation distributing 3,147 meals daily.'[5] Other cities and towns introduced similar schemes on a smaller scale. Such efforts were often done not out of a feeling of benevolence or even paternalism, but as a pragmatic step to address or prevent disturbances. In the Carse of Gowrie in spring 1800, there followed 'a period of considerable tension and threatened violence caused by concerns about movement of grain out of the area through landowners selling to merchants'.[6] In other parts of the country different actions were taken depending on local circumstances to appease discontent. In Edinburgh in spring 1800, premiums were even offered by the town council to farmers who brought their goods into the city to be sold.

Major landowners were again at the forefront when it came to contributing to funds and encouraging others to do likewise. Reports of such generosity helped to spur smaller contributions from others, who were either beholden to them or sought to be held in good favour. Private funds were required as the usual sources of relief from towns or parishes were in many instances entirely depleted and simply unable to cope with the demand put upon them. 'By late 1800 the funds of the Glasgow general session were said to be exhausted' and 'by the summer of 1801, in Aberdeen at least funds for supplying meal and coals had run out, although the public kitchen continued to operate'.[7]

Disturbances that did break out were mainly dealt with locally by constabulary and by the volunteer forces that were now increased in size. The council in Paisley established a constabulary to specifically deal with the riots that had occurred. They were made up of what were described as respectable citizens, who were nonetheless equipped with batons. In other places, including Edinburgh, Leith and Dundee, the enhanced volunteers dealt with the outbreaks of discontent, although in Ayr military support was required. In most areas the volunteers and local constabulary were not only sufficient in number, but willing to act and able to cope.

However, this was not always the case. In Peterhead at the start of the century, the local volunteers refused to protect a cargo of meal being shipped from the port. They argued that whilst they were willing to protect property in the town, they were not prepared to assist merchants in shipping meal out of it. In Auchtermuchty, volunteer members refused to confront rioters from within their own community and in Errol in Perthshire a group of women disarmed the local volunteers and a group of men resigned from the corps rather than intercede when a confrontation arose. Beyond these instances though, dissension and rebellion within the local volunteer regiments was limited.

Views and attitudes towards poverty and the poor were also transforming. Paternalism continued with the benevolence of the supposed great and the good continuing through demonstrations of public generosity. However, alongside this there was also a hardening of attitudes in favour of the protection of private property. This was something that had never really been challenged by the radicals who had sought universal franchise rather than a redistribution of wealth. This would later change but was initially seen as being almost inviolate. Perhaps this was because personal possessions were so limited and as a result were viewed as being almost sacrosanct, or that as the elite possessed all of the wealth this could be changed by political power being reformed.

This attitudinal change manifested itself in a variety of ways. A hardening of views towards poaching and other such activities set in. Partly, this was a result of the commercialisation of land but also followed the growing stratification of society and an increase in intolerance, if not hostility, to the freedom of action of employees, tenants and local inhabitants in general.

The changing mood was also reflected across far wider sections of society and was perhaps also linked to a rise in religious evangelism. The provision of relief was still supported and indeed arguably increased, though perhaps this was through necessity. However, it was an early portent of distinctions being made between the deserving and undeserving poor that have continued ever since. Soup kitchens were popular provisions as those who were able to pay were expected to contribute, even if they could only do so modestly. The investigations conducted by those running relief schemes into the circumstances of those applying could be intrusive and demeaning. As well as following the rising religious tide, such measures also allowed for tighter social control by an establishment that was petrified about the prospect of the breakdown of public order as had occurred in revolutionary France.

The religious revival that extended across Europe also spread to Britain and throughout Scotland and this played its part in defusing tension. The revival commenced in the 1790s but accelerated as the new century dawned. Originating in the central belt, it then spread north. As well as inciting a new religious fervour, this revival also had other societal consequences. Although the spiritual beliefs it espoused were radical, the movement neither challenged the social order nor the economic order. Rather, as with other such events around this time, the revival meant that people became more enthused and energised, but they remained publicly restrained beyond their own personal behaviour and worship. Perhaps this also helped to dissipate the mood for radical change or was even a reaction to the failure of the radical cause. Although there is insufficient information about the exact role that religion played, it certainly appeared to fill a void for some individuals or even plug a gap in entire communities. In some areas religious dedication superseded the demands for immediate political change.

Meanwhile, the established church was craven in its support for the government, as it had been throughout this period. Specific actions by some local ministers in support of the landed elite in the opposition to radicalism, were matched by the actions of the church leadership in deference to the authorities. In the early years of the French Revolution, when public support had been considerable and the repression of the Friends of the People was ongoing, Robert Arnot, the Moderator of the General Assembly of the Church of Scotland, had written to Robert Dundas pledging the Kirk's obedience and obsequiously praising Britain.[8] Further letters followed, including one after the discovery of the Pike Plot, when tensions were high and showing loyalty was deemed to be essential. This no doubt justified the link between political radicals and dissenting churches as a rejection of the supine actions and attitude of the established church.

Political changes were also introduced around this time, although the Tories would not reach the peak of their political control of Scotland until 1802, when they won forty-three out of forty-five seats. However, as Henry Meikle also explained, 1802 was to be the start of an era that would lead to the First Reform Act in 1832.[9] Change was achieved through constitutional routes and the leading players were once again from amongst the wealthier sections of society. As the crushing of the radicals brought about the decline of the threat of internal rebellion, it also saw a recovery in Whig political activity and fortunes. Although it had never gone away in London where Whig parliamentary representatives remained, such calls had most certainly been muted in Scotland as a result of the war and the public backlash towards the French Revolution.

As conflict dragged on and war weariness set in, along with the economic problems it brought, the Whigs once more began to find their voice. This, in turn, encouraged others outside the parliamentary chamber to echo those within it. There was a realism about the arguments being made, with a recognition that so long as Britain and France were at war then major change was unlikely to happen. It was, though, an opportune time to return to the political fray and lay the groundwork for future reform.

Such was the progress that the Whigs made during this time, that the party even had a brief period in government in 1806, following the death of William Pitt the Younger. The administration under William Grenville was dubbed the 'Government of all the talents' but only lasted for a year. The group made little progress on either peace or the economy and the party soon fell from power and remained so for years to come. However, the administration did abolish slavery in 1807, even if political reform at home was never achieved. The election of the Whigs, albeit brief, also reverberated in Scotland where Tory hegemony was even greater, and the political circles that operated were even smaller. As the leading Whig lawyer Henry Cockburn described, the party's victory was 'a most salutary event' and one which showed that the Tories were not invincible.[10]

Even before this electoral shock, the Tory establishment suffered a severe blow when the apparently invincible Henry Dundas fell from grace. By this time he had become a peer as Viscount Melville and was

First Lord of the Admiralty from 1804–05. An inquiry had been commissioned into the management of the Admiralty in 1802. Dundas had carried out some welcome reforms whilst he was in office, but he had also been Admiralty treasurer some years before and suspicions had grown about financial irregularities. He was impeached in 1806, and although he was ultimately acquitted, his reputation was permanently tarnished. With the death of his political mentor Pitt in the same year, Dundas never again held high office and he died in 1811. However, Tory control persisted – aside from the brief interlude in 1806 – and his nephew Robert Dundas continued the family dynasty, although he lacked the same ability and prestige of his uncle.

However, the demise of Dundas proved a fillip to Whigs in Scotland even if more radical spirits remained subdued. Former reform advocates awoke from their slumbers. Many of those who had disappeared from view or renounced their convictions began to return, despite the fact that they were promoting moderate reform rather than revolution. Many, if not most of such individuals, were from the wealthier sections of society, and those who had initially been enthused by the American Revolution, as well as the early stages of the French Revolution, and who were seeking political power to match their new-found wealth and status. The fear and disgust felt in response to the radical and violent turn of events in France, allied to similar concerns over the direction of the cause in Scotland, had seen reformers distance themselves from the cause of the French Revolution. But by this point they felt that it was safe to return and the war and economic difficulties offered up opportunities, which were matched by the Whig revival.

An early manifestation of this development was the publication of the *Edinburgh Review*, which first appeared in 1802 and became an outlet for Whig views. It was followed by other liberal journals, and also prompted a reaction from Tory interests to counteract the influence of such publications. With few opposition MPs in Scotland and the lack of a parliamentary chamber, the focus for political debate was at the Bar. Advocates traditionally made up the core of political representatives and even political activists, as demonstrated by Muir himself. During this time a Whig and reform-minded group reappeared that attracted many younger members of the legal profession. As with the creation of liberal journals this provoked concern amongst the Tories as many young privileged men began consorting with liberals. Scotland was changing and reform was returning to the political agenda, even if the radical cause was still subdued.

What of the political martyrs themselves? What of their fate? Muir, as described in Chapter 13, had a remarkable tale to tell before his early death in 1799. The fates of many of the other radicals was far less exciting, but even more tragic. Palmer, Skirving and Margarot had been transported along with Muir in 1794, aboard the convict ship the *Surprize*, which sailed from Woolwich in April 1794. As the fears following the uncovering of the Pike Plot had mounted, the authorities decided to remove the convicts from the country, lest they be an incitement for revolutionaries. Gerrald, who was the last to be tried in March 1794, was imprisoned in London until he was transported on the *Sovereign*, a ship that sailed in May 1795.

Such journeys were fraught with risk and danger, however whilst sailing and once they had arrived in the new world, the political martyrs were treated better than most convicts who had been transported. Both the nature of their crimes and their social class marked them out. Indeed, they had previously – though not always – been afforded particular privileges when they were incarcerated. Visits from leading London Whigs often replicated what had happened in the Tolbooth in Edinburgh and elsewhere. Funds were also raised for them from radicals in London and across the country, which meant that they travelled with resources that allowed for better treatment.

During this period capital punishment applied for many crimes for those individuals who were transported they were most often being punished for economically related offences, such as minor theft or prostitution. More serious crimes, such as major theft or rape, would usually result in the death penalty being imposed. In many ways transportation operated as a removal of the poor from society through involuntary emigration, or as a form of ethnic cleansing, as is sometimes alluded to today. Some who were transported were taken on dedicated convict ships, others on vessels that were simply adapted to take either a human cargo or larger numbers of passengers, with little consideration for anything other than security.

Not only were the passages long and arduous with the danger of tempests and storms on the great oceans, but both the design of the vessels and the navigational charts for the seas and channels were limited. Risks to all, including the crew, were everywhere. The cruelty of cramming prisoners into tightly restricted spaces was only surpassed by the barbarity of the slave ships that operated during the same era. Ill health plagued many prisoners before they even boarded, either as a result of the slums from which they had come or the prisons in which they had been rotting. Months at sea in bad conditions and with a poor diet exacerbated matters. The vessel that took Mealmaker to Australia was worse than many; forty-three of the 400 prisoners died at sea, but death before landing was common.

Muir and his fellow political martyrs enjoyed greater freedom and comfort whilst aboard their vessels than most convicts, and they paid for this from the funds provided for them. This did ensure a more pleasant passage, notwithstanding the circumstances of their voyage. The journey for the first four embarked was largely uneventful other than for a rather strange allegation that they had planned a mutiny, with the intention then being to sail the ship to France. Skirving and Palmer were implicated as apparent ringleaders with the accusation being made by the first mate or the superintendent of convicts, but the precise basis of this claim remained obscure. There have been suggestions that this was part of a personal animus towards them from a man who was known to be a British loyalist. In any case, the evidence against them was limited. Much information had been extracted from individuals who had been flogged, which also cast doubt on the accuracy of such evidence. All in all, it appears that the case was rather flimsy and both the two martyrs and the others involved appear hard done by.

Muir sought to intercede on his friend's behalf and made legal arguments and submissions about the lack of evidence and the manner in which the investigation was conducted. But this held no sway with the captain who exercised his arbitrary, if not draconian powers whilst at sea, and wanted to take no chances with his revolutionary cargo. Skirving and Palmer were placed in custody in a cabin below deck for the rest of the journey. The other individuals allegedly involved were more harshly treated and were flogged or placed in chains.

No mutiny took place but it caused a divide amongst the martyrs themselves with Margarot being side-lined, if not ostracised, by the others. Margarot had been praised by the captain for his behaviour whilst condemning the others, which resulted in Skirving and Palmer suggesting that their erstwhile colleague may have implicated them. Again, the evidence is limited but a division arose between them and suspicions remained about Margarot ever after.

Landfall for the convict vessels was at Botany Bay, part of what is now greater Sydney, and for the first four departed they reached their destination on 25 October. Disembarking must have been a relief for everyone aboard after so long at sea. The penal colony itself had not long been established after the American War of Independence closed off previous preferred sites in the southern states of America. The first batch of prisoners arrived at the colony along with Captain Arthur Phillip, who would soon be the first Governor of New South Wales, on 26 January 1788, the date now celebrated as Australia Day.

Some prisoners were in chain gangs and operated under military guard but most were free to move about, although they were usually required to complete work. The intention after all was to encourage the expansion of the colony, albeit primarily predicated on penal labour, and this required business and farming acumen, whether from free emigrants or prisoners who possessed skills. Prisoners could also stay on after their sentence had been served and seek to make a new life for themselves.

Nowadays the colony is perceived as being a British version of the notorious Devil's Island – which was a prison island located in French Guiana – but this was far from being the case. Abuses did take place and harsh punishments were meted out. However, a crude rule of law was enforced and discipline was applied. The military were present to guarantee order and would intercede to ensure its maintenance, but even then they were subject to civil authority. The colony was therefore far from lawless and was different from prison as we understand it today.

Poverty and degradation afflicted some, but the conditions for convicts were in many ways better than those faced by working people in Britain. Likewise, opportunities to socially and economically progress were greater than had existed for many in their homeland. It was for these reasons that many stayed on and prospered after their sentence. Scottish prisoners in particular, who were almost invariably literate and numerate, were able to settle and improve their lives. However, the plight of others and in particular the Irish was often more extreme, where language difference and the lack of education worked to impede social mobility. There was also a lot that depended on the attitude of the individuals and how they reacted to their new environment.

But for those who were committed to a new society and political order, such as the political martyrs, this was not what they had imagined their life to be like. Moreover, the skills they had and the work they had been trained for did not readily transfer to the new land. They had and no doubt still sought to transform their old land, rather than colonise a new one. Political prisoners were in the minority and many of the ordinary felons transported would have lacked the education or literacy that was possessed by the radicals. When Muir and his colleagues arrived in Australia there were few if any other individuals who were there because of their political views. The Tolpuddle Martyrs were still decades away from making their sad journey, although after the 1798 rebellion there were some United Irish prisoners who had been transported. By this time though Muir had escaped, but the other radicals remained.

The martyrs were also from the wealthier section of society. For some there would have been a natural social distance between them and the other prisoners. As with political prisoners in later years and in other societies, they may also have been viewed as slightly odd by those who were transported for ordinary criminal offences. However, there is no suggestion that any animosity or antagonism was either felt towards them or disrespect shown by them.

As a colony rather than simply an army camp, primacy was supposed to be with the civil authority. Ironically, shortly after their arrival in Australia, the Governor of New South Wales would be a Scot. John Hunter from Leith assumed the post in 1795 after a successful career in the Royal Navy, which included exploring the waters around the continent, remaining there until 1799. He later returned to Britain and settled in his native Leith and his statue now stands there at the Shore. Following their arrival the martyrs were provided with a simple brick cottage and they were able to use the funds they had brought with them to buy land. As they were allowed to roam relatively freely it was their intention to either enter into farming or some other business, as they did not all have the experience or desire for the land or agriculture.

Muir escaped in February 1796, and soon after two of his fellow martyrs would pass away. Skirving and Gerrald died within days of each other in March 1796. According to convict records Gerrald passed away on 16 March and Skirving on 19 March. Both never really adapted to their new lives in the penal colony, though Gerrald's stay was brief given his ill health.

Arriving in late November 1795, Gerrald also used some of the funds he had been provided with by supporters to acquire a small cottage and garden. However, he did not have much of an opportunity to enjoy them or even experience much of colony life. The harsh regime during his imprisonment had taken its toll before he even departed Britain. This was worsened by the lengthy sea journey and resulted in him being plagued by ill health throughout his brief exile. He suffered from tuberculosis and survived for less than six months in his new home; despite treatment from the military doctor and the tender care of Palmer, he died on 16 March 1796, aged just thirty-three.

On his arrival Skirving quickly acquired a reasonably substantial land holding, amounting to some 100 acres, on ground that he named New Strathruddie. Presumably, his background in farming and interest in agriculture allowed him to settle in quickly, although even he struggled with the new soil. He also appears to have forsaken any involvement in the radical discussions and intrigue that took place covertly in the penal colony, and which no doubt strengthened Muir's desire to escape. Skirving seems to have preferred his own company and a private life. This is also explained by both poor health and depression that he suffered from, which was brought about by enforced separation from his wife and children. As a result, his punishment was to be an altogether unhappy time. A bout of yellow fever in January 1796 weakened him before he finally succumbed to dysentery on 19 March, just days after Gerrald, and aged just fifty-one.

Before the end of the year two of the political martyrs had died and one had escaped; another, George Mealmaker had joined them on the Australian penal colony. However, Palmer, who had received the shortest sentence of all, of only seven years, was soon to be liberated as the period of punishment commenced when the sentence had been imposed by the court and not the date of transportation. Accordingly, he was released in September 1800. Not only had he survived his term of enforced exile but he also positively thrived, and became prosperous. He had chosen to start a business rather than work the land, and had acquired a boat to trade in and around the colony. The venture proved remarkably successful and he demonstrated a considerable flair for commerce. The business grew in size and scale and had numerous boats trading with the Norfolk Islands, and even secured assistance from the authorities.

Palmer was supported in his efforts by his friend James Ellis who decided to join him in Botany Bay. Ellis was originally from Dundee, but was living in Paisley when Palmer was arrested and was linked to the minister through the radical cause. Reluctantly on his part, he was required to give evidence against Palmer at his trial. Perhaps then it was as a result of guilt as well as friendship, that he chose to join his mentor in exile and accompanied him as a voluntary settler. He was to prove a loyal and steadfast friend.

With Palmer's sentence served, it was his intention to sail home along with Ellis on one of their ships, which would allow them to trade along the way. In this way they could pay for the venture and earn some money. However, Palmer's good fortune did not last and the voyage was plagued by bad luck. Delay and difficulty in New Zealand to obtain a cargo was followed by being unable to land in Tonga where a war was ongoing. When continuing on they made for the Fiji Islands but struck a reef on the way, which required them to stay longer than they had hoped as repairs were carried out. After departing Fiji, they then headed for Macao but storms forced them ashore on the Mariana Islands. The islands were a Spanish colony and once again, as Britain and Spain were at war and as with Muir in California, the beleaguered radicals were taken into custody. Despite being treated decently by the Spanish governor, Palmer still succumbed to dysentery and died on 2 June 1802, aged fifty-five.

It was tragic that Palmer had endured transportation and survived in exile but then died on an island, still thousands of miles from home. His loyal friend James Ellis arranged to have his body buried on the beach, as a cemetery was unavailable for non-Catholics. A few years later, though, Palmer's bones were exhumed by a visiting American sea captain and he was finally reinterred in a cemetery in Boston, Massachusetts. Sadly, Ellis also died soon after and the wealth that the pair had accumulated fell to Ellis's relations, as neither had married nor had children.

The unacknowledged martyr, George Mealmaker, also did not survive the ordeal of transportation. He was sentenced after the others in 1798, and was given fourteen years rather than seven as was given to Palmer, and he too never made it home. Tragically for Mealmaker, his departure on a convict ship from England came just weeks before a change in attitude on the part of the authorities, which had seen the sentences for other members of the United Scotsmen either being remitted or reduced. The belief by the authorities that Mealmaker was the organisation's leader and their haste to punish him as a warning to others, meant that he was quickly processed through the court system. Convicted and sent south to await a transportation ship, he festered in the hulks that held such unfortunate prisoners and for unknown reasons his removal was initially delayed. This may have been as a result of the authorities simply awaiting the right vessel, after accumulating sufficient bodies to embark or for other colonial or military reasons. Eventually though, Mealmaker was dispatched on a ship the *Royal Admiral* in May 1800.

Despite the delay, Mealmaker did not receive a reprieve. It was by then more than two years since his conviction and the United Scotsmen had been suppressed. The attitude of the authorities had become more relaxed, even if they still retained a tight grip on security. By the summer of 1800 it was believed that the threat to the established order had passed and the government decided that they could vary the sentences of many of the supposed troublemakers. Some, such as Angus Cameron, had already been allowed to simply disappear and of the eight others who were awaiting transportation, only Mealmaker was eventually sent to Botany Bay. For others, banishment from Britain or other reduced sentences applied.

Unfortunately for Mealmaker his ship had already sailed, both literally and metaphorically, and no attempt was made to countermand orders or notify any change. Had he not already been on the high seas, it may well have been that a new life in France or America could have been his fate. But it was not to be and instead he sailed forlornly to his exile in Australia.

Mealmaker would not have known the cruel hand that fate had dealt him when he first landed in Botany Bay on 20 November 1800.[11] Letters and communications in later years, from friends and family, must have brought home not just his physical isolation but also the extent to which he was singled out from amongst the United Scotsmen. Whether as a result of this or simply through a continuation of his radical beliefs, Mealmaker never settled in Australia and soon had run-ins with the authorities.

After obtaining a dwelling in Sydney Cove, Mealmaker appears to have made contact with Palmer before he departed and also with Maurice Margarot, who had adjusted to his new settings but retained his radical beliefs. Perhaps, it was through these Scottish contacts that Mealmaker went on to meet with exiled United Irishmen. It was these liaisons with the United Irishmen that brought him to the attention of the governor.

A new governor was now in charge of New South Wales. Captain Philip King would have considered that Mealmaker was keeping bad company and would have been wary of the newly arrived Scot. As another Royal Navy officer, King had succeeded John Hunter in becoming the third to hold the post of governor in 1800 and remained in office until 1806. King was to develop mining and whaling concerns, and also sought to introduce weaving into the colony.[12]

Mealmaker's clashes with the authorities began within months of his arrival. He appeared before the criminal court in February 1801 charged with perjury for supporting a convict's wife, who had alleged that money belonging to her had been taken by the captain of the ship which had brought her to the colony. Evidence against him was given by John Macarthur who was a voluntary settler and was by then well on his way to becoming a major landowner and sheep farmer. Now a celebrated figure in the country's early settlement, Macarthur ironically had Scottish roots. He was born in Plymouth, England, and his father had in fact been a Jacobite who had fled initially to the West Indies after the 1745 rebellion. Despite the testimony from the influential Macarthur, Mealmaker was acquitted.

However, Mealmaker was soon to reappear before the court, and in March 1802, he was dragged from his bed by armed soldiers. This time plans for a rebellion were suspected by the authorities and Mealmaker was implicated. In fact, the rebellion appears to have been instigated by the United Irishmen.[13] Although Mealmaker was a marginal figure this was sufficient to ensure his arrest, but at trial he was once again acquitted. Whilst there may very well have been substance to the allegations made, the evidence against him came only from testimony from tortured prisoners and the prosecution case collapsed. Although Mealmaker had declined to represent himself during his trial in Scotland, in his new home in Australia he became a barrack-room lawyer and even petitioned the King following his second acquittal. Perhaps, this was his way of continuing to rebel against the establishment.

Despite these difficulties, some opportunities and good fortune still came Mealmaker's way as the new governor was keen to establish a weaving industry on the colony. A master weaver had been recruited from England but had died on the voyage out. Attempts were made using Irish convict labour but these failed as their skills and experience were inadequate, despite their protestations. Attention then turned towards the radical weaver. With his services in demand, Mealmaker was able to negotiate a salary, a cottage with a servant and a garden. In return, he set to with a will and delivered all, if not more than, the governor could have hoped for. By the end of 1804, nine looms were operating and the quality of the fabric produced was commented on favourably by English traders. In being allowed to return to his craft, Mealmaker likely regained some of his pride and self-esteem, whilst also improving his living conditions.

But his progress soon faltered and with it any mitigation of his plight, and Mealmaker's decline continued. King was succeeded as governor by Captain William Bligh, of HMS *Bounty* notoriety. Under Bligh's rule, relationships with the military on the colony worsened and an army mutiny over the rum trade occurred in January 1808. Just before this event a fire had destroyed at least some of the looms that had been established by Mealmaker and in the political crisis that ensued, the weaving industry collapsed. Mealmaker did not appear to have been bitter or blamed Bligh and even subscribed to a letter that supported the governor's policies, although a few caveats were added that would benefit settlers. As the leading Australian historian Michael Roe has whimsically described, Mealmaker's involvement in this matter en-sured that the Scottish radical 'contributed to the first popular demand for constitutional rights ever voiced in Australia' in a very minor way.[14] He was rebellious until the end, and within a few weeks he was dead.

Despite his successful spell in the weaving industry, Mealmaker was unhappy throughout his exile. He never fully settled or reconciled himself to his fate and the opportunities that others saw in the new land were of little interest to him. As a man of great ideas and firm convictions separated from his friends and family, it must have been a lonely existence for him. As a result, he turned to drink to drown his sorrows and alcoholism played a part in his death. His wife had not heard from him for many years, which is surprising given his early loyalty and is likely linked to the depression he experienced. In 1811 a minister in Dundee enquired on her behalf about her husband's fate with the government. They in turn contacted the colony, and received the following reply in October 1811:

Sir,

In obedience to your Excellency's Command I beg leave to inform you as far as comes within my knowledge respecting how and what time George Mealmaker a native of Scotland who was Transported some Year since came by his death.

The abovenamed George Mealmaker Died in the factory at Parramatta in March 1808. Supposed to have been suffocated by drinking Spirits; at the time of his Death he possessed no property not even as much as defrayed his Funeral expenses.

I have the Honor to be Your Excellency's Most obedient Servant,

Isaac Nichols[15]

As he stated in his speech to the jury upon his conviction, Mealmaker's wife and children were cared for by 'the God who feeds the ravens'. His wife outlived him by thirty-five years, and lived until November 1843. Of all the political martyrs, in many ways Mealmaker suffered the most and it is tragic that today, his name is neither inscribed on the memorial in Edinburgh nor marked in his native city of Dundee.

Only one martyr made it home alive and that was Maurice Margarot, who was paradoxically the one who had fallen out with his comrades during the voyage. There is no obvious reason for his survival and it may well just have been down to a healthy constitution and good fortune. His treatment was similar to that of the others and he was certainly not afforded any special privileges.

But perhaps he was just a little more experienced in travelling and living abroad than the other radicals, having been born abroad and educated in Geneva. Although, his experience of colonies and being a settler was no greater than any of the others, and it is hard to see how his earlier experiences could have prepared him for the conditions in the new world. It is more likely that the fact his wife sailed with him as a voluntary settler made creating a new life easier and spared him the hardship of separation that afflicted Skirving and Mealmaker. He was also a strong and driven character, who was always willing to challenge authority. Therefore, his survival may also have been a result of his ongoing confrontations with the authorities, upon which he positively thrived.

Despite lingering suspicions about his role in Palmer's and Skirving's confinement on the *Surprize*, upon his arrival Margarot soon set about challenging the colonial establishment. This included arguing that transportation had discharged his sentence and therefore any restrictions on him in the colony should be lifted. This and other such protestations were given short shrift by the governor but this did not stop him continuing with his arguments throughout his sentence.

Early on Margarot was implicated in reports to the governor about potential sedition and plans for rebellion as he was associated not just with other radicals but with the United Irishmen who had begun to arrive. As with the other martyrs, he had obtained a cottage and bought a small farm, and it soon became a meeting house for radicals and a hotbed of sedition. His home was promptly raided by the authorities and papers documenting his political sentiments were seized. In March 1804 he was implicated in the Castle Hill Rebellion, which was carried out predominantly by United Irishmen. Many were killed and the ringleaders executed, but as Margarot was only on the fringes of the group, he escaped punishment. However, shortly after this he was sentenced to hard labour, which may well have been a punishment for his suspicious activities, even if nothing was proven at the time. Whether this was a salutary lesson to him is not known, but he appears not to have come to the attention of the authorities thereafter. His rebellious spirit was likely undaunted but wiser counsel prevailed, and he served out the rest of his sentence quietly until he was released.

Margarot returned to Britain in 1810, once again accompanied by his wife, who had also survived the ordeal of transportation, and he then recommenced his lambasting of the authorities. He gave evidence to parliamentary committees and enquiries once he was back in London and denounced corruption in the penal colony and the behaviour of the military. Unlike Palmer, he had not made any money during his ordeal and returned in penury. As Palmer's energies had been focused on commerce, Margarot's had remained fixed on radical politics.

Much of his remaining life in Britain was therefore simply spent trying to eke out an income and survive. However, some of his actions bordered on the bizarre, and included writing a letter in May 1811 to Henry Dundas seeking compensation. He used the letter as an opportunity to allow Dundas to atone for his sins for having him transported. The political despot had in fact died just before the letter was due to be sent and Margarot instead forwarded it to Dundas's son with a covering letter. Needless to say, the request was summarily rejected.

Margarot's political activities continued unabated upon his return. He published several radical pamphlets, and it has been suggested that he visited France to encourage Napoleon to invade Britain, though no action was taken against him by the authorities. His subsequent return to Scotland was more worrying for the establishment. In 1812 he ventured north for the first time since his arrest in 1794 and caught up with radical friends and contacts from that time. In Paisley, Margarot dined with Archibald Hastie, who had been a delegate to the British Convention of the Friends of the People and who was detained after the Pike Plot, but had remained at the centre of radicalism in the area. Moving on to Edinburgh, Margarot met with William Moffatt, the lawyer, who had assisted Muir during his trial and would later be involved in the erection of the memorial to the martyrs. The other individuals that he encountered during his sojourn were also known to the authorities from their past involvement in radical politics. On his return to London he was reported as saying to his associates that 'he found the good old conventional & Republican Party in that part of the Kingdom to be as determined as ever'.[16]

His activities undoubtedly worried the authorities, who kept a watchful eye on his movements throughout his visit with regular memorandums sent to the Lord Advocate and the Home Secretary. As well as journeying to Scotland, he also travelled around the north of England where unrest was growing, and his arrival in Scotland co-incided with a huge weaver's strike in the Glasgow and Paisley areas. Both Luddism and political agitation were provoking discontent south of the border and the economic difficulties caused by the Napoleonic Wars were similarly fuelling discontent in Scotland.

Margarot was often injudicious, even brazen, about his voluble condemnation of Britain and his support for Bonaparte. Despite there being no attempt to detain him, there were considerable concerns that he was acting as an emissary for a radical revival. With the ongoing industrial disputes, his activities caused consternation, the Home Secretary noting that 'there are at this time in Scotland materials for this man & his associates to work upon, which are highly favourable to their malignant designs'.[17]

The Sheriff of Renfrewshire interviewed many of those that Margarot had visited and came to the conclusion that the returned radical was an envoy attempting to revive the cause of parliamentary reform. This position has been supported by historians who have researched Margarot, such as Gordon Pentland, and the evidence backing that view is compelling.[18] Several of those who were detained and interrogated during this time had letters in their possession from Major John Cartwright, who was a leading figure in the revival of the reform cause south of the border and who had been touring northwest England in 1812. Scotland also featured in his later speaking tours, during which many individuals questioned by the Sheriff of Renfrewshire hosted the visiting English radical. As has been accurately deduced by Pentland, Margarot 'the returned exile, the victim of persecution, was the perfect vehicle' to attempt to 'reorient and revive the parliamentary reform movement' in Scotland.[19]

After returning south, Margarot continued to be monitored by the authorities but he does not appear to have raised their concerns nor did he ever return to Scotland. He died in poverty in December 1815, but remained a radical until his final days, despite the fact that suspicions lingered about his intentions and activities when aboard the *Surprize*. However, there is no evidence that he was ever a government informant; thrawn and difficult he may have been, but loyal to the cause he most certainly was.

The death of Margarot marked the end of the lives of the political martyrs. Ironically, and indeed rather unjustly, this occurred just at a time when the radical cause was about to be revived. For although the murmurings of discontent had been subdued, a legacy still remained and many individuals were simply biding their time. By 1815 the time had come to rekindle the revolutionary fire.

CHAPTER 15

RADICALISM REIGNITED

As the nineteenth century progressed, the country largely settled down; groups such as the Society of the United Scotsmen had either been wiped out or had ceased their activities and disappeared into the anonymity and safety of their communities. The trial of Thomas Wilson from Fife in 1802 closed this radical chapter, although informants at this time reported attempts to suborn volunteers in Dundee. It appeared as though the rebels wished to perform one final flourish before their ultimate disbandment.

For even in the year of Wilson's trial there was evidence of on-going subversive activities.[1] Economic problems once again acted as a stimulant for the United Scotsmen, despite its reduced state and increasingly secret operation. A slight increase in membership numbers had been noted during this time and even in the Fife villages of Auchtermuchty and Strathmiglo – which were every bit as much the radical hotbeds as the weaving communities in the west of Scotland – according to the secretary who had been detained by the authorities, there were reputed to be 2,000 members of the group. Although this figure is rather incredible given the overall national membership just a few years before, it could have been that sympathisers were assumed to be members following the clampdown on the administration of oaths in the 1790s.

Information obtained by the government at the time also suggested

that in making returns to the national committee of the United Scotsmen, those collating were asked to differentiate between those who
had and did not have military training. The latter group would have
been quite large due to the amount of individuals who had either
served in the army, enlisted as volunteers or been conscripted into the
militia. Dundee and Perth in particular recorded significant numbers
of members who had military experience.

Members of the organisation also knew that they were still working
in conjunction with other sister organisations that existed in England
and Ireland. Agents linked to the United Irishmen continued to liaise
with cells made up of their own members within British Army units
that were stationed in Fife and with local members of the United
Scotsmen. Any attempts to launch armed action came to nothing,
but there does appear to have been outbreaks of what was described as
'Defenderism' in Fife. Defenderism involved the sabotage of property
and, as the term originated in Ireland, its use may indicate that it was
those individuals who had fled from Ireland who were responsible
for such acts, although it could have also just been carried out by
United Scotsmen who had copied some of the tactics used in Ireland.
Whoever was responsible for such activities, they were told to desist
by more senior members.[2]

However, peace between Britain and revolutionary France was secured when the Treaty of Amiens was signed in March 1802, and with
it any hopes of a French invasion were finally ended. By this time
the authorities considered that the only real danger from the United
Scotsmen would come about as part of an invasion. In the absence
of this threat, the influence of the group was largely contained. This
would have had a major effect on the spirit of the remaining members
and helps explain why the movement's activity largely ceased around
this time.

This did not mean that the radicals had simply disappeared. In 1803
the Lord Advocate noted that 'the Societies in Scotland were all alive

again, and their activities in centres like Perth continued to be carefully monitored, though their central leadership was as impenetrable as ever'.[3] However, any real threat had been greatly reduced, which explains why the authorities had become more relaxed.

Of course, this did not mean that the government was going to end its vigilance towards – and repression of – malcontents. As was noted, 'The Lord Advocate opposed any demobilisation of Volunteer cavalry regiments "composed of the higher" orders: he wanted the arms of disbanded regiments stored at remote forts as opposed to "open towns"'.[4] To compare this with a modern equivalent, which is used with reference to acts of terrorism, security would remain in place even though the threat level had been reduced.

This also helps explain the more lenient sentences that were being imposed and the altogether more liberal position adopted by both the prosecution and the courts. For example, Thomas Wilson's sentence of one month's imprisonment followed by two years' banishment was remarkably light, given the severity of punishments that had been imposed on other radicals just a few years before. Although he was found guilty of sedition and of being a member of the United Scotsmen just as the earlier Scottish radicals, his punishment was much less severe.

The more tolerant approach was replicated when the poet Thomas Campbell, who was mentioned earlier in Chapter 8 for having walked from Glasgow to Edinburgh to witness Gerrald's trial, was arrested in 1801 after returning from being abroad. The Sheriff of Edinburgh interrogated the young man but released him without either charge or punishment, and reported that 'Like many of his class he entertains rather free notions on political subjects but I do not suppose he has carried them further than loose conversations'.[5] Discussions about discontent and even expressions of moderate dissent had obviously become acceptable, although anything more would have likely led to the imposition of sanctions by the authorities.

But other than these minor undercurrents, revolutionary activities all but ceased and radical support was muted following the changes in revolutionary France. The spectre of war also soon returned, as the French Revolutionary Wars were promptly followed by the Napoleonic Wars. Although the enemy remained the same, the circumstances of the conflict had changed dramatically. Sympathy for the aims of the enemy was replaced as a result of the hardening of regard for France and for its dictatorial leader Napoleon.

The French Revolutionary Wars started in 1792 and ended in 1802 with the signing of the Treaty of Amiens. The Napoleonic conflicts spanned the years 1803–1815. The latter wars are broadly considered to be made up of five distinct conflicts over that period as coalitions and alliances changed. Peace came and went, but Britain was at war with France almost constantly throughout this time. Napoleon's defeat in 1814 and banishment to Elba, before his eventual escape and subsequent defeat at Waterloo in 1815, finally brought this tempestuous period to an end.

This era of almost perpetual war came at a huge cost to the economy. Not only was there a heavy price to be paid for military engagement, but the conflict had a huge impact on trade. Social and economic conditions deteriorated. Of course, some individuals enjoyed a boom, in particular those who worked in crafts that were in high demand as a result of military requirements. But for most there was a slow grinding down of standards of living as money tightened and trade reduced. Unemployment and hunger stalked the land.

Problems were compounded when peace finally prevailed in 1815, as soldiers returned from war only to discover that there was neither work nor support available for them. Poverty and unemployment therefore overshadowed the clamour for political change and for many the thoughts about creating a new society were superseded by worries about survival.

This was the backdrop that had helped to diminish radical fervour that previously existed. Occasionally a report on insurrectionary activity came to the attention of the authorities, but in many ways these were more noticeable because of how rare they were. Once again, there were often Irish links to such incidents, although it was no longer the United Irishmen who were implicated, but the Defenders. As mentioned before, the Defenders were a largely Catholic group that formed an alliance with the United Irishmen in the failed 1798 Rebellion.

In 1807 reports were received by the authorities from informants, which alleged that Defenders were operating in Ayrshire. Although papers were discovered relating to the group, there was little evidence of any other activity or of an extensive network that existed across the country.[6] Little seems to have followed the discovery of the existence of the group by the authorities, which indicates that although they were monitoring the situation, they were not overly concerned by it. Another report in 1811 described how the group appeared to be largely though not exclusively made up of Irish émigrés and was in contact with other organisations in Ireland and England.[7] However, by the following year the authorities were satisfied that there was no immediate threat and the organisation was likely to either fade away or could swiftly be dealt with if necessary.[8]

As the economy was beginning to undergo a transformation, changes were also taking place in working-class communities. The movement from rural land to urban communities across all of Scotland was accelerating. Mechanical inventions and rudimentary technology were beginning to revolutionise the industrial process, but the issues of unemployment and poverty persisted. In many ways this foreshadowed the battles between capital and labour that were to come, although this was more often defined in those years as being a conflict between the 'master' and the 'servant'. Trade union membership increased as industrialisation increased and industrial processes developed. Weavers and colliers were joined by other tradespeople, such as cotton spinners, shoemakers and papermakers, in uniting for mutual protection, as assaults upon early industrial rights by the establishment mirrored the attack on the political rights that had occurred years before in the 1780s.

It was against this backdrop that a major strike occurred in 1812. Margarot had been on the fringes of the events when he visited Scotland following his exile and his presence caused considerable concern amongst the authorities. Once again, the government was ruthless, this time in defence of the interests of the manufacturers rather than the landowners, although frequently they were the same individuals. In some ways this event epitomised the growing industrial struggle, but it also heralded a return to radical political campaigning.

Cotton spinners in Glasgow and in nearby towns in west Scotland had been seeking an improvement in their pay and their working conditions. Magistrates were asked by the workers to set new pay scales for the trade. However, there were doubts surrounding the legal competencies of the justices to make this adjustment, and as the process was also bitterly opposed by the cotton employers, the case ended up in the Court of Session. The judges in the High Court decided that it was within the powers of the local justices to set new pay scales. The magistrates had in fact already set new and improved pay rates but despite this, the manufacturers refused to pay the increased wages. A strike was called and an estimated 40,000 individuals ceased work in the factories across the city and in neighbouring towns.

Rather than seeking to enforce the court's decision, the government moved against the strike leaders. By this time Archibald Colquhoun, who was another Tory and part of the Dundas circle, had become Lord Advocate. His father had been Provost of Glasgow and he himself had served as Sheriff of Perth during the revolutionary years. His fear and dislike of radicals was therefore well established and he sought to act decisively against what he saw as being a politically motivated dispute.

Although the strike was peaceful, the existence of correspondence with similar organisations in England was evidence enough for Colquhoun to believe that sedition was being planned. Suspicions were further fuelled by information, as was mentioned earlier, about Margarot visiting the area at the time and meeting with former colleagues from the British Convention. There appears to be no basis for Colquhoun's concern as the communications between the groups were not subversive in nature and Margarot's efforts were at best exploratory. However, Colquhoun's paranoia was worsened by the prejudices of the employers of the strikers who exacerbated his fears with suggestions of rebellion.

As a result, the homes of the strike leaders were raided and arrests were made. Ringleaders were charged under the Combination Laws that had been brought in over a decade before to crush the embryonic trade union movement. Despite the perversity of having earlier decided in the workers' favour, the court connived with the government and the manufacturers, and sentenced the strike leaders to eighteen months' imprisonment. The liberalism that had prevailed after peace with revolutionary France once again was supplanted by old prejudices. This served as a salutary lesson to the radicals that it was necessary to have political organisation alongside industrial action.

The defeat was compounded by growing social and economic problems as another trough in the economic cycle began. The Corn Laws enacted in 1815 put pressure on the poor and benefited the rich, as they protected the home-grown product of landowners and restricted access to cheaper imported grain for workers. The laws resulted in riots across the country, in Glasgow, Perth, Dundee and in other industrial communities. To the discontented this could only have served as a reminder about the need to gain political power, as well as acting as a driver to return to the radical fray.

And a return to the fray there would be. Margarot's visit to Scotland was made in an attempt to lay the ground to relaunch the earlier political campaigning, rather than as part of his involvement in the strike by the cotton spinners. As John Brims has highlighted, sympathies for the radical cause had not disappeared:

Beneath the surface calm of politics in the first decade and a half of the nineteenth century lay not only a small number of revolutionary conspirators but also a great mass of men whose hearts and minds had been won over to the democratic cause in the 1790s and who when circumstances changed, would be ready to stir once more and demand their rights.[9]

During his trip to Scotland, Margarot seems to have been acting either as an ambassador or outrider for Major John Cartwright, mentioned in Chapter 14. However, it was still a few years before the radicals that Margarot had met, along with others, surfaced politically and that Major Cartwright made his appearance north of the border. In the summer of 1815, the veteran English radical travelled to Scotland and was delighted at the reception he received. From 'Lanark and Greenock to Edinburgh and Aberdeen' he found 'an unequivocal desire on the part of the mass of the people ... to promote reform by signing petitions'.[10] His speaking engagements during the tour were extensive; he visited the old radical heartlands in the west of Scotland, Fife and Tayside and up into the northeast of the country. He also held several meetings in the big cities, such as Edinburgh and Glasgow, and visited the radical communities in the likes of Renfrew, Paisley, Coupar Angus and Forfar.

Cartwright's visit acted as a spark, which reignited the radical flame amongst many individuals who had been active in the 1790s, but for whatever reason had turned away from radicalism. Reformist stalwarts, including old activists from Perth and the lawyer William Moffatt in Edinburgh, helped plan Cartwright's tour and many other individuals returned to the cause. In 1816 Archibald Hastie chaired a meeting in Paisley, which demanded universal suffrage; in reports to the government he was later described as being the leader of reformers in the area. Former activists continued to return to fight for the issues they had fought for in the 1790s.

Once again universal suffrage and annual parliaments were called for, with the centre of power remaining in London. There was neither suggestion of, nor calls made for, a revocation of the Treaty of Union. The Scottish republicanism of Thomas Muir was replaced by the original demands of the Friends of the People. Moreover, despite the backdrop of social and industrial turmoil, political power rather than economic equality was sought; property rights were certainly without challenge, if not sacrosanct. Defeating the vested interests of the landowners was seen as being sufficient to provide the change that the discontented sought, and at this stage there were no calls for the redistribution of wealth or land. All this was to be achieved peacefully and constitutionally in an approach that replicated the aims of the Friends of the People rather than the Society of the United Scotsmen. However, again similarly to the events in the 1790s, some more extreme revolutionary groups did start to organise in the west of Scotland in around 1816.

Once again, the constitutional reformers were initially at the forefront of the movement, building on the upsurge in support that followed in the wake of Cartwright's visit. In 1816 a major rally was organised in Glasgow, which faced obstruction from the Tory council, as was the case with the obelisk in Edinburgh decades later. Reformers had been meeting and organising in the city and many were well-known traders and merchants. They included John Russell, a manufacturer in the city; John Ogilvie, a china merchant in Jamaica Street; John McArthur, an ironmonger in Argyle Street; William Watson, a manufacturer in George Street; and William Lang, a printer in Bell Street, as well as others from more humble trades, such as Benjamin Gray, a shoemaker in Nelson Street, and John McLeod, a cotton spinner in Tureen Street.

Their original plan was to hold a rally on Glasgow Green, which was common then as now, but the Lord Provost threatened to disperse the crowd with the military if necessary. Accordingly, the group then proposed to hold the meeting at an inn where the landlord was known to be a reform sympathiser. However, again after hearing of the plan, the Lord Provost and the landowner objected and forced the publican to withdraw his consent. Into the breach stepped James Turner, a shoemaker's son, who had started out as a tobacco shop owner but then became a successful merchant in the city. He possessed land outside the city boundaries – over which the Lord Provost and council had neither say nor influence – and he offered it as a location for the rally. His field at Thrushgrove, which is now part of the Royston area of Glasgow, was the setting for a huge rally and an event that demonstrated that the radical cause was well and truly alive.

In October 1816 the rally finally took place, with another leading English reformer as the main speaker. This time it was William Cobbett, the publisher of a radical paper that had become extremely popular amongst the English working class called the *Political Register*. Over 40,000 attended the rally, with many sporting caps of liberty, the long soft hat associated with the French Revolution; this highlighted the fact that although sympathy for France had faded, that for the principles of the revolution most certainly had not. Others carried brushes, to symbolise the sweeping away of political corruption in the land. Such behaviour seems quite light-hearted now, but back then it was radical, if not provocative.

Accordingly, the event took place under the watchful eyes of the authorities, who had the army stationed in the city barracks primed and ready to strike at any sign of disturbance. The authorities were looking for any excuse to send in the dragoons that were readied and prepared to gallop out if the signal was given by those monitoring the proceedings. The authorities had either forgotten or had chosen to ignore the events at Tranent less than two decades previously, and this served as a prelude for Peterloo a few years later. However, the meeting passed peacefully, the crowd was loud and boisterous but otherwise well behaved, and afforded no excuse for any intervention, militarily or otherwise. Although Thrushgrove might not have been a long walk for those living in nearby Glasgow, it also attracted people from far and wide.

The rally, along with Major Cartwright's tour the year before, marked the revival of the radical cause in Scotland. The speaking tour focused on those areas that had been the most radical in the 1790s and it was in these towns that the reformists awoke from their slumbers. The campaign's motivation was best encapsulated in a report sent by the Lord Advocate to the Home Secretary in December 1816. The report concerned a meeting held at the Kilbarchan Relief Church where one of the speakers was noted as stating: 'A spark was kindled at the French Revolution which the enemies of freedom think they have extinguished, but still it burns, and every fresh occurrence fans the flames.'[11]

Both newly formed and reconstituted societies were still overwhelmingly committed to achieving their aims through peaceful measures. The early activities of most individuals, as well as being the focus of the majority of the meetings that were held, centred on preparing for or supporting petitions backing parliamentary efforts for reform. At this time Sir Francis Burdett, an English MP and a prominent reform supporter, was pushing for universal suffrage through motions in the House of Commons and his efforts were bolstered by widescale public demand. The petitions related to the cause were public and the meetings were largely open; there was neither any attempt made to be secretive or clandestine. Although the mood amongst radicals was no doubt watchful and wary given past experiences.

The peaceful make-up and intentions of the reformers and radicals was well known to the Lord Advocate and the authorities that were monitoring them. But just as Cartwright's tour and the Thrushgrove rally encouraged the radicals, it sent shivers of fear down the back of the establishment. Those in charge may have held their fire at Thrushgrove, but they still intended to crush the growing dissent. Moreover, as earlier, the Lord Advocate and the authorities believed that the radicals were intent on inciting a revolution. These feelings were hardened by reports received about secret committees and clandestine societies that had been established. They may have been few in number and far less than the peaceful organisations, but their existence was enough to justify the fears of the authorities and legitimise their repression.

The secret societies had evolved, especially in the radical heartlands in the west of Scotland. Such groups became modelled on the Society of the United Scotsmen and were based on a cell structure, replete with oaths of loyalty, secret signs and handshakes to identify members and with specifically stipulated revolutionary aims. Such societies not just espoused the moral arguments for universal franchise, but were prepared to use physical force to defend themselves and to achieve their aims. However, although they had grown they were still limited in number and even more limited in terms of access to arms.

As had happened previously, informants were infiltrated into organisations to monitor proceedings. One report in December 1816 stated that 'secret committees of the disaffected, consisting chiefly of the ringleaders of the combination in 1812, and of such members of the seditious societies of 1793 as were still alive, had been formed in different quarters of Glasgow, Ayrshire, Dumbarton and Stirlingshire'. The note alleged that delegates from England had visited the Glasgow committee and that this committee, after discussing the organisation of the United Irishmen, and of the 'traitors in Scotland in 1795' had resolved to adopt the plan of the former, so as to form a disciplined force utilising all the available arms within reach.[12]

Whether this report was false or simply embellished is not known. It is reasonable to assume that though there was truth in such claims and that the secret societies had re-formed, they were neither as many nor as threatening as was suggested. However, with a Lord Advocate who was receptive to rumours of rebellion, the authorities were not going to take any chances.

These events also must be seen in the wider context of what was happening across Britain, as much of the new radicalism was emanating from the industrialising areas across the country. Riots were occurring in London and in other towns and cities as the economy crashed once again. Penury, if not starvation, was a reality for many, but one particular incident was to be the prelude for a national clampdown, which reverberated north of the border. On 28 January 1817 the Prince of Wales, heir to the throne and soon to be crowned George IV, was attacked in his coach as he returned to Buckingham Palace, following the state opening of Parliament. His rather debauched lifestyle made him an unpopular figure, and he became almost an incitement to violence during that difficult period. Whether his carriage was hit with a stone or a bullet was never ascertained, but the audacious attack sent out shockwaves and resulted in the re-imposition of draconian legislation.

The news of the attack reverberated north of the border and an already anxious Lord Advocate no doubt felt compelled to act to ward off revolution. Thus, February 1817 saw twenty-six radicals arrested across the country, as the authorities swooped into action. The charges were varied and generally did not make any links between those accused or allude to any suggestions of a plot. The evidence largely related either to seditious comments or writings, or the administration of secret oaths. This gave the impression that those who were detained were simply the individuals who were known to the authorities, rather than those actually involved in any planned insurrection or threat to the state.

However, things had changed in the Scottish courts since the previous trials – notwithstanding the decision in the cotton spinners' strike. Whilst the laws may have remained much the same, the attitude of the courts had transformed remarkably. Gone was Lord Braxfield with his prejudices and vindictiveness. Whilst far from being radical, the new High Court bench displayed greater fairness in its actions and general behaviour. By then there were even some former Whig supporters who sat as judges. This meant that there would be a far more balanced outcome when the accused came to trial.

First to appear in court on 5 March 1817 were Alexander MacLaren, a weaver, and Thomas Baird, a shopkeeper. MacLaren was accused of having delivered what was described as a 'violent speech' in Kilmarnock and Baird for printing it in a pamphlet. Although MacLaren made reference to 'the spirit of Bannockburn', he primarily called for parliamentary reform and denounced the system under which they lived. The weaver continued:

> We are ruled by men only solicitous for their own aggrandisement; and they care no further for the great body of people than as they are subservient to their accursed purposes ... Shall we, I say, whose forefathers defied the efforts of foreign tyranny to enslave our beloved country, meanly permit on our day without a murmur a base oligarchy to feed their filthy vermin on our vitals, and rule us as they will? No, my countrymen! Let us lay our petitions at the foot of the throne, where sits our august Prince, whose gracious nature will incline his ear to listen to the cries of the people, which he is bound to do by the laws of the country. But should he be so infatuated as to turn a deaf ear to their just petition, he has forfeited their allegiance. Yes, my fellow townsmen, in such a case, to hell with allegiance![13]

Rebellious in tone and content MacLaren's speech may have been, but revolutionary it was not, other than in the way that it warned about failing to listen, which at this time would have been more than enough to be considered seditious. The presiding judge at the trial was Lord Adam Gillies, who had been a prominent Whig before being appointed to the bench, and though the two accused were ultimately convicted of sedition, the jury urged clemency. Whether as a result of this or because of his own judgement, the sentence imposed by Gillies was only six months' imprisonment for each. A far cry from transportation to Botany Bay.

The more liberal regime was demonstrated in another trial that involved Andrew McKinlay, another weaver who was charged with treason and having administered secret oaths. The legal arguments made by defence counsel meant that the prosecution had to withdraw the charges initially laid and serve new ones. This was only to be the beginning of what was to prove to be a catastrophic case for the prosecution. When the trial eventually proceeded in the July a witness was called who had been involved in the alleged crime and had been persuaded to give King's evidence. When he was formally asked if he had been offered any inducement for his testimony, his reply stunned the court who had been anticipating the usual denial. He firstly confirmed that he had been induced to testify and when this question was followed with by whom, he identified the Advocate Depute who was prosecuting the case and went on to add that it had also been offered in the presence of the Sheriff of Edinburgh and that he had been promised a good situation abroad after the conclusion of the trial. Needless to say, the case collapsed with the judges rightly angered and the prosecution hugely embarrassed.

Other accused individuals would also benefit from the court's new actions and attitude. The second trial for sedition involved the Reverend Neil Douglas, an elderly preacher of a dissenting church in Glasgow, who Berresford Ellis and Mac A' Ghobhainn have suggested was both a friend of Skirving and Gerrald and a delegate at the Friends of the People conventions, although his name was not recorded at the first two meetings. However, his commitment to the cause was not doubted and his sermons were both radical and popular.

Douglas had been charged with sedition, including for having made disparaging comments about the Prince of Wales. The charges against him stated that he asserted that 'His Royal Highness, the Prince, was a poor infatuated devotee of Bacchus'. Other remarks that he allegedly made were similarly biblically or classically themed, although he also suggested that 'we could not deem the battle of Waterloo a subject of congratulations for many reasons' before going on to cite the restoration of the old monarchical order.

Perhaps, the jury was sympathetic because the preacher was sixty-seven years old and described by the lawyer Henry Cockburn as being 'old, deaf, dogged, honest and respectable'.[14] Or alternatively the jury may have viewed the comments as being mild and within the limits of what was legal, as was the basis of his lawyer's defence. For whatever reason Douglas was acquitted, with the jury indicating not only a change in the attitude of the judiciary, but also in the make-up of the juries. Gone were the days of the selection of Goldsmiths' Hall members for the jury, which was reflective not just of a more relaxed attitude on the bench but more liberal sympathies across the land.

If there had been any conspiracy planned by these secret societies the arrests most certainly brought them to an end, albeit temporarily. Any planned insurrection would also no doubt have been affected by the general repression imposed across the land, as similar punitive actions were also taken in England. Given that radicalism had been revived following the high-profile visits of leading English reformers, the dissipation of spirit there must surely have lapped over into Scotland. For though these secret societies may have been formed in a manner mimicking counterparts from Ireland, it became evident that links with radical organisations in England were increasing.

This is understandable given a variety of factors, from the proscription of the United Scotsmen and United Irishmen, through to the religious differences that existed between a largely Calvinist Scotland and a Catholic Ireland, which was no doubt accentuated by the sectarian fallout after the failed 1798 rebellion; to the expansion of industrialisation and the forging of ever-closer links across the Scottish and English border between working classes with shared interests.

Irish radicals remained involved but were very much on the fringes. Those who persisted were generally revolutionary in outlook and willing to use physical force as a strategy. Their purpose was mainly to seek allies for future insurrections whether within the Irish émigré community or amongst other like-minded individuals that would rise with them. This was a philosophy that would continue for more than a century to come.

As the second decade of the nineteenth century progressed, revolutionary France – which had motivated the earlier political martyrs – was replaced by industrial Britain as the inspiration for Scottish radicals. Lacking encouragement from abroad and subdued by the government at home, evolution more than revolution became the path for radicals; although a rebellious spirit remained within them.

Of course, the Scots operated largely independently and in their own distinctive way. They were never simply homogeneous Scottish regions or subgroups of larger English bodies. Distinct societies and separate institutions in Scotland necessitated this and the situation was complicated by the vastness of the country. But, closer cooperation with societies in England was beginning and events south of the border had a pivotal role as the legacy of the martyrs played out.

CHAPTER 16

EVENTS IN ENGLAND

This book concerns Scotland during the revolutionary era and neither later events in England, nor even the 1820 Rising are directly
related. Moreover, these occurrences were both extensive and significant, and merit books and studies in their own right. However, the
legacy of the Scottish political martyrs and the others who struggled
during the 1790s lingered and inspired those involved in subsequent
events, which provided both a direct link in the case of some and an
ideology more generally with others. Consideration of such events is
therefore necessary to complete the tale of the revolutionary years.

For as the cycle of prosperity continued in terms of both war and the
economy, so the popularity of the reform cause ebbed and flowed. The
crackdown on radicals in 1817 was followed by a return to the fray of advocates for change, as unemployment grew and social problems mounted.
With those who supported a more confrontational approach still recovering from the previous spate of arrests, the focus in Scotland, initially at
least, returned to more moderate and constitutional campaigners.

The old burgh reform movement was rejuvenated by yet another
example of government ineptitude, combined with the continuation
of flagrant electoral abuse. For 1817 also brought public anger over
burgh elections, with concerns over the selection of the Montrose
Town Council spilling over into other communities. Issues in the
Angus town meant that the Lord Advocate had to issue a new charter

governing the structure and conduct of the area, which was slightly more democratic than the form of self-selection that had preceded it. Although he was concerned by the possible implications of conceding the new format, the Lord Advocate felt that failing to act would have had worse consequences. The new incumbent as political ruler of Scotland at this time was Alexander Maconochie (Lord Advocate 1816–19), who was yet another member of the landowning classes, although he had already proved himself spectacularly inept during the prosecutions of the radicals that same year.

However, the moderate changes introduced did not resolve the issue but made it worse. Other towns soon sought similar progressive changes, and meetings were held in Edinburgh and elsewhere as the burgh reform movement was re-energised. The government reacted by refusing further requests and by hunkering down against any additional changes, and no doubt rued its supposed liberality.

Reform-minded burghs litigated to try and obtain similar changes, but their attempts were rejected by the Court of Session, which emphasised the fact that although there had been progress, the court still remained a pillar of the establishment. This was evidenced in correspondence between Robert Dundas, the former Lord Advocate who at the time sat on the Scottish bench as Chief Baron of the Exchequer, and Lord Sidmouth, the then British Home Secretary. Although he was no longer in power, Sidmouth still sought Dundas's counsel, perhaps as a result of a lack of trust in Maconochie. In November 1817 Dundas wrote to his London colleague and advised:

> Having been led into one error at Montrose is no reason why we should repeat it in the other burghs ... There is no part of the United Kingdom that has prospered more than North Britain for above a century past, with the exception of a small mistake we made in 1745, and I have no relish for experimental changes by wholesale.[1]

Leaving aside the description of the barbarity of Culloden and the tragedy that unfolded in the highlands as 'a small mistake', this statement makes clear the continued opposition of the establishment to even modest changes in the franchise. Compounding this crass insensitivity was a reference to prosperity in the north of Britain. This may have been the case for the elite and the burgeoning middle class as the empire and trade expanded. Growing prosperity allied to increased opportunity at home and abroad saw huge wealth that was accumulated by landowners and many individuals made their fortunes. But this did not apply for the working classes where poverty and unemployment were rife. These social and economic issues would become the driver of further calls for political reform and once again the mantle would be passed from reformers to radicals.

The radical revival erupted in January 1819 when George Kinloch, who was known as the 'radical laird', addressed a large crowd in Dundee and spoke about the burdens on the poor through war and excessive taxation, along with the need for universal suffrage. The link between political reform and the changing social and economic conditions was being made; and demands for change would only escalate as hardship grew.

By August 1819 unemployment had increased and so had agitation for change, especially in the textile areas, such as Glasgow, Paisley and Dundee, which were rightly viewed as hotbeds of sedition. But this also applied in other areas as campaigning was stepped up, by both burgh reformers and more radical groups, although a clear chasm was growing in the attitudes and actions of the Whig reformers and the working-class radicals.

Demands for change were already being made in England. That summer an atrocity was perpetrated in Manchester that would reverberate north and south of the border and have an explosive outcome in Scotland. On 16 August 1819 the Peterloo massacre unfolded, which bore some similarities with Tranent but on a far larger scale. More importantly the tragedy received much greater public awareness, but ominously there was also a vastly more severe government reaction.

The Manchester Patriotic Union, which was an organisation that supported political reform, had been increasing its activities as unemployment and poverty afflicted the growing industrial metropolis and the towns clustered around it. Plans for a meeting in early August caused concerns across the country, as well as locally. The Home Secretary wrote to local magistrates and warned them against the gathering and suggested that action be taken to stop it. The authorities appeared to have got their information from some intercepted correspondence, which wrongly suggested the existence of insurrectionary activities.

However, it should be noted that military drilling had been ongoing in the area and elsewhere in England especially in the north, as it had in parts of Scotland, and unemployed ex-servicemen and other discontented groups had been preparing for a more confrontational approach. A royal proclamation had even been issued the same month against the practice of drilling, which was widespread in the area. An initial meeting that was planned for 9 August was thus banned by the local magistrates. However, with leading orators having already arrived for the rally, including the celebrated Henry Hunt who was to be one of the principal speakers, it was decided to proceed with the event the following week.

The meeting held on 16 August was neither halted nor impeded by the authorities, although both troops and Yeomanry forces were mobilised. Between 60,000 and 80,000 people gathered at St Peter's Field on the outskirts of the town to hear speeches, which was a substantial crowd at that time even for a fast-growing conurbation. Local magistrates who had been monitoring the situation were panicked by the scale of the demonstration and called on the Yeomanry to arrest Hunt. Mayhem ensued as the militia units charged into the tightly packed crowd, only for the paramilitaries to become enveloped within the throng, which was understandable given the lack of space for either friend or foe to manoeuvre.

As at Tranent, the cavalry then joined in and men, women and children were gunned and cut down. As the crowd fled, the army attacked and then pursued them. Control seemed to be lost both by the military command and the soldiers themselves. Eighteen people were killed and between 400 and 700 wounded before the slaughter finally came to an end. In a further replication of events in Scotland, and adding insult to injury, it was the demonstrators who were then arrested and Henry Hunt and other organisers were rounded up.

In a sardonic reference to Waterloo, the events at St Peter's Field were christened 'Peterloo' and the name has stuck. The effect was significant south of the border, but the event also reverberated north of it, as radicals responded in rage and fury and the authorities reacted with repression. As news reached Scotland there was anger amongst radicals and reformers alike. Newspaper reports on the atrocity were eagerly read, even if some comments about the demonstration were sanitised or even condemnatory. Radical pamphlets and publications served to expose the full horror of the event and the links that had been established between reform groups allowed for oral testimony about what had actually happened to be quickly passed on.

Demonstrations followed in many parts of Scotland. In early September there was a major demonstration in Glasgow as radicals in the city expressed their rage and sorrow, and the protests continued across the country. On 3 November a meeting was held in Kirkcaldy where over 5,000 people attended to make their condemnation of Peterloo abundantly clear. Resolutions were passed that called for reform but again the crowds were eager to emphasise that their intentions were peaceful, which may have been a necessary precaution given the likelihood of the authorities to respond with violence. The following week on 10 November, almost 10,000 people gathered at Magdalen Yard in Dundee. Despite being banned, some flags and banners were carried by a number of demonstrators. The words emblazoned on the signs clearly denoted their sympathies and demands: 'For the Sufferers of Manchester' and 'We Only Want Our Rights in a Peaceable and Constitutional Manner'.[2] Others carried broken teapots and glasses, and even fragments of small bones, which were meant to symbolise the luxuries that the poor were denied. The radical laird, George Kinloch, once again addressed the crowd and advocated for the universal franchise, whilst attacking the events in Manchester. Having learned a lesson from other demonstrations and doubtless to avoid a confrontation, the magistrates stayed away from the event, but a warrant was later issued for Kinloch's arrest. Shortly after, 20,000 people attended a meeting in Kilmarnock where reference was made to Kinloch and thanks given.

The most serious outbreak of disorder took place in Paisley and by this time the authorities were mindful of the need to avoid a clash with the protesters. On 11 September, less than a month after the Peterloo atrocity, a protest meeting was held on Meikleriggs Muir at the southern edge of the Renfrewshire town. This was a regular venue for radical rallies as it afforded easy access both from the town and Glasgow, but also for the communities further to the west in Renfrewshire or to the south in Ayrshire. One such event on 17 July 1819 saw almost 30,000 gather to hear demands for parliamentary reform and the granting of the ability to vote for all.[3]

The event on 11 September had fewer attendees than the earlier meeting, with estimates varying between 14,000 and 18,000, but this was still a significant turnout given the circumstances and the size of the local population. The gathering was planned for 4 September but bad weather forced it to be postponed for a week; in addition, the Sheriff of Renfrewshire had also sought to ban it.

Therefore, when the rally was finally held it proceeded with an air of tension, accompanied by anger both at events in England and the situation in Scotland. The solemnity of the occasion was confirmed by the platform party who were dressed in funereal black, and with the banners carried by the crowds also being edged in black. People attended from Glasgow and from all across Renfrewshire and Ayrshire. The rally passed off peacefully and the chairman Alexander Taylor stated that they did not want revolution, but just a reform of parliament.

However, for some parts of society mere reform was no longer sufficient and a meek response to harassment had become entirely unacceptable. Young men in particular were inflamed by news of the massacre and many were no longer prepared to stand by and be bullied or attacked by the authorities.

This increasing militancy and willingness for confrontation became evident when the rally on Meikleriggs Muir concluded and the crowd began to disperse. Despite the demonstration having been prohibited, the authorities had taken no action to stop it, whether through fear at the scale of the crowd or as part of a desire to avoid a clash. However, a confrontation was almost inevitable given the increasing tension and unease in the air. As a section of the rally returned towards Glasgow, special constables attempted to grab the group's flags and banners, which had also been prohibited. A riot then ensued and disturbances continued in the town for almost a week.

Despite the Riot Act being read out, and indeed proclaimed on numerous occasions, the authorities were unable to restore order. Moderate reform leaders also called for calm but their pleas likewise went unheeded. The military were then called in and repeated clashes took place between cavalry and rioters, with crowds numbering up to 4,000 to 5,000 on the streets. As was the case in Tranent – but on an even larger scale – the narrow streets and alleys in the town afforded a ready means of escape for the rioters but prevented access to soldiers on horseback. Described as being audacious and self-confident, the local protesters were joined in the evenings by other crowds from the surrounding villages who would then return home as night fell. Gun shops were raided and arms and ammunition were taken, and some larger houses and even the council chambers were attacked by the demonstrators. A curfew was even called and finally calm was restored after five days, most likely as a result of the increasing strength of the military presence and the exhaustion of protesters.

Glasgow saw similar trouble in the aftermath of the confrontation as the rally was being dispersed. Rioting occurred over several days especially in the east end of the city in weaving areas, such as Bridgeton and Dalmarnock. Many of those who had been involved in the fracas when leaving Paisley continued to vent their anger once they arrived home. Many others, however, also joined in as the rage of working people boiled over. Troops, Yeomanry and constables were again mobilised and deployed. Although the disturbance was less extreme than in Paisley it was still significant enough to be reported on widely and caused alarm amongst the authorities.

In the aftermath two young men were convicted for being involved in the riots in Paisley. One pled guilty and received a sentence of four months' imprisonment and the other was convicted after trial and imprisoned for nine months. Other individuals who had been involved simply took off abroad before they were arrested and faced prosecution, as had occurred during the early revolutionary years. Alexander Taylor, who had chaired the meeting, headed for Canada rather than face certain imprisonment, despite the fact that he made it clear that peaceful reform was what was being sought.

However, what was more noticeable than the immediate retribution taken against those involved in the riots, and more ominous for radicals in the longer term, was the mobilisation drive by the authorities that followed the rally. Troops were garrisoned in the town as a result and a barracks was later built in the area. In the interim, in addition to the military presence, the Earl of Glasgow, who was Lord Lieutenant of Renfrewshire, held a meeting on 5 November to raise a regiment of Yeomanry Cavalry and enlist a volunteer corps. It was reckoned that the strength of this militia unit alone reached almost 1,000, which encapsulated the growing fear felt by the establishment. Other areas likewise saw an expansion of the Yeomanry. This measure was most certainly not about repelling any foreign invaders and no such fiction was even suggested. The precaution was taken entirely to protect the wealth and privilege of the landowning elite from revolution or rebellion amongst 'the lower orders'.

The establishment across all of Britain, not just in the west of Scotland, was once again becoming increasingly worried about the situation and for their personal safety. According to Berresford Ellis and Mac A' Ghobhainn, Lord Charles Hope, the Lord President of the Court of Session, wrote to Lord Melville and stated that 'all disguise is now thrown off – even the flimsy pretence of radical reform is laid aside – a complete revolution and plunder is their avowed object'.[4] Scotland's most senior judge went on to suggest almost apocalyptically that conflict was coming. The authorities were preparing to put down any attempts at rebellion and had enlisted other sections of the wealthy and privileged in society to assist them.

Once again, the state, as well as arresting radicals, brought in further repressive legislation; in many ways this replicated what had happened in Scotland during the revolutionary years. By the end of 1819 what were known as the Six Acts had been brought in. The legislation was described by the historian, Élie Halévy, as being part of a 'counter revolutionary terror', as the establishment responded ferociously.[5] For after Peterloo disturbances had broken out in the north of England that soon spread into the Midlands and beyond. All seventeen counties were affected and magistrates in these areas who feared a further loss of control sought parliamentary support and action. Lord Sidmouth, the Home Secretary, responded by having Parliament recalled in late November and by the end of the year the Six Acts had been enshrined in law, which granted sweeping powers to the state and its local representatives. Repression was unleashed.

Newspapers were gagged and radical publications restricted. Trials were accelerated and sentences increased. Powers of search for weapons were augmented. Anyone found drilling was liable to be arrested and punished by transportation. Meetings of over fifty people on matters relating to church or state required permission from local magistrates. North of the border the laws were ultimately only applied in Renfrewshire and Lanarkshire, which showed where the authorities considered the threat to be primarily located.

But as the authorities made preparations and took action so too did the radicals. For the militant mood was spreading across the land. Despite the crackdown in England with the arrest of radicals and the introduction of legislation, military drilling increased and organisations met to plot a more coordinated response. Many radicals had served in the army and knew how to handle weapons, even if they did not possess them. The mood in the west of Scotland was similar, and many people began organising themselves in a similar way.

Organisations across Scotland, though predominantly in the west of the country, were by this time cooperating and preparing. Although there was no re-formation of the Society of the United Scotsmen as such, many of those involved would have been past members. Many were called 'union societies', which was more of an early reference to working-class unity rather than the political union between Scotland and England. They existed on both sides of the border but operated entirely separately. They were most active in the areas that had previously been United Scotsmen strongholds, and particularly in the weaving villages of the west of Scotland. They became more cohesive towards the end of 1819 and as well as acting as political platforms there were also suggestions that members were practising military drills and acquiring arms.

As in earlier years, information about such groups was limited given the homogeneity and clannishness of the towns and villages where they operated. However, the authorities knew that discontent was spreading and preparations for organisation were being made, even if they did not quite know what for. Paisley and the surrounding villages were an example of this, with the revolutionary spirit of the 1790s being revived with enthusiasm. As explored in Chapter 15, Archibald Hastie, a delegate to the British Convention of the Friends of the People in 1793, chaired a radical meeting in the Paisley West Relief Church in 1816. The following year Kilbarchan was described as a 'nest of radicals' and other communities could be described similarly as previously quiet radicals began to openly express their views.[6] But it was not only talk but practical action that was being taken.

On the day of the Peterloo demonstration on Meikleriggs Muir another meeting was held, in the Unitarian church, where it was agreed that a coordinating committee for radical organisations in southwest Scotland be established, as well as the founding of a newspaper. Similar discussions were ongoing in Glasgow, Lanarkshire, Ayrshire and beyond as a wider Scottish network was established. Radical meetings were held across Scotland, with Edinburgh and Kilmarnock holding events the size of which caused concern amongst the authorities. Other large-scale demonstrations took place in the likes of Ayr, Neilston and Airdrie as the discontent in the west of the country escalated. In Glasgow in early December 1819 the Yeomanry were called out as an insurrection was feared in the city. Troops were deployed across the town and field guns were strategically positioned as rumours about a planned rebellion reached the authorities. In the end nothing serious transpired, although there appeared to be a suspicious number of strangers in the city, which seemed to give some credence to the rumours. At the same time radicals openly paraded in Kilsyth, with drilling ongoing elsewhere.

Weapon searches increased as a result of concerns held by the authorities about the growing combativeness shown by working people. The Home Secretary expressed a fear that the people had secured military field guns, which would have been a quantum leap from pikes and pistols. In response, Lord Sidmouth wrote to the Lord Lieutenants and called for vigilance and action over cannons owned by landowners that could have been put to use if they were acquired by insurrectionists.

As 1819 ended, there were further arrests of radical leaders in Scotland as another clampdown began. George Kinloch, the radical laird and a leading reformer in Dundee, was due to stand trial in December having been arrested for allegedly giving seditious speeches. Despite or because of his wealthy origins the establishment marginalised him and the novelist Walter Scott apparently alluded that Thomas Muir had been punished for far less.[7] Sensing his fate and certain doom, Kinloch fled, first to England and then to France. At the same time a radical paper that had been launched in October 1819 called *The Spirit of the Union*, a reference to the union societies, was suppressed in January 1820 after only a few editions. Its editor, Gilbert McLeod, was tried on charges of sedition and transported for five years, which highlighted how Kinloch's decision to flee was wise.

The arrest of Kinloch and McLeod signalled that the repression experienced during the revolutionary era was well and truly back. But the response to it this time was different, which reflected that times had changed and that lessons had been learned. Many radicals had concluded by this time that their beliefs would need to be defended and fought for. Peterloo had confirmed this. Unlike in the early part of the 1790s, there would be no passive acceptance of oppression or compliant tolerance for punishment like the martyrs. Physical force radicalism was coming.

With the wealthier radical leaders being arrested or disappearing for their own safety, both the combatants and the stage was changing. It was the working class rather than the lawyers and the wealthier reformers that were organising and preparing for rebellion. This time the battlefield would not be in the law courts and fought with eloquent speeches, but in the poorer communities of the west of Scotland with pikes and pistols. The conflicts occurred primarily in Glasgow and Paisley, but also in the surrounding industrial towns and weaving villages. Both the radicals and the establishment were now set on a trajectory for confrontation. Tension was rising on both sides of the border and the Scottish societies were linking up with their English and Irish counterparts. Conflict was inevitable.

As social and economic conditions worsened, discussions were held by groups both within Scotland and across Britain and Ireland about instigating an armed rebellion. A major meeting was held in Nottingham in December 1819 when radicals from both sides of the border attended alongside representatives from Ireland. Delegates from many societies in Scotland attended, including John Neil for Renfrewshire.[8] In his report he disclosed what was planned and provided an insight into the thinking of those involved. Other delegates likewise reported to their societies and colleagues both in Scotland and elsewhere.

Neil explained that a rebellion was being planned for April 1820 and recounted that thousands of people were to be involved, with soldiers and workers in arsenals expected to defect to the side of the revolutionaries. This was reminiscent of what had happened in revolutionary France and would occur in revolutions generations later, when armed forces united with the people. The prelude for the rising was a general strike across the land. On the back of this it was assumed that revolution and insurrection would follow, although arms were to be acquired both to defend the strike and to help the revolt to spread.

A provisional government was to be established in Scotland, as well as in England and Ireland. This appeared to have been seen as a temporary measure pending parliamentary reform and the establishment of the universal franchise on a Britain-wide basis. The provisional government was to all intents and purposes a form of local revolutionary command, rather than an indication of a nationalist agenda. As the Scottish societies were distinct and operated independently it was decided that control would initially need to be exercised separately north of the border. But whilst it was clear that the Scots were operating independently, the scheme was still planned as part of a pan-British rising.

To provide some reassurance to Scottish radicals that they were neither alone nor without support south of the border, Neil explained that Scotland was only to rise when 180,000 Englishmen were already on the march. To indicate that the events were unfolding as hoped in England, the signal for rebellion to begin in Scotland was to be the nonarrival of the regular mail coach from England in Glasgow on 1 April. A 'general congress of delegates' from all the reform societies was held near Paisley on 22 February, where presumably final plans were resolved. Songs were sung and oaths were sworn as comradeship was forged. A delegate was also dispatched to the north of England to advise about Scotland's readiness.[9]

However, the intentions of English radicals for a general rising were blown apart by events that unfolded the day after this caucus of Scottish comrades. For on 23 February 1820 the Cato Street Conspiracy was uncovered in London. This was a plot to assassinate the entire British Cabinet, including the Prime Minister Lord Liverpool, who ironically had been in charge of the military at the time of the Tranent massacre. The plot was planned by a revolutionary group who subscribed to the radical views of Thomas Spence, who had died just a few years before. Spence sought not just universal franchise but also called for more radical social and economic changes, including public ownership and the redistribution of land.

The conspiracy got its name from the street near Edgware Road in London, where the flat in which the plot was planned was located. The intention was to attack the members of the Cabinet when they were dining at a house in central London, which would spark a revolution. However, there was little done to ensure that a rising followed the attack and the operation appears to have been entirely separate from the plans discussed in Nottingham in December 1819. The intentions were known to the authorities, who had already infiltrated the small organisation, and the plan was instigated by an agent provocateur, which allowed the authorities an excuse for widespread suppression.

On 23 February police raided the flat where a fight took place and a police officer was killed in the commotion that ensued. Some plotters were captured and others were rounded up shortly thereafter. Arthur Thistlewood, who was viewed as being the lead conspirator, and four other men were executed by being hanged and then beheaded, the last such occasion this punishment was used in England, although not in Britain. Five others were transported to Botany Bay, as the Scottish radicals had been before them.

Whilst the organisation was radical, it was on the periphery of the more mainstream groupings. Like many such organisations in years to come and in other countries around the world, the Cato Street conspirators operated entirely separately and to their own agenda. In some ways their plan was more nihilistic than revolutionary and there is no evidence that the group was involved in the plans for a revolt in April. The plan to eliminate the British Cabinet may have been daring for this revolutionary group but it was to be disastrous for the radical cause.

The already severe repression was increased through the new powers that were available under the Six Acts. It was not just those linked to the Cato Street Conspiracy; across the English radical and reform cause that further arrests and incarcerations occurred. Round-ups of known agitators took place and the arbitrary powers ensured that the radical cause was even more harshly suppressed than it ever had been before. The plans for a widescale rising in England were doomed.

But this information was not known by the radicals north of the border and nor would it have concerned those who were intent on rising anyway. The 1820 Rising would still proceed in the west of Scotland, where the revolutionary beacon still burned bright for many.

CHAPTER 17

THE 1820 RISING

There is a great deal of mythologising that has surrounded the 1820 Rising, in addition to disagreements amongst historians over the actual purpose of the uprising. Some writers, in particular Berresford Ellis and Mac A' Ghobhainn but also Peter Mackenzie, have portrayed the event as an insurrection in support of Scottish independence.[1] In this way they have asserted that it was almost a continuation of Thomas Muir's demands for a Scottish Republic. This has been challenged by other commentators such as F. K. Donnelly who has argued that the revolt was part of a wider movement across Britain.[2]

Donnelly and other historians have explained how in reality it was a general strike, albeit organised as a pretence for instigating revolution. Tom Johnston has described it as a 'strike for political freedom – a strike which the bulk of the participants expected would end in a bloody but successful revolution'.[3] This was a rising against oppression where the enemy was just as much the Scottish aristocracy with their Yeomanry and militia, as it was the British Army or government. Class rather than country was the driver for most, even if some espoused Scottish republican sentiments.

Some commentators have also blamed both the inception of the scheme and its failure on government informants and agent provocateurs, with their supposed intention being to encourage actions that could then be ruthlessly crushed by the authorities. Whilst others have argued that the plan was incited by radicals themselves and that it failed because of a variety of factors, including poor planning, bad luck and, perhaps most importantly of all, the overwhelming power of the establishment that confronted the activists. However, firstly it is necessary to understand what actually happened.

Despite the catastrophe that had unfolded south of the border after the discovery of the Cato Street Conspiracy, revolutionary preparations continued apace in Scotland. Military drilling continued as those who had been in the military sought to train those who had no experience. Arms were also made, in addition to being sought locally and from further afield. Training took place at night and in secluded spots and the manufacture and acquisition of arms was also clandestine. However, the authorities must have still known that something was being planned.

The coordinating committee for Scotland was raided in late March 1820 and some arrests were made, replicating the crackdown that was ongoing south of the border. News quickly spread and some radicals in Paisley fled, but returned when it was clear that nothing incriminating had been discovered. Although this was a false alarm in some ways, it indicated that the authorities were aware that something was being planned.

Government spies were gathering information, even though many of the societies and communities were closed to such outsiders. Limited information was still received by the authorities although this varied according to the locality. Glasgow, no doubt due to its size and more transient population, was a more lucrative source than Paisley or the weaving communities where strangers were viewed with greater suspicion.

Likewise, government agents were no doubt operating and seeking to promote disinformation, as well as encouraging actions that could be reported on and then crushed. However, the events that took place in April were largely planned by the radicals themselves. The date had been set and though much was ill-conceived and coordination was lacking, the rising occurred as a result of the deliberate actions of the reformists.

On Saturday 1 April 1820 proclamations were posted up overnight all across Lanarkshire, Renfrewshire, Ayrshire, Dunbartonshire and Stirlingshire. The document was entitled: 'Address to the Inhabitants of Great Britain & Ireland' (a copy of the proclamation is included in Appendix C). The document stated:

> Friends and countrymen, Roused from that torpid state in which We have been sunk for so many years, We are at length compelled, from the extremity of our sufferings, and the contempt heaped upon our petitions for redress, to assert our rights, at the hazard of our lives; and proclaim to the world the real motives which (if not misrepresented by designing men, would have united all ranks), have reduced us to take up arms for the redress of our common grievances.

As well as stating why they were acting, the address called for a general strike and urged workers to stay at home from 1 April. The document also made it clear that the group sought to overthrow the system and that they were prepared to fight for this outcome. Any suggestions that the proclamation was created by agent provocateurs in Glasgow are rather far-fetched, given the sentiments that were expressed and the fact that the documents were distributed over a considerable area, which must have necessitated the cooperation of multiple groups.

The strike was initially remarkably successful. The day after the proclamations were posted was a Sunday and a day of rest for most at that time, but it offered an opportunity to further publicise the call for a strike. Monday 3 April was therefore the first working day after the strike had been called and it garnered solid support across the west of Scotland. It has been estimated that 60,000 people ceased work that day and given the size of the population of just under 2.1 million, it was in many ways a general strike, and became a prelude to events that would follow more than a century later.[4] In Paisley and the surrounding villages, almost every individual did not go to work and in Glasgow the Lord Provost noted in a letter to the Home Secretary: 'Almost the whole population of the weaving classes have obeyed the orders contained in the treasonable proclamation by striking work.'[5]

The call to stay away from work was overwhelmingly supported in the weaving sector and in related trades, such as cotton spinning. But it was also supported across the wider community; of those who were later tried for striking offences their listed occupations included labourers, blacksmiths, grocers, tailors and others. However, support amongst colliers and agricultural workers was far less widespread. This was likely as a result of the fact that such communities were often separate from the weaving areas and because landowners or mine owners usually held greater control over their employees through possible sanctions or retribution, than the more independent weavers. The strike also never really extended out to the counties in the west of Scotland. Other radical areas in Fife and Angus remained quiet, presumably they were either unaware of the strike or unconvinced that it had merit.

In Glasgow there would have been an eerie sense of tension as many factories lay idle and shops remained shut as had been demanded. Troops were described as being 'mustered there as if for a siege' and thousands of soldiers were on the streets of the city.[6] The Royal Bank was barricaded with sharpshooters positioned inside as a precaution. Other prominent buildings were also heavily guarded. Many of the wealthy inhabitants of the city had either departed or had arranged for their families to be evacuated from the city, having them sent down the coast or to other areas that were considered safe. However, the warring parties kept their distance from each other and there was only one clash between cavalry and some 300 radicals later that evening.

Although as the troops patrolled some other areas they discovered that certain parts of the city – especially the nearby villages and communities away from the centre – remained firmly in the control of the radicals and the soldiers were forced to warily watch events from a distance.

The striking men found activities to keep them occupied and military drilling took place in many parts of the city, with reports of it occurring in several districts including on Glasgow Green, Dalmarnock and Tollcross. As well as ensuring that the call to strike was being complied with, steps were also being taken to prepare for the planned insurrection. Weapons were acquired after foundries and forges were raided and pikes were made.

In Paisley, 300 armed men ensured the closure of the mills on Monday 3 April and the same happened in other towns and villages with groups of men hanging around and calling on others to join the strike.[7] A major meeting, more akin to a rally, was held in Maxwellton Street. In Johnstone, calls were made for the mills to close as the proclamation was read out in the town centre with hundreds listening on. In Kilbarchan a militia man was overpowered and his weapon taken. There were reports of patrolling soldiers who discovered men making pikes in Kilbarchan where a forge had been made, of strikers being forcibly dispersed in Stewarton and of several hundred men assembling in Balfron and Galston. Outbursts of dissent, if not open rebellion, were popping up through all Ayrshire and into the southwest. There were even reports of drilling as far north as on the outskirts of Perth.

However, the authorities had been on their guard and did not stand idly by. The strikers were faced with a military presence that had been significantly reinforced over recent days and weeks. Troops had already been 'quartered strategically at Glasgow, Paisley, Dumbarton, Kilmarnock, Hamilton and Airdrie in line with recommendations from local elites'.[8] Yeomanry and soldiers had also been brought across to the west from elsewhere in Scotland. Cannon were placed with army units on one side of the river in Glasgow to protect and cover the Clyde bridges. Other units were located outside the city, in Paisley and in other communities. Further regiments were also moved through to the Glasgow area to provide an additional military presence. Loyalist groups offered supplementary support to the military and local powers. The establishment was prepared to meet any unrest that might proceed from the strike or any rebellion that might follow it.

As well as the visible military presence, the government posted up their own proclamations on 3 April. This was a response to the striker's address, and imposed a curfew on citizens and also called on them to illuminate their windows to provide as much light as possible if the street lamps were put out. This measure would presumably help the military locate any radicals if trouble broke out, and it indicated that the authorities were anticipating unrest. The following day, 4 April, an address was also posted that offered a reward for the capture or information leading to the capture of those involved in the disturbances. However, this document was distributed on the same day on which the rebellion had been planned and trouble soon broke out, even if it was not to the extent that had been hoped by the revolutionaries.

According to the plans, armed risings were to follow the strike, commencing on Tuesday 4 April, if the mail coach from England failed to arrive in Glasgow, which would indicate that a rebellion had started south of the border. Its failure to arrive in Dumfries en route to Glasgow would also provide an early signal to the revolutionaries in the southwest and Ayrshire.

However, the coach arrived on the Tuesday morning on schedule and as a result many strikers simply drifted away disappointed, believing that they had been betrayed or that other problems had arisen in England. Notwithstanding this, some individuals decided to proceed with the rising. This may have been because they were not properly informed and simply assumed that all was going to plan, however, in some instances the radicals knew that the signal had not arrived, but chose to continue with the revolt. Passions would have been high and the opportunity to fight for their cause must have been irresistible; as a result some radicals decided to confront the ruling elite and the military, regardless of the support they had or the risk involved.

Therefore, the rebellion was not coordinated in the way that had initially been intended and was significantly smaller in scale than had been hoped. Nonetheless, it still caused huge problems for the authorities. Large parts of Ayrshire were abandoned by landowners and other members of the elite, given the numbers of radicals involved and the limited military presence in the area. In Paisley, although there was a large military presence, the authorities were unable to provide assurances to requests from landowners in outlying areas who were worried about their safety. Their limitations were confirmed by raids that took place on big houses on the outskirts of the town by groups of radicals seeking arms. Arms were seized from some properties, but when one group reached Foxbar House they discovered it barricaded. Shots were fired from the house and as some of the radicals already had weapons a gunfight took place. One radical was killed and several were wounded before the gang fled, aware that the cavalry would soon be coming.

On 4 April in Glasgow a group headed for the Carron Company Ironworks at Falkirk where they intended to acquire guns and other weapons. The men assembled and planned to meet a contingent from Anderston before heading east. For whatever reason, the latter had returned home and did not arrive. Nevertheless, a group of twenty-five men set off, led by Andrew Hardie, an unemployed weaver and a former militia man. At Condorrat they met John Baird, another weaver and former soldier who had served in the Peninsular War, along with another small group. The assembled company then marched overnight and travelled through Castlecary where they obtained some breakfast at an inn. They progressed on and arrived in

Bonnybridge where they attempted to garner additional recruits, but without success.

A government informant had apparently infiltrated the group and confirmed to the military precisely where Hardie, Baird and their band were, although the Carron Ironworks had always been the target. Moreover, on their way they were noticed both by passers-by and off-duty soldiers and Yeomanry. The presence of the informant within the group was a confirmation that the scheme was poorly planned rather than evidence of the work of an agent provocateur. By the time the group reached Bonnymuir on the morning of 5 April, troops and Yeomanry forces were aware of the group's movements and were searching for them. By this time the group had apparently realised that there was no general rising and that the cause had little support, and were therefore simply resting up before returning home. But the stage was set for what has become known as the Battle of Bonnymuir.

In reality it was no contest. The wet and weary radicals who had marched overnight, armed with only pikes and a few guns, versus the fresh cavalry troops who had been stationed in nearby Kilsyth, armed with swords and muskets. Whether the radicals attacked the troops first or simply acted to defend themselves has caused debate amongst historians. From the information available, it appears that when the radicals saw the soldiers coming, they made preparations to fight and shots were exchanged with a few casualities sustained on both sides; a lieutenant suffered a pike wound to his right hand and a sergeant was shot and stabbed by a pike. Regardless of which side acted first and how committed the radicals were, they were no match for profession-al soldiers and were soon overpowered by the hussars, with nineteen taken prisoner. The report made on the weapons that were taken from the radicals disclosed five muskets, two pistols and eighteen pikes. This was hardly a match for the well-armed troops but is testimony to the courage and commitment of the radicals.

The initial reports that reached Glasgow suggested that the strikers had won, which resulted in rejoicing in the streets and showed the support that existed for the radical cause, in spirit if not in kind. In Bridgeton and Calton between 400 and 600 armed radicals paraded but they soon dispersed when the truth became known. Other incidents of armed rebellion had been ongoing elsewhere, for example, 100 armed men took control of Strathaven.[9] However, only some two dozen of the participants were then prepared to march on Glasgow where they were led to believe that a rising was taking place.

On the morning of 6 April the small band of radicals left Strathaven under the command of James Wilson, who was then aged sixty-three but who had been an active member of both the Friends of the People and the Society of the United Scotsmen. The party marched with banners proclaiming 'Scotland Free or a Desert' and 'Strathaven Union Society 1819', but when they reached Rutherglen they were warned by local radicals about the situation and it became evident that there was no general uprising and they returned home.[10] Some other members of the group, including Wilson, turned back early, after sensing that something was wrong.

Some historians have suggested that the march was organised by government agents and there is evidence that disinformation was spread by the authorities.[11] However, the controlling of the village was planned by the radicals and the scheme to travel to Glasgow was also genuine, even though it did not receive extensive support. Wilson's home became the centre for operations and the plans to take initial control of the village and then march to Rutherglen were organised there. As has been pointed out by other commentators, the fact that none of the group were captured after reaching Rutherglen or before, can either be viewed as entirely fortuitous or that any involvement of informants must have been limited. In reality, it is likely that the intentions of the rebels were genuine and that spies had infiltrated the group and had provided misleading information.

Irrespective of how the events came to pass, ten men were identified as being involved in the rising in Strathaven and they were all detained by the evening of 7 April, including James Wilson. They joined their comrades in jail who had already been captured at Bonnymuir and others arrested elsewhere. By this stage the insurrection was petering out. For although control was lost in parts of the country and a stand-off had initially taken place in Glasgow, the overwhelming power of the military machine soon crushed any signs of dissent, let alone rebellion.

By 5 April, as the Battle of Bonnymuir was unfolding, the army had moved into Paisley. House-to-house searches were conducted and arrests were made. The neighbouring weaving villages were also raided by troopers and the radical flame was being extinguished, almost as quickly as it had been lit. Even though not all of the residents in this part of the country had been involved in the rising, a code of silence was adopted, which meant that the evidence available to the courts was limited. Some radicals who were fearful of what their fate might be did as others had done before and fled to America; some departed from Greenock and others from Ardrossan.

In Glasgow the radicals also quickly realised that the rebellion was not proceeding as planned. An attempt by radicals from Bridgeton to march on Kirkintilloch on 7 April was abandoned, as defeat was finally recognised. Any arms were then hidden or disposed of along with any incriminating papers and pamphlets. The stand-off that had taken place with the military folded as the army mobilised and the revolutionaries took cover. The superior weaponry and overwhelming power wielded by the authorities emphasised the fact that all was lost.

Although the failure of the rising was recognised and many radicals put down their weapons, there was still fight left in some and strenuous efforts were made to protect those who had been involved. On 8 April there were further disturbances in Greenock. A 120-strong contingent of Port Glasgow volunteers were marching to Greenock jail with five radical prisoners from Paisley when they came under attack. The raid was initially uncoordinated and carried out by sympathetic members of the public, although it is likely that the radicals were involved in instigating a rear-guard action in defence of their colleagues.

The militia had to fight their way through to the jail as the crowd thronged about them and pursued them all along the route; the short journey from their base in Port Glasgow to Greenock turned into a running fight. The soldiers would have been relieved when they reached the jail mostly unscathed but their troubles were far from over, as they were then required to fight their way back out as an angry mob surrounded the jail. As in Tranent and Paisley, the protesters used the streets and closes to their advantage. However, as in Tranent the reprisals from angry and wounded soldiers were also brutal and eight people were killed and ten more wounded as the militia opened fire. The firing was indiscriminate, as women and young children were amongst the victims in the bloodbath that ensued. Despite the brutality of the soldiers, or perhaps because of the anger it provoked, the jail door was beaten down, the prison stormed and the prisoners were released.

However, this was to be the final flourish of the 1820 Rising. By 9 April the west of Scotland was largely pacified and trouble had ceased, only to be replaced by a closing of ranks in the radical communities. The situation was perfectly captured by Alexander Boswell, who was the commander of the Ayrshire Yeomanry. He noted in a letter to the Home Secretary: 'The ferment for two days … was excessive over the whole manufacturing district but finding that the rising could not take place and learning that the troops were now determined to act with severity, at least the semblance of a great change has taken place.'[12]

Boswell also commented that 'the most contaminated villages' had been the weaving villages of Newmilns and Galston, which he described as 'poisoned since the year 1794 and the evil has fester'd ever since'.[13] This dedication to the radical cause was replicated across the country, in cities and towns like Glasgow and Paisley and other weaving villages like Duntocher, Strathaven and Kilbarchan, where as one participant later commented, 'in the street where I resided, the inhabitants were all radicals throughout'.[14] But despite the radical strength in some communities and the long-standing support for revolutionary sentiments in many other areas the attempted revolution failed to ignite sufficient support and was snuffed out. Other areas that were watching and waiting the progression of events, not just in the west, but in areas in the east such as Fife and Angus, likewise abandoned whatever plans for a rising they may have had. Some trouble and discontent continued, but only on an isolated and sporadic basis. As troops fanned out across the country and arrested those suspected of being involved, the overwhelming power of the state was on show. Dissent became increasingly subdued and open displays of opposition were muted. The 1820 Rising was over.

Much of the evidence put forward by historians arguing that the rising was part of a Scottish insurrection simply confirms how distinctive and powerful the radical cause was in Scotland, rather than confirming that there was a widespread desire for a Scottish republic.[15] The singing of 'Scots Wha Hae' at radical meetings or on marches was simply evidence of ordinary people enjoying a popular song, which had sentiments that befitted the struggle of the people, rather than espousing a desire for independence. The provisional government was designed as a revolutionary command structure rather than a form of secessionist government. Slogans such as 'Scotland Free or a Desert' related more to despotic Scottish landowners rather than rule from England.

There were references made to spy reports that suggested an intention to establish a Scottish republic; for example, an 'audacious plot to sever the Kingdom of Scotland from that of England and restore the ancient Scottish Parliament' was uncovered by the government.[16] However, such aims were somewhat contradictory to the efforts that had been ongoing over the past few years, as was regularly reported in Gilbert McLeod's *The Spirit of the Union* before it was suppressed and he was transported. Even the strike proclamation posted up across the west of Scotland made reference to Britain and Ireland, whilst referring to 'Britons'.

It would seem that such reports related to at most a few individuals or groups, but it could also simply have been an attempt at embellishment by an informant to further blacken the name of the radicals. Accusing such figures of seeking to divide the United Kingdom increased the nature of the threat. In many ways this linked the contemporary Jacobins with the older Jacobites, who were equally hated and feared by the Hanoverian establishment. Spies and infiltration of radical groups undoubtedly existed, but at least one supposed major agent was shown to have been falsely accused.

Given the sequence of events surrounding the 1820 Rising, it is hard to dispute Donnelly's analysis that the radicals were not part of a secessionist movement. The rising proceeded independently and the societies involved operated separately from those in England. But their aim was to effect reform across Britain, despite the fact that Scotland was a very different country to England. In this way, Tom Johnston's analysis was correct. The 1820 Rising was a planned strike from which it was hoped that a revolution might spring. The enemy were the landowners who ruled Scotland despotically and the rising was initially intended to occur across all of Britain. This analysis is also supported by those who have made more nationalist interpretations; Berresford Ellis and Mac A' Ghobhainn referred to attacks on landowners in areas that did not participate in the general rising as being indicative of long-standing hatred.[17]

Moreover, limited risings did also take place in the north of England – although they were smaller in scale than in the west of Scotland – which again supports the argument that an insurrection was planned across the United Kingdom. On 1 April an uprising was intended in Huddersfield during which the military garrison was to be attacked and the mail coach to Scotland intercepted as the signal for the radical comrades north of the border. The rising was ultimately abandoned for unknown reasons, perhaps as a result of the spreading of disinformation or perhaps due to lack of support. But several thousand armed men did initially march on the town with the intention of rebelling.

On 11 April, 500 men marched from Barnsley towards Huddersfield as they also believed that the rising was to proceed. Many of the crowd were armed but after finding little support they once again abandoned their plans. Armed men also assembled and marched for revolution in Wigan, Accrington and Carlisle, although again the hordes soon dissipated. In Sheffield a pistol was fired in the air by a protestor, but this was the only shot fired in the disturbances that took place across Yorkshire and Lancashire as general strikes and rallies also took place in Halifax, Dewsbury and elsewhere.

The risings that did take place were ultimately 'ill coordinated and confused' but they most certainly were planned.[18] Government agents may well also have been at work but the strikes and the risings that occurred were organised in support of an agenda that had been previously agreed. The fact that the strikes garnered the support of 60,000 individuals out in the west of Scotland indicated the level of enthusiasm that existed for the cause and the fewer numbers involved in the failed risings that followed highlighted the failures and difficulties that had occurred. Whether as a result of those initial failures or simply through other insurmountable obstacles, the risings neither had the success that some had hoped for nor did they harness the true level of radical support that existed in the country. Perhaps, for some individuals who were committed to reform and even radical change, but who abjured revolution, it was a step too far. For others in the west and elsewhere who were supporters of physical force resistance, they decided to wait before deciding whether to join in. And it quickly became clear that neither a rebellion was happening in England nor was there much chance of success in Scotland, so they became passive observers.

However, whatever mistakes and failures were made, the revolution was always doomed. The strength of the establishment was overwhelming and over a course of months and years preparations had been made to put down any insurrection. Although radicalism had flourished and was undoubtedly strong in many parts, there was also a growing loyalist sentiment and reform rather than revolution was more widely sought. Those who did participate in the rising were both committed and courageous, but ultimately they were always destined to be defeated by the military power of the state supported by the elite in society. The imbalance in numbers and arms at the Battle of Bonnymuir was the starkest embodiment of the discrepancy in resources and power between the radicals and the authorities.

The final chapter of the revolutionary years was drawing to a close. But those who had challenged the establishment in the 1820 Rising still had to face retribution, as had their predecessors in the 1790s. Once again it was both swift and brutal.

CHAPTER 18

AFTERMATH AND EPILOGUE

Eighty-eight radicals were brought before the courts across Scotland, charged with treason for their part in the 1820 Rising. Forty-seven were tried at special courts under oyer and terminer, the English procedure used in the treason trials of the 1790s. It is unclear why this procedure was utilised during this period as there was no need to circumvent a senior judge as had been the case with Braxfield. It may simply have been used because a precedent had been set and given the seriousness of the charges, such a special procedure was deemed to be appropriate. Many other individuals faced charges locally as round-ups continued and arrests were ongoing. As before, some people simply disappeared before their trial, and often fled abroad, rather than risk appearing in court.

This time round many of the accused were acquitted, which showed how the juries had become less partisan; in some cases jury members were even sympathetic for those brought before them. However, the judicial bench remained as unremittingly hostile as it had been in the decades before, even if it was not as flagrantly biased as that under Braxfield.

Some radicals were granted clemency and the opportunity to rebuild their lives by going overseas. But for the ringleaders no mercy was shown. As with the prosecutions in the previous century the punishments were severe and brutal.

The Battle of Bonnymuir, despite being little more than a skirmish, was the focus for severe retribution. Although the press reports – even those by pro-Tory papers – emphasised the fact that few individuals were involved and the limited nature of the confrontation, it still equated to taking up arms against the state. And this was not going to be tolerated by the authorities in any shape or form. The trial was presided over by the Lord President Charles Hope and the prosecution was conducted by the Lord Advocate, Sir William Rae, which highlighted the significance placed upon the case. Eighteen prisoners appeared before the court in Stirling, and all were represented by lawyers when proceedings commenced.

First to be tried on 13 July 1820 was Andrew Hardie. Evidence about the confrontation was provided by soldiers and civilians. Francis Jeffery, a noted reform-supporting lawyer, represented Hardie. However, little could be offered in defence and it was hardly surprising that the jury was out for only ten minutes before it returned guilty verdicts on two of the charges, although acquitting Hardie on two others. The following day John Baird was in the stand and the evidence and defence was similar. Although the jury took slightly longer this time to reach their decision, their verdict was still the same. Sensing the futility of the proceedings the other prisoners then changed their pleas to guilty in the hope that the acceptance of guilt would go in their favour. The court then adjourned until 31 July for sentencing.

Before sentencing, the ringleader of the Strathaven rising James Wilson appeared for trial in Glasgow on 20 July, faced with four charges of treason, as with Baird and Hardie. The Lord President and Lord Advocate were once again presiding and acting. Other participants who appeared with Wilson were ultimately either found not guilty or discharged. However, the elderly weaver was found not guilty on three charges but guilty of seeking to levy war against the King.

The evidence against him included being identified whilst marching towards Glasgow with a sword in his hand, involvement in the manufacture of pikes and advising others about how to acquire guns. As in previous trials from the 1790s evidence that he possessed radical books and pamphlets were also used. Notwithstanding the guilty verdict, the jury still unanimously requested that mercy be shown towards Wilson, which confirmed that radical views were viewed as being less of a threat at this time and also that the risk of revolution was taken less seriously.

The trial took two days to conclude and when the jury returned on Friday 21 July, it was already early evening. Accordingly, the court adjourned until the following Monday and on 24 July James Wilson returned for sentencing. When asked if he had anything to say, the ageing radical responded with an altogether stoic but defiant speech, which was brave and eloquent:

> My Lords and gentlemen, I will not attempt the mockery of a defence. You are about to condemn me for attempting to overthrow the oppressors of my country. You do not know, neither can you appreciate, my motives. I commit my sacred cause, which is that of Freedom, to the vindication of posterity. You may condemn me to immolation on the scaffold, but you cannot degrade me. If I have appeared as a pioneer in the van of freedom's battles – if I have attempted to free my country from political degradation – my conscience tells me that I have only done my duty. Your brief authority will soon cease, but the vindictive proceedings this day shall be recorded in history. The principles for which I have contended are as immutable, as imperishable, as the eternal laws of nature. My gory head may in a few days fall on the scaffold and be exposed as the head of a traitor, but I appeal with confidence to posterity. When my countrymen will have exalted their voices in bold proclamation of the rights and dignity of Humanity, and enforced their claim by

the extermination of their oppressors, then and not till then, will some future historian do my memory justice, then will my name and sufferings be recorded in Scottish history – then will my motives be understood and appreciated; and with the confidence of an honest man, I appeal to posterity for that justice which has in all ages and in all countries been awarded to those who have suffered martyrdom in the glorious cause of liberty.[1]

As with the speeches from the dock during the earlier radical trials this statement simply acted as an incitement to the bench. The Lord President thundered that Wilson had perpetrated the most horrendous of crimes in seeking to wage civil war. As for the jury's request for mercy he said he would transmit it to the government but it was his obligation to impose the most severe punishment. He then sentenced Wilson to be hung and beheaded on 30 August.

Wilson, in a final heroic riposte, stood up and stated:

I am not deceived. You might have condemned me without this mummery of a trial! You want a victim; I will not shrink from the sacrifice. I have neither expected justice nor mercy here. I have done my duty to my country. I have grappled with her oppressors for the last forty years and having no desire to live in slavery, I am ready to lay down my life in support of these principles which must ultimately triumph.

At Stirling on 4 August the focus once again returned to Bonnymuir. Before Baird and Hardie along with their sixteen comrades were sentenced, hearings took place for the accused from Falkirk and Camelon who had been involved in related activities. Negotiations had seemingly already taken place between defence lawyers and the prosecution as four pleaded guilty, whilst the others were freed. The court then moved to sentence all twenty-two that were before them. A harangue was once again given by the bench about the heinousness of treason and the consequences that must follow. Some hope for mercy was offered to a few of the radicals, but Baird and Hardie were singled out. Lord President Hope stated 'to you Andrew Hardie and John Baird I can hold out little or no hope of mercy'. All twenty-two were then sentenced to be hung and beheaded.

On 30 August 1820 James Wilson was taken to be executed at Jail Square in Glasgow. After seeing the number of people who had gathered (estimated by some as being as many as 20,000) he stoically and rather proudly said to his executioner: 'Did y' ever see sic a crowd, Tammas?'[2] Despite a commotion after a cavalry officer charged into the crowd having suspected a rescue attempt, the execution proceeded and the sullen crowd hissed and booed as a hood was placed over the old weaver's head and a rope placed around his neck. The gallant old radical was hanged and then beheaded. Adding insult to injury, he was then buried in a pauper's grave despite requests by the family to take his mutilated body home. However, that night, some of Wilson's friends dug up his remains and reburied him secretly in his home village of Strathaven, where he still rests.

Baird and Hardie followed their comrade to the grave on 8 September, when they were executed. A crowd numbering some 2,000 gathered at Stirling and the military was deployed to watch for trouble as other troops escorted the radicals from the castle where they had been held. As they stood on the scaffold the radicals were cheered by the crowd. Baird stepped forward and declared:

> Friends and countrymen, I dare say you well expect me to say something to you of the cause which has brought me here; but on that I do not mean to say much, only that what I have hitherto done, and which brought me here, was for the cause of truth and justice.

Hardie then exclaimed: 'I die a martyr to the cause of truth and justice.' The crowd roared their applause and nervous soldiers raised their guns, but they soon quietened down and the troops relaxed. Hardie sought to calm proceedings further by advising them to go home and read their bibles. The execution then proceeded and both radicals were hanged and then beheaded. Their severed heads were held up by the executioner who shouted: 'This is the head of a traitor.' This angered the crowd, and once again the anxious soldiers drew their weapons.

This brought an end to the bloody executions. These were the last occasions that such a barbaric sentence was imposed either in Scotland or indeed in Britain. The others involved who were sentenced to a similar punishment had their death convictions commuted, although one James Clelland, a Glasgow blacksmith, received this news just days before he was due to die. His minister successfully intervened to save him from a gruesome fate.

But it was to be no free pardon, instead Clelland and eighteen others were transported to Botany Bay, seven of them, including Clelland, for life and twelve others for fourteen years, including Alexander Johnston who was a fifteen-year-old weaver from Glasgow (the names of those transported are included in Appendix D). One other prisoner who was convicted with them was released and avoided being transported.

Of these nineteen, more than half were weavers and the others were mainly skilled tradesmen. As their defence advocate stated at their trial, these individuals had been driven 'by great sufferings and privations'. Most of them were from the west of Scotland although two were from Camelon and others were from St Ninians in Stirling and Balfron. Two of the deportees, William Smith and Thomas Mc-Culloch, were from Ireland although the latter moved to Scotland as a child. Whether there was any direct or family link with the Society of United Irishmen is unknown, but their arrival in Scotland came at a time when many Irishmen were fleeing after the failed rebellion.

The convicted prisoners were transported in two separate groups with some going to Botany Bay and others sent to Van Diemen's Land (which would later become Tasmania).

Other individuals involved in the rising were more fortunate with their juries failing to convict them. In Dumbarton on 27 July the jury acquitted Robert Munro, the first of several charged for treason over incidents at Duntocher. However, although this group had been involved in preparations and the creation of pikes, they had not actually turned out for the rising. On this basis the jury refused to convict and the crown declined to proceed against the others.

In Ayr on 9 August three men from Mauchline were acquitted for their actions in their hometown. For some unknown reason one pled guilty and was sentenced to death, but this sentence was later revoked. It appeared as if the blood lust had been sated with the convictions of Baird, Hardie and Wilson and that many jurors felt sympathy towards the accused.

This latter empathy was shown in Paisley during another trial on 1 August. The case involved James Speirs and John Lang, who had read out the strike proclamations in Johnstone and made calls for the mills to shut. Others who faced trial included John Neil, who had attended the meeting in Nottingham in 1819 when a pan-British insurrection had first been discussed. Speirs's case proceeded first and evidence was presented about his involvement, however, some of the testimony seemed to confirm that pressure had been brought to bear on the witnesses by the prosecution. After deliberating, the jury returned with a verdict of acquittal on all charges, other than that concerning his involvement in the strike. An argument then followed with the presiding judge who told the jurors that their verdict was incompetent and that they could only find Speirs guilty or not guilty rather than impose their own decision. Having sent the jury away to reconsider, they returned and once again infuriated the judge by acquitting Spiers. The cases against Lang and others were then abandoned as the prosecution realised that a conviction would not be obtained. Spiers and the other acquitted celebrated with their jubilant supporters, and like many other radicals emigrated the following day to the United States to begin a new life.

With this the trials were over and the establishment had delivered its retribution. However, although the perpetrators of armed insurrection had been crushed, sporadic outbursts of violence and disorder continued. Some consisted of attacks on landowners and members of the aristocracy, such as the attempt by the young Perth radical James Murray to assassinate the Duke of Atholl.[3] On 30 July he managed to gain access to the duke's home by arranging a meeting about his personal grievances. When inside the house he put his hand in his pocket as if to produce documents, but instead drew a pistol. However, he was overpowered by the duke and his aides before he could fire and was arrested. He was subsequently convicted and was transported to Van Diemen's Land in 1821.

Reprisals were also carried out against witnesses in the trials. On 8 September following Baird and Hardie's execution, the home of a Glasgow justice of the peace who had been involved in the arrests was attacked by armed men. The official was absent when the mob arrived at the house and they satisfied themselves with ransacking the premises. Further attacks also took place that evening in Stirling where shots were fired at other witnesses who had given evidence. A few days later there were also reports of armed men who sought to set fire to a mill and other instances of industrial discontent in the west central belt of the country.

However, despite these minor eruptions of unrest the days of physical force radicalism were over. Society and the economy were changing and the political battlegrounds were evolving. As the Industrial Revolution took hold and the British Empire expanded, the extension of franchise and the rights of workers became the major issues for the evolving working class. Chartism and trade unionism became new causes that were pursued, and political and industrial activism replaced agitation and cries for revolution.

The establishment also realised that after repressing the uprising, concessions were required. The authorities had managed to see off rebellion, but they could neither sustain the level of control indefinitely nor refuse the increasing demands for reform for much longer. Moreover, whilst opposing physical force radicalism united the wealthier sections of society, other demands for change were being made by the growing middle classes. Throughout 1820 there was also increased activism amongst moderate reformers. The continued growth of this group was confirmed at a rally held in December 1820 on Calton Hill in Edinburgh, described as 'the very citadel of Toryism'.[4] At the event 17,000 people signed a petition calling on the King to dismiss his ministers.

Demands for other changes were also made, especially in the legal sphere given its important status amongst the wealthy in Scotland and as a result of its importance in the absence of a Scottish Parliament. Concern had been growing about punishments and actions that were tantamount to those during the days of Lord Braxfield. For example, the transportation of the radical editor Gilbert McLeod caused serious concern, particularly as this kind of punishment did not apply south of the border; as a result, calls for judicial and legal reform mounted.

A Whig MP introduced a Bill on jury reform in 1821, which would ensure jurors were selected by ballot and provide the accused with the right of peremptory challenge. Despite a rear-guard opposition by some Tories, the Bill was enshrined in law later that decade. In 1825 the sentence for sedition was changed so that it corresponded with that in England and in 1830 court procedures were altered to speed up proceedings and reduce delay.

The 1820s also saw the restoration of old Jacobite titles to those who had them forfeited or taken after Culloden. This may have been part of the romanticising of the Jacobite period that occurred during this time, but it could also have been part of an attempt to create unity across the landowning elite in the face of rising radicalism. Nonetheless, political reform could not be postponed much longer and the demands for an extension of the franchise became overwhelming.

The First Reform Act was finally enshrined in 1832. As a response, Andrew Hardie's mother placed a poignant card in her window in commemoration of her son:

> Britons, rejoice, Reform is won!
> But 'twas the cause
> Lost me my son.[5]

However, reform had only been partially won, as despite Mrs Hardie's sad lament her son would still have been denied the vote. The legislation only increased the Scottish electorate from 4,500 to 65,000 out of a population of 2.3 million. Members of the working class and all women were still excluded from this expanded franchise and despite the passing of further pieces of legislation, it would be several generations before the battle was finally won for universal male suffrage in 1918. However, Andrew Hardie's sacrifice and that made by all of the other radicals had been vital to achieving this limited progress. There was still a long way to go and many more struggles to be fought. But some success had been achieved in the face of not just opposition but overt repression.

Many moderate and even some radical reformers were elected in Scotland, as the almost complete Tory ascendancy began to collapse. George Kinloch, the radical laird, who was forced to flee the country as the events of 1820 began to unfold, was able to return. Having been pardoned as calm descended in the late 1820s, he was elected MP for Dundee in December 1832, as the first elections after the reform were held. The progress and irony of the situation was not missed by him.

The newly declared MP pointed out that on 24 December 1819 he had been outlawed as a rebel at the Mercat Cross in Edinburgh and on the same day in 1832 he had been 'proclaimed the chosen representative of the people of Dundee'.[6]

Working-class representation was still a long way off, but other progress was also made by those who had struggled and suffered. In 1836 the individuals who had been transported in 1820 were finally pardoned. Two, Thomas McFarlane and Andrew White, returned to Scotland. McFarlane, who had marched with Baird and Hardie and been wounded at the Battle of Bonnymuir, was fêted by fledgling Chartist societies and other working men's associations.[7] The radical memory was being recalled as new challenges were faced.

This was an opportunity to seek to preserve Scotland's radical history, as the soft power and fictional narrative began to take root through the erection of statues and the changing of street names. The return of those who had struggled provided a link to the radical martyrs for the Chartist cause. As well as being celebrated by reform societies, McFarlane was introduced to leading radical figures and was even taken on a tour of the sites from 1820, including where his former comrades had been executed. White also helped to build a link to the events of 1820, although to a lesser degree. This connection was not only promoted by the Chartist cause but would also be used by the Labour movement in Scotland later on. Banners evoking the memory of the martyrs became common at Chartist and then Labour rallies. The founder of the Independent Labour Party Keir Hardie even claimed to be distantly related to his namesake Andrew Hardie, although this appears to be based more on sentiment rather than genealogy.[8] Similarly, later on, radical supporters of Scottish independence have carried banners stating '1820' and 'Scotland Free or a Desert'.

This led to the campaign to commemorate the lives of the radical martyrs and ultimately to the erection of the memorial in Old Calton Cemetery. Tragically, as time has passed the story of these individuals has fallen from memory, aside from a resurgence in the veneration of Thomas Muir. Other key figures who were equally heroic remain unrecognised and their sacrifice and suffering has been left unacknowledged. Yet, they laid the ground upon which others have followed and started the battle for the rights of working people that continue to this day. Their story deserves to be told as it is the history of the people, although it is the lords and ladies who opposed and oppressed the masses whose names adorn Scottish streets and whose statues stand in our parks.

The martyrs also straddle the modern divide in radical Scottish politics between supporters of the Constitution and those who advocate for Scottish independence, yet they should be revered across the political spectrum. A few radicals, such as Muir, did fight for a Scottish republic, but most wanted universal franchise and reform of the British Parliament. Some who support the independence cause may be disappointed by this, but why should that be?

Scotland, notwithstanding the Treaty of Union and indeed arguably because of it, with its preservation of distinct institutions in church law and education, was and remains a distinct society with its restored devolved Parliament. Those who campaigned, struggled and even fought for revolutionary change did so within their own separate organisations. The solution to the oppression they faced and the poverty they lived through was to seek political change in Parliament in London. Whether the institution would have remained had revolution been successful can only be speculated upon. Political nationalism has grown as the difficulties faced in the administration of two different societies has increased, as was evidenced at the time of the Scottish radicals with the American War of Independence.

Those who oppose Scottish independence should also recognise that the radicals were proud of and confident in their Scottish identity. Whilst the kilt and the highland games have been successfully assimilated into Scottish culture and much of the romanticism instigated by

Walter Scott and others persists today, the drive to supplant a Scottish identity with a northern British one has failed.

As mentioned, the mantle that was passed on during the revolutionary period from the Friends of the People to the Society of the United Scotsmen and on to those who rose in 1820, has continued to inspire other radicals who have followed. Further Reform Acts were introduced in 1867 and 1884, which saw the right to vote further extended, although it was not until 1918 that most working-class men were granted the ability to vote.

Their legacy was maintained by those who formed the Scottish Labour Party in 1888, which merged with the Independent Labour Party in 1894. The roots of the Red Clydesiders in the twentieth century stretched back to the early radicals and the groups shared some notable similarities, particularly in their ties to dissenting churches. Both the contemporary Scottish Labour Party and the Scottish National Party have sought to portray themselves as the heirs to this radical tradition.

Universal franchise has been obtained but other issues targeted by the later radicals remain. The common enemy for those who either sought Scottish independence or radical reform in London were the ruling oligarchy of wealthy landowners. It was this group who owned the land and in whose interests the nation was run. What is more of a tragedy than the idea of the memory of the martyrs being forgotten is the fact that land in Scotland continues to be owned by a minority group, some of whom are the descendants of the enemies of the original Scottish radicals.

As was written by Tom Johnston over a century ago, 'so long as a dozen families own one half of Scotland, so long will countless families own none of it, and be under continual necessity of cringing before and begging'.[9] Progress has been made in land reform but huge swathes of Scotland are still owned by a small privileged elite.

People often assume that the land issue that runs so deep into

Scottish society was driven by the haunting memory of the Highland Clearances. However, the deep-rooted antagonism towards the landowners comes not just from what they did in the north of the country, but also what they did in the lowland areas. It is little wonder that after the modest extension of the right to vote in 1832, only one Tory was returned as an MP in Glasgow until 1886. The Liberals also dominated in Scotland for seventy years between 1850 until 1922, until the Independent Labour Party swept in.

As Johnston also wrote, 'the histories of our land have been mostly written to serve the political purposes and flatter the conceits of our aristocracy'.[10] This is a harsh rebuke for many hard-working historians who have strived to record the events of our past as accurately as possible, and obscures and downplays the role that the church and the legal sphere have played as arms of the state in the suppression of a history of the people. It has been perception rather than the histories and historians that have marginalised and forgotten our radical past.

Recalling our radical history is essential, it is out there but it must be promoted. Some progress has been made in this domain, but our appreciation of these key figures is far from what it should be. The statues in Scottish cities largely remember the lords and their battles, rather than the radicals and their struggles. It should be Muir, Palmer, Skirving, Margarot, Gerrald and Mealmaker who are memorialised.

This book is a modest attempt to honour the sacrifice and preserve the history of the Scottish radicals. Efforts to acknowledge their memory are once again long overdue. Councils of a more radical hue across Scotland should ensure that these individuals are remembered. It is our duty to maintain their commemoration and to continue their struggle. As Thomas Muir said in his speech from the dock and as was echoed by the other martyrs throughout this tumultuous period, the cause of the people 'is a good cause – it shall ultimately prevail – it shall finally triumph'.

APPENDICES

The following documents included in the appendices have been taken from a number of sources. Some were held in the National Records of Scotland and others were found in historical accounts, including those by Peter Berresford Ellis and Seumas Mac A' Ghobhainn, and Margaret and Alastair MacFarlane. The formatting and styling has been kept as it would have appeared in the original.

APPENDIX A

CONVENTION DELEGATES
FIRST CONVENTION

Sederunt of the Delegates of the Associations of the Friends of the people met in Convention at Edinburgh, Tuesday, 11 December 1792.

Mr Hugh Bell in the chair.

Thomas Muir, esq, Vice-President.

Wm. Skirving, esq, Secretary.

Mr Muir, after a short introductory speech, moved that the delegates verify their powers. Mr Skirving then rendered the commissions. These were by letter and some of them began 'Citizen President'.

Calton of Glasgow; David Russell.

Anderston; Allan McLean.

Glasgow; Colonel Dalrymple, William Dalrymple, A. Riddell, George Crawford.

Canongate, No 2; John Stronach, Alex Aitchison.

Canongate No 1; Thomas Muir, George Malcolm, William Campbell, Alex Bell, John Buchanan, J. Fortune, J. Thomson Callender, John Thomson, William Wallace, J. Taylor.

Dundee; Thomas Muir.

Anstruther Easter; James Darcy.

Kilbarchan, Lochwinnoch, and two other societies; George Lee.

Pathead of Kirkcaldy; Robert Cork, Matthew Shiells.

Stirling; Alex Forrester, William Clark, William Gibson, Robert Marr, William Paterson, William Taylor.

Forfar; Rev Thomas Fyshe Palmer.

Paisley United Societies; James Alcie, David Graham.

Nine societies in Perth;

William Bisset, William Miller, Alex Paul, Johnston, McNab, Patrick Grant, Rev Wilson, George Miller, Wyllie.

Cowgate, Edinburgh; John McIntyre, Simon Drummond, John Gourlie, John Miller, Rev Mclean and some others.

Portsburgh, Edinburgh; Lord Daer, William Skirving, Robert Fowler, Allan, Hardie and some others.

Dunbar; Thomas Mitchell, Sawers, Cowan.

Belhaven; Alex Oliver, Kilgour.

Shotts; Rev Ebenezer Hislop.

Hamilton; Joseph Miller, Bailie Vanie.

Lodge Room, Blackfriars Wynd, Edinburgh; John Reid, Alex Crawford and some others.

Gorbals, Glasgow; John Wilson, James Smith.

St Cyrus; William Christie, William Walter.

Finnie; William Wallace.

Strathaven; William Aitken.

Dunfermline; James Boyd, Alex Stewart.

Leslie; William Skirving.

Candleriggs, Glasgow; Robert Smith

Montrose; William Robb jnr.

Paisley; James Ellis, Dan Blane.

Lawnmarket, Edinburgh; William Romanes, John Gourlay, and three others.

Taylors Hall, Potterow; John Clark, William Alexander, T. Ritchie and six others.

Glasgow; John Gray.

Seven Societies, Kilmarnock; William Wyllie, William Muir.

Lodge Room, New Town; Gordon Murray, Kain, Walter Veitch, Phin.

Glasgow, High Street; John Bruce.

Glasgow Balmanns Street; George Stayley.

Dundee; William Bisset, William Webster.

Penicuik; Smith, Tait.

Dovehill and Saltmarket, Glasgow; George Hill.

Gallowgate, Glasgow; A. McVicar.

Dalkeith; Carfrae, Caldwalls, Mofat, Ritchie, Gray.

Musselburgh; William Begg, A. Carmichael.

Grinston's Tavern, Glasgow; William Hart, William Riddell, George Waddell.

Kirkintilloch; James Baird.

New Town and Calton of Edinburgh; W. Christie, White, Watt.

Abbeyhill; Alex Nisbet.

Original Association of Edinburgh; Izett, Hugh Handyside, James Farquhar, Walter Russell, Sam Paterson, Robert Forsyth, Lothian, Alex Ritchie, James Inglis, Livingston, Berry, Mitchell Young, Galloway, Dr Yuille, Taylor, Lancashire, Hutchison, Cleghorn, Dalrymple, Allan, Dunn, Smith, Campbell.

Pathhead No1; No Delegates.

Pathhead No2; No Delegates.

Campsie; Henry.

Water of Leith; A delegate.

New Society, Mather's Tavern, Edinburgh; Bartlett, McAsline.

Linlithgow and Linlithgow No2; Joseph Reed, Stephen Mitchell, Joseph Calder, Malcolm Ewan, George Ross.

Saltcoats; one delegate.

SECOND CONVENTION

List of Societies represented at the Second General Convention of the Friends of the People, 30 April to 3 May 1793.

Kilwinning; Robert Barr.

Miltioun, Campsie; James McGibbon.

Galston, Newmills etc; John Wallace.

Dundee; James Peat.

Strathaven; John Smith.

Dunfermline; James Masterton, James Boyd, Andrew Mercer, Adam Pringle, David Young, James Dun, George McLatchie, George Freer, Andrew Paterson, Ebenezer Brown, Thomas McLash, James Tod, George Innes.

Hawick; James Turnbull.

Operative Society, Edinburgh; John Thynne.

Glasgow Societies; Walter Hart, Henry Rose, John Sinclair.

Paisley Societies; William Moodie, William Mitchell, James Kelly, Archibald Hastie, John Tayler, John Tannyhill, William Wood.

Linlithgow; Stephen Gibson.

Newton; James Sommerville.

Whitburn; John Stark.

Selkirk; Alex Dobson.

Dalkeith; Peter Lyden, Thomas Taylor, William Howieson.

Canongate, No 1 and 2 Edinburgh; Robert Yuill, Alex Aitchison,

Archibald Wright, John Thomson, John Stronach, Alex Fortune, Alex Carse, Alex Miller, William Simpson, Robert Ruthven.

New Town, Edinburgh; John Wilson, Walter Davidson, Robert Wright, David Bertie, John Reid, Alex Ingram, Alex Knox, John Bruce, Alex Bremner.

Penicuik; James Smith, James Anderson.

Linktown; James Mather.

Auchterderran; Robert Wemyss (letter of apology).

Kilmaurs; James Lambroughton.

Canongate Society of Edinburgh; Alex Reid, Archibald Binny, John McIntyre, John Gourlay, George Callum, Mitchell, Young, Charles, Isaac Salter.

Musselburgh; William Wilson, Duncan Charles.

New Town and Calton, Edinburgh; James Muirhead, James Smith, William Philip, Robert Christie, George Watt.

Water of Leith; John Rymer, William Farquharson.

Fenwick; James Fulton.

Cowgate No 3, Edinburgh; John Laing, David Taylor, William Robertson, James Calder, James Weir, William Stark, John Tweedie, John Hamilton, John Spalding, Alex Adams, Charles Stirling, Peter Moffatt, Neil Campbell.

Kilmarnock; Rev James Robertson.

Portsburgh, Edinburgh; Robert Jardine, John Thomson, George Anderson, James Tweedie, Peter Wood, James Thomson, David Sinclair, William Skirving, William Moffatt.

Montrose; Rev McFarlane, James Glen.

Mid Calder; Adam Wilson.

Anstruther; Mitchell Young.

Twelve United Societies in Perth; Robert Sands, Thomas Smith, David Jack, William Thomson, Moses Wylie, Andrew Dott, David Johnston.

Pathhead; George Drummond.

APPENDIX B

UNITED SCOTSMEN RESOLUTION AND RULES
THE RESOLUTION

In the present age, when knowledge is making rapid strides among mankind and neighbouring nations have been under the necessity of ameliorating their condition, owing to the stubbornness and perfidy of the governments under which they tired, by despising and rejecting the reiterated and just calls of the people for reform. It becomes us as friends to peace and good order, at the present awful crisis, when we are engaged in an unprecedented, bloody and expensive war, to investigate with calmness and deliberation into the system of our government, on purpose to discover its errors and defects: so that whatever abuses may exist, they may be rectified by a timely reform and the life calamities, which have befallen, a neighbouring nation may be prevented.

Conscious of the rectitude of our association and intentions, and regardless of the threats of the venal and uninterested, we will enquire into our grievances with a determined and manly freedom, knowing that we have no other object in view, but the peace and happiness of our native country. Possessing such ideas, we cannot but exclaim with astonishment, what a multitude of ages have mankind been kept in complete ignorance with respect to their natural rights! – Rights of which no association of men have a power to deprive them, whatever foolish titles they may assume. Was the human race created with reasoning facilities by the Supreme being, for no purpose than to be possessed and made tools by corrupt governments, for the destruction of their own species? No – it was for a more noble end.

We disdain the principle of corrupt courtiers and their sale titles who propagate such nefarious doctrine. Mankind are naturally friends to each other, and it is only the corruptions and abuses in governments that make them enemies. We profess ourselves friends to mankind, of whatever nation or region. National and party distinctions have been erected and supported by tyrannic men, on purpose to maintain their unjust usurpations over the people.

We will ask any unprejudiced person, if the people in Britain are fairly, fully and equally represented? Have the people in general any control or concern in the election of the Magistrates in the different Burghs in Scotland? Are clergymen in many parts of Scotland forced on the people against their inclination? Are there any intricacies or inequalities in law procedure that could be rectified? We decline enumerating many other abuses, all of which could be removed by a timely and radical reform in the House of Commons!

We abhor and detest all riots and tumults. Our armour shall be reason and truth, which we will not swerve from on any account. Our whole aim is to procure Annual Parliaments and Universal Suffrage. Till this is done, we declare to the world that we will never desist till we procure this our national right, the want of which is probably the source of all our nation's grievances.

Impresses with these sentiments, we have collectively and voluntarily agreed to form an association to be called the United Scotsmen; and we do pledge ourselves to our country and mutually to each other to carry into effect by all just means the following.

Resolution

An Equal Representation of all the People in Parliament.

I)   This society is constituted for the purpose of forwarding a brother of affection, a communion of rights, and a union of power among Britons of every description – for the purpose of obtaining a complete Reform in the Legislature, founded on the principles of civil, political and religious liberty.

II)   The members of this society shall not be confined to any description of men, but extended to all persons who may be deemed eligible.

III) Every candidate for admission into this society shall be proposed by one member and seconded by another, both of whom shall vouch for his character and principles and be balloted for before he can be admitted a member.

IV)   Each member shall pay not less than 6d on entering the society, and not less than 4d per month during his continuing in the said society.

V)   The one half of the income to be paid into the hands of the Secret Committee, the other half to the defraying of expenses of Delegates attending their duty in different committees.

VI)   The Officers of this Society shall be a Secretary and Treasurer who shall be chosen by ballot and continue in office two months.

VII) No member shall speak more than twice to one question without leave from the Chairman, who he shall address standing.

VIII) A President to be chosen by ballot at each meeting whose business it shall be to keep order and not to enter into debate.

IX)   When any society amounts to sixteen members, they divide into two societies, the new society taking along with them a secretary properly constituted.

APPENDIX C

PROCLAMATION AT 1820 RISING
ADDRESS TO THE INHABITANTS OF GREAT BRITAIN AND IRELAND

Friends and countrymen,

Roused from that torpid state in which We have been sunk for so many years, We are at length compelled, from the extremity of our sufferings, and the contempt heaped upon our petitions for redress, to assert our rights, at the hazard of our lives; and proclaim to the world the real motives which (if not misrepresented by designing men, would have united all ranks), have reduced us to take up arms for the redress of our common grievances.

The numerous Public Meetings held throughout the country has demonstrated to you, that the interests of all classes are the same, that the protection of the life and property of the Rich Man is the interest of the Poor Man, and, in return, it is the interest of the rich to protect the poor from the iron grasp of despotism; for when its victims are exhausted in the lower circles, there is no assurance, but that its ravages will be continued in the upper; For once set in motion, it will continue to move till a succession of Victims fall.

Our principles are few, and founded, on the basis of our constitution, which were purchased with the Dearest Blood of our ancestors, and which we swear to transmit to posterity unsullied, or perish in the attempt, Equality of Rights (not of Property) is the object for which we contend; and which we consider as the only security for our liberties and lives.

Let us show to the world that We are not that Lawless, Sanguinary Rabble which our oppressors would persuade the higher circles we are – but a Brave and Generous People, determined to be Free, Liberty or Death is our motto, and We have sworn to return home in triumph – or return no more!

Soldiers,

Shall You, Countrymen, bound by the sacred obligation of an Oath, to defend your Country and your King from enemies, whether foreign or domestic, plunge your Bayonets into the bosoms of Fathers and Brothers, and at once sacrifice at the Shrine of Military Despotism, to the unrelenting Orders of a Cruel Faction, those feelings which you hold in common with the rest of mankind? Soldiers, Turn your eyes toward Spain, and there behold the happy effects resulting from the Union of Soldiers and Citizens. Look to that quarter, and there behold the yoke of hated Despotism, broke by the Unanimous wish of the People and the Soldiery, happily accomplished without Bloodshed. And shall You, who taught those Soldiers to fight the battles of Liberty, refuse to fight those of your own Country? Forbid it Heaven! Come, forward then at once, and Free your Country and your King from the power of those that have held them too, too long to thraldom.

Friends and Countrymen, The eventful period has now arrived, where the Services of all will be required, for the forwarding of an object so universally wished, and so absolutely necessary. Come forward then, and assist those who have begun in the completion of so arduous a task, and support the Laudable efforts, which we are about to make, to replace to Britons, those rights consecrated to them, by Magna Charta and the Bill of Rights, and Sweep from our Shores, that Corruption which has degraded us below the dignity of man.

Owing to the misrepresentations which have gone abroad with regard to our intentions, we think it indispensably necessary to DE-CLARE inviolable, all Public and Private Property. And, We hereby call upon all Justices of the Peace, and all others to suppress Pillage and Plunder, of every description; and to endeavour to secure those Guilty of such offences, that they may receive that Punishment, which such violation of Justice demand.

In the present state of affairs, and during the continuation of so momentous a struggle, we earnestly request of all to desist from their Labour, from and after this day, the First of April; and attend wholly to the recovery of their Rights, and consider it as the duty of every man not to recommence until he is in possession of those Rights which distinguishes the Freeman from the Slave ; viz: That, of giving consent to the laws by which he is to be governed. We, therefore, recommend to the Proprietors of Public Works, and all others, to Stop the one, and Shut up the other, until order is restored, as we will be accountable for no damages which may be sustained; and which after this Public Intimation, they can have no claim to.

And We hereby give notice to all, those who shall be found carrying arms against those who intend to regenerate their Country, and restore its Inhabitants to their native Dignity: We shall consider them as Traitors to their Country, and Enemies to their King, and treat them as such.

By order of the Committee of Reformation
For forming a Provisional Government
Glasgow 1 April 1820

Britons – God – Justice – The wishes of all good Men are with us – Join together and make it one Cause, and the Nations of the Earth shall hail the day, when the Standard of Liberty shall be raised on its Native Soil.

APPENDIX D

RADICALS TRANSPORTED TO BOTANY BAY AFTER 1820 RISING

NAME	OCCUPATION	LOCATION	PENALTY IMPOSED
John Anderson	Weaver	Camelon	Life
John Barr	Weaver	Condorrat	Fourteen years
William Clackson or Clarkson	Shoemaker	Glasgow	Fourteen years
James Clelland	Blacksmith	Glasgow	Life
Andrew Dawson	Nailer	Camelon	Life
Robert Gray	Weaver	Glasgow	Life
Alexander Hart	Cabinet maker	Glasgow	Fourteen years
Alexander Johnston	Weaver	Glasgow	Fourteen years
Alexander Latimer	Weaver	Glasgow	Fourteen years
Thomas McCulloch	Stocking weaver	Glasgow	Fourteen years
Thomas McFarlane	Weaver	Condorrat	Life
John McMillan	Nailer	Camelon	Life
Benjamin Moir	Labourer	Glasgow	Fourteen years
Allan Murchie	Blacksmith	Glasgow	Life
Thomas Pike or Pink	Muslin slinger	Glasgow	Fourteen years
William Smith	Weaver	Glasgow	Fourteen years
David Thompson	Weaver	Glasgow	Fourteen years
Andrew White	Bookbinder	Glasgow	Fourteen years
James Wright	Tailor	Glasgow	Fourteen years

BIBLIOGRAPHY

BOOKS

Armstrong, Murray, *The Liberty Tree: The Stirring Story of Thomas Muir and Scotland's First Fight for Democracy* (Edinburgh: World Power Books, 2014).

Berresford Ellis, Peter and Seumas Mac A' Ghobhainn, *The Scottish Insurrection of 1820* (Edinburgh: J. Donald, 2001).

Cobbett, William, *Cobbett's Complete Collection of State Trials and Proceedings for High Treason and Other Crime and Misdemeanours from the Earliest Period to the Present Time* (S. I.: T. C. Hansard, 1809–1826).

Devine, Thomas, *The Scottish Nation 1700–2000* (London: Penguin, 2000).

Elliott, Marianne, *Wolfe Tone* (Liverpool: Liverpool University Press, 2012).

Halliday, James, *1820 Rising: The Radical War* (Stirling: Scots Independent, 1993).

Harris, Bob, *The Scottish People and the French Revolution* (London: Routledge, 2015).

Hughes, Robert, *The Fatal Shore: A History of the Transportation of Convicts to Australia, 1787–1868* (London: Vintage, 2003).

Hume Brown, Peter, *History of Scotland, vol. III* (Cambridge: Cambridge University Press, 1900).

Hunter, James, *Last of the Free: A Millennial History of the Highlands and Islands of Scotland* (Edinburgh: Mainstream Publishing, 2010).

Johnston, Tom, *The History of the Working Classes in Scotland* (Glasgow: Forward Publishing Co, 1974).

Johnston, Tom, *Our Scots Noble Families* (Glasgow: Forward Publishing Co, 1913).

Logue, Kenneth, *Popular Disturbances in Scotland 1780–1815* (Edinburgh: Donald, 1979).

Lynch, Michael, *Scotland: A New History* (London: Vintage Digital, 1992).

McFarland, E. W., *Ireland and Scotland in the Age of Revolution: Planting the Green Bough* (Edinburgh: Edinburgh University Press, 1994).

MacFarlane, Margaret and Alastair, *The Scottish Radicals – Tried and Transported to Australia for Treason in 1820* (Stevenage: SPA, 1981).

McKean, Charles, Bob Harris and Christopher A. Whatley (eds), *Dundee: Renaissance to Enlightenment* (Dundee: Dundee University Press, 2009).

Mackenzie, Peter, *Reminiscences of Glasgow and the West of Scotland, vol. III* (Glasgow: Tweed, 1868).

Mathieson, W. L., *The Awakening of Scotland: A History from 1747–1797* (Glasgow: James MacLehose & Sons, 1910).

Meikle, Henry, *Scotland and the French Revolution* (Glasgow: James MacLehose & Sons, 1912).

Parkhill, John, *The History of Paisley* (Paisley: Robert Stewart, 1857).

Pentland, Gordon, *The Spirit of the Union: Popular Politics in Scotland, 1815–1820* (London: Pickering & Chatto, 2011).

Sherry, Frank A., *The Rising of 1820* (Glasgow: William Maclellan Ltd, n. d.).

Smout, T. C., *A Century of the Scottish People 1830–1950* (London: Collins, 1986).

Tennant, Charles, *The Radical Laird: A Biography of George Kinloch, 1775–1833* (Kineton, Roundwood Press, 1970).

Wells, Roger, *Insurrection: The British Experience 1795–1803* (Gloucester: Alan Sutton, 1983).

Whatley, Christopher A., David B. Swinfen and Annette M Smith, *The Life and Times of Dundee* (Edinburgh: John Donald, 1993).

ARTICLES

Brims, John, 'The Scottish Democratic Movement in the Age of the French Revolution' PhD thesis, University of Edinburgh, 1989.

Clark, Sylvia, 'The Crime of Rebellion', Paisley Library.

Curtis, Neil, 'The Place of History, Literature and Politics in the 1911 Scottish Exhibition', *Scottish Literary Review* (2015), vol.7, no. 1, pp. 43–74.

Donnelly, F. K., 'The Scottish Rising of 1820: A Reinterpretation', *Scottish Tradition* (1976), vol. 6, pp. 27–37.

Honeyman, Valerie, '"A very dangerous place?": Radicalism in Perth in the 1790s', *The Scottish Historical Review* (2009), vol. 87, issue 2, pp. 278–305.

Kidd, Colin, 'The Kirk, The French Revolution, and the Burden of Scottish Whiggery', in Nigel Aston (ed.), *Religious Changes in Europe 1650–1914: Essays for John McManners* (Oxford: Clarendon Press, 1997), pp. 213–34.

London Corresponding Society, 'An Account of the Treason and Sedition Committed by the London Corresponding Society', (London: J. Downes, 1794).

Miller, James, 'Tranent 1797', Scottish Mining Website, http://www.scottishmining.co.uk/506.html (accessed January 2020).

Morrison, R., 'Account of the Trial of Thomas Fyshe Palmer', Dundee Library.

Pentland, Gordon, 'Patriotism, Universalism, and the Scottish Conventions, 1792–1794', *History* (2004), vol. 89, no. 295, pp. 340–60.

Pentland, Gordon, 'Radical Returns in an Age of Revolutions', *Études écossaises* (2010), vol. 13, pp. 91–102.

Pentland, Gordon, 'The Challenge of Radicalism to 1832' in T. M. Devine and Jenny Wormald, *The Oxford Handbook of Modern Scottish History* (Oxford: Oxford University Press, 2012), pp. 439–54.

Pentland, Gordon, 'The Posthumous Lives of Thomas Muir', in Gordon Pentland and Michael T. Davis (eds), *Liberty, Property and Popular Politics: England and Scotland 1688–1815: Essays in Honour of H. T. Dickinson* (Edinburgh: Edinburgh University Press, 2016), pp. 207–23.

Roe, Michael, 'George Mealmaker, the Forgotten Martyr', *Journal and Proceedings* (Royal Australia Historical Society, 1958), vol. 43, pp. 284–98.

Tyrell, Alex and Michael T. Davis, 'Bearding the Tories; The Commemoration of the Scottish Political Martyrs 1793–94', in Alex Tyrell and Paul Pickering (eds), *Contested Sites: Commemoration, Memorial and Popular Politics in Nineteenth Century Britain* (Aldershot: Ashgate 2004), pp. 25–56.

Tyrell, Alex, 'The Earl of Eglinton, Scottish Conservatism and the National Association for the Vindication of Scottish Rights', *Historical Journal* (2010), vol. 53, pp. 87–108.

PRIMARY SOURCES

The *Caledonian Mercury*.

National Records of Scotland, Register House, Edinburgh.

The Netherlands Institute for Military History, the Hague.

'Report of the Secret Committee of the House of Commons. Ordered to be Printed on the 15th of March', London, 1799.

The Working Class Movement Library, Salford.

ACKNOWLEDGEMENTS

There are many people to thank for their assistance and guidance along the journey that this book has taken me on. Academics such as Dr Gordon Pentland and Alex Tyrell were generous with their time and indulged my academic ignorance. Emeritus Professor Michael Roe was equally helpful from afar.

Librarians and institutions were also just as kind in their support. Both the National Library and the National Records of Scotland were key sources and the staff were similarly supportive. Local libraries in Perth, Dundee and Paisley were invaluable and their staff were ever helpful and provided crucial guidance and encouragement. The Working Class Movement Library in Salford was also of great assistance. Dr van der Spek at the Netherlands Institute for Military History entertained my lack of linguistic knowledge and provided invaluable information. I am grateful to my friend Catriona Black for introducing me to him.

My editor James Lilford has done a sterling job in a very tight timescale and improved my rough copy immensely. He even endured my limitations with technology with great forbearance for which I am truly grateful.

My friend John Woods reviewed my draft and made helpful comments that were of great assistance.

To each and every one I pay tribute, along with my wife Susan who supported me throughout this venture.

I hope that the book does justice to those who fought for the rights of the Scottish working people as we owe so much to them and they deserve to be remembered.

NOTES

CHAPTER 1: THE MONUMENT

1   Thomas Devine, *The Scottish Nation 1700–2000* (London: Penguin, 2000), p. 153.

2   The *Caledonian Mercury*, January 1798.

3   Tyrell, Alex and Michael T. Davis, 'Bearding the Tories; The Commemoration of the Scottish Political Martyrs 1793–94', in Alex Tyrell and Paul Pickering (eds), *Contested Sites: Commemoration, Memorial and Popular Politics in Nineteenth Century Britain* (Aldershot: Ashgate 2004), pp. 25–56.

4   Ibid.

CHAPTER 2: IN SEARCH OF THE REVOLUTIONARY STORY

1   Murray Pittock, *Culloden* (Oxford: Oxford University Press, 2016) and *Jacobitism* (Basingstoke: Macmillan, 1998).

2   Tom Johnston, *The History of the Working Classes in Scotland* (Glasgow: Forward Publishing Co, 1974).

3   Roger Wells, *Insurrection: The British Experience 1795–1803* (London: Collins, 1986), p. 21.

4   John Brims, 'The Scottish Democratic Movement in the Age of the French Revolution' PhD thesis, University of Edinburgh, 1989, p. 142.

5   Kenneth Logue, *Popular Disturbances in Scotland, 1780–1815* (Edinburgh: Donald, 1979), p. 7.

6   Peter Mackenzie, *Reminiscences of Glasgow and the West of Scotland* (Glasgow: Tweed, 1868), p. 16.

7   W. L. Mathieson, *The Awakening of Scotland, a History from 1747 to 1797*, p. 104.

8   Ibid.

9   Ibid.

10 Ibid., p. 105.

11 Tom Johnston, *Our Scots Noble Families* (Glasgow: Forward Publishing Co, 1913), p. 33.

12 Kenneth Logue, *Popular Disturbances in Scotland 1780–1815*, p. 9.

13 Peter Hume Brown, *History of Scotland, vol. III* (Cambridge: Cambridge University Press, 1900), p. 386.

14 Fergal Keane, *Wounds: A Memoir of Love and War* (London: William Collins, 2016), p. 100.

15 Kenneth Logue, *Popular Disturbances in Scotland 1780–1815*, p. 133.

16 Ibid., p. 10.

17 Ibid., p. 10.

CHAPTER 3: A DISCONTENTED LAND

1   Smout, T. C., *A Century of the Scottish People 1830–1950* (London: Collins, 1986).

2   John Brims, ibid., p. 19.

3   Ibid., p. 25.
4   Ibid., p. 25.
5   Ibid., p. 31.
6   Ibid., p. 37.
7   Colin Kidd, 'The Kirk, The French Revolution and the burden of Scottish Whiggery', in Nigel Aston (ed.) *Religious Changes in Europe 1650–1914: Essays for John McManners* (Oxford: Clarendon Press, 1997), p. 224.
8   Ibid., p. 38.
9   Ibid., p. 111.
10 Many of those who returned as MPs in 1922 had similar links with Campbell Stephen, who was a United Free Church minister, and others, including David Kirkwood, were members and even elders of the church.
11 Bob Harris, *The Scottish People and the French Revolution* (London, Routledge, 2015), p. 40.
12 Kenneth Logue, *Popular Disturbances in Scotland 1780–1815*, p. 30.
13 Peter Hume Brown, *History of Scotland, vol. III*, p. 380.
14 John Brims, 'The Scottish Democratic Movement in the Age of the French Revolution', p. 174.

CHAPTER 4: THE KING'S BIRTHDAY RIOTS AND OTHER DISTURBANCES
1   Kenneth Logue, *Popular Disturbances in Scotland 1780–1815*, p. 134.
2   Ibid.
3   Ibid.
4   Ibid., p. 146.
5   Ibid., p. 134.
6   James Hunter, *Last of the Free: A Millennial History of the Highlands and Islands of Scotland* (Edinburgh: Mainstream Publishing, 2010), p. 237.

CHAPTER 5: THE FRIENDS OF THE PEOPLE AND THE TREES OF LIBERTY
1   Henry Meikle, *Scotland and the French Revolution* (Glasgow: James MacLehose & Sons, 1912).
2   John Brims, 'The Scottish Democratic Movement in the Age of the French Revolution', p. 181.
3   Ibid., p. 180–81.
4   Ibid, p. 204.
5   Valerie Honeyman, '"A very dangerous place?": Radicalism in Perth in the 1790s', *The Scottish Historical Review* (2009), vol. 87, issue 2, pp. 278–305.
6   Kenneth Logue, *Popular Disturbances in Scotland 1780–1815*, p. 148.
7   Ibid., p. 149.
8   Bob Harris, *The Scottish People and the French Revolution*, p. 116.
9   Kenneth Logue, *Popular Disturbances in Scotland 1780–1815*, p. 149.
10 Christopher A. Whatley, David B. Swinfen and Annette M. Smith, *The Life and Times of Dundee* (Edinburgh: John Donald, 1993), p. 130.
11 National Records of Scotland, RH/2/4/74.

CHAPTER 6: THE FIRST NATIONAL CONVENTION AND REPRESSION UNLEASHED
1   Bob Harris, *The Scottish People and the French Revolution*, p. 56.
2   Henry Meikle, *Scotland and the French Revolution*, p. 103.
3   Bob Harris, *The Scottish People and the French Revolution*, p. 56.
4   John Brims, op. cit., p. 319.
5   National Records of Scotland, RH/2/4/74.

CHAPTER 7: MUIR AND PALMER STAND TRIAL
1   Peter Hume Brown, *History of Scotland, vol. III*, p. 380.
2   Murray Armstrong, *The Liberty Tree: The Stirring Story of Thomas Muir and Scotland's First Fight for Democracy* (Edinburgh: World Power Books, 2014).

3   Valerie Honeyman, '"A very dangerous place?": Radicalism in Perth in the 1790s'.
4   Henry Meikle, *Scotland and the French Revolution*, p. 125.
5   Ibid., p. 136.
6   Ibid., p. 135.

CHAPTER 8: THE BRITISH CONVENTION MEETS
AND THE OTHER MARTYRS STAND TRIAL

1   Henry Meikle, *Scotland and the French Revolution*, p. 141.
2   Bob Harris, *The Scottish People and the French Revolution*, p. 91.
3   Ibid., p. 101.
4   E. W. McFarland, *Ireland and Scotland in the Age of Revolution: Planting the Green Bough* (Edinburgh: Edinburgh University Press, 1994), p. 113.
5   John Barrell, *Imagining the King's Death: Figurative Treason, Fantasies of Regicide 1793–1796* (Oxford: Oxford University Press, 2000), p. 151 referenced in Bob Harris, *The Scottish People and the French Revolution*, p. 101.
6   Henry Meikle, *Scotland and the French Revolution*, p. 142.
7   Bob Harris, *The Scottish People and the French Revolution*, p. 119.
8   Ibid., p. 120.
9   Henry Meikle, *Scotland and the French Revolution*, p. 144.
10   John Brims, 'The Scottish Democratic Movement in the Age of the French Revolution', p. 248.
11   Henry Meikle, *Scotland and the French Revolution*, p. 145.
12   John Brims, 'The Scottish Democratic Movement in the Age of the French Revolution', p. 548.
13   Ibid., p. 552.

CHAPTER 9: A CHANGE IN TACTICS AND THE PIKE PLOT

1   Henry Meikle, *Scotland and the French Revolution*, p. 155.
2   Valerie Honeyman, '"A very dangerous place?": Radicalism in Perth in the 1790s'.
3   National Records of Scotland, RH2/4/74.
4   Bob Harris, *The Scottish People and the French Revolution*, p. 103.
5   National Records of Scotland, RH/2/4/74.
6   National Records of Scotland, RH2/4/75.
7   John Brims, 'The Scottish Democratic Movement in the Age of the French Revolution', p. 552.
8   Henry Meikle, *Scotland and the French Revolution*.
9   Ibid., p. 151.
10   E. W. McFarland, *Ireland and Scotland in the Age of Revolution: Planting the Green Bough*, p. 117.
11   Mary Thale, *Selections from the papers of the London Corresponding Society 1792–1799* (Cambridge: Cambridge University Press, 2009), p. 177, referenced in Bob Harris, *The Scottish People and the French Revolution*, p. 105.
12   Tom Johnston, *Our Scots Noble Families*, p. 227.
13   SC 58/22/72, referenced in Bob Harris, *The Scottish People and the French Revolution*, p. 104.
14   E. W. McFarland, *Ireland and Scotland in the Age of Revolution: Planting the Green Bough*, p. 117.

CHAPTER 10: GEORGE MEALMAKER AND
THE SOCIETY OF THE UNITED SCOTSMEN

1   Henry Meikle, *Scotland and the French Revolution*, p. 155.
2   Charles McKean, Bob Harris, Christopher A. Whatley (eds), *Dundee: Renaissance to Enlightenment* (Dundee: Dundee University Press, 2009), p. 198.
3   Henry Meikle, *Scotland and the French Revolution*, p. 154.
4   Ibid., p. 154.
5   Michael Roe, 'George Mealmaker, the Forgotten Martyr', *Journal and Proceedings* (Royal Australia Historical Society, 1958), vol. 43, pp. 284–98, p. 287.
6   Ibid., p. 286.

7   Peter Berresford Ellis and Seumas Mac A' Ghobhainn, *The Scottish Insurrection of 1820* (Edinburgh: J. Donald, 2001).

8   Tom Johnston, *The History of the Working Classes in Scotland*.

9   E. W. McFarland, *Ireland and Scotland in the Age of Revolution: Planting the Green Bough*, p. 152.

10   Ibid., p. 158.

11   Roger Wells, *Insurrection: The British Experience 1795–1803*, p. 95.

12   McKean, et. al., *Dundee: Renaissance to Enlightenment*.

13   Michael Roe, 'George Mealmaker, the Forgotten Martyr', *Journal and Proceedings* (Royal Australia Historical Society, 1958).

14   Notes from D. Cameron interrogation, April 1798, HO/102/16/208-9, referenced in Roger Wells, *Insurrection: The British Experience 1795–1803*, p. 96.

15   National Records of Scotland, RH2/4/83.

16   National Records of Scotland, SO JC 26/297.

17   Henry Meikle, *Scotland and the French Revolution*, p. 187.

18   E. W. McFarland, *Ireland and Scotland in the Age of Revolution: Planting the Green Bough*, p. 154.

19   Roger Wells, *Insurrection: The British Experience 1795–1803*, p. 97.

20   E. W. McFarland, *Ireland and Scotland in the Age of Revolution: Planting the Green Bough*, p. 155.

21   National Records of Scotland, RH/2/4/80.

22   The *Caledonian Mercury*, 11 January 1798.

23   Ibid., 13 January 1798.

24   E. W. McFarland, *Ireland and Scotland in the Age of Revolution: Planting the Green Bough*, p. 187.

25   Bob Harris, *The Scottish People and the French Revolution*, p. 159.

26   NAC JC 26/293 referenced in Bob Harris, *The Scottish People and the French Revolution*, p. 163.

27   Ibid.

28   Michael Roe, 'George Mealmaker, the Forgotten Martyr', p. 284.

CHAPTER 11: THE MILITIA ACT RIOTS

1   'Scot Corr', vol. i, 18 October 1782, referenced in Henry Meikle, *Scotland and the French Revolution*, p. 178.

2   'Scot Corr', vol. vii, referenced in Henry Meikle, *Scotland and the French Revolution*, p. 179.

3   Bob Harris, *The Scottish People and the French Revolution*, p. 171.

4   Ibid., p. 167.

5   National Records of Scotland, RH2/4/81.

6   National Records of Scotland, RH2/4/82.

7   Bob Harris, *The Scottish People and the French Revolution*, p. 174.

8   Kenneth Logue, *Popular Disturbances in Scotland 1780–1815*, p. 79.

9   Bob Harris, *The Scottish People and the French Revolution*, p. 170.

10   Ibid., p. 174.

11   Kenneth Logue, *Popular Disturbances in Scotland 1780–1815*.

12   E. W. McFarland, *Ireland and Scotland in the Age of Revolution: Planting the Green Bough*, p. 194.

13   Ibid., p. 180.

CHAPTER 12: THE MASSACRE OF TRANENT

1   Kenneth Logue, *Popular Disturbances in Scotland 1780–1815*.

2   Ibid., p. 93.

3   Ibid.

4   Ibid.

5   William Cobbett, *Cobbett's Complete Collection of State Trials and Proceedings for High Treason and Other Crime and Misdemeanours from the Earliest Period to the Present Time* (S. I.: T. C. Hansard, 1809–1826).

6   National Records of Scotland, RH/2/4/83.

7   National Records of Scotland, RH2/4/82.

8   Kenneth Logue, *Popular Disturbances in Scotland 1780–1815* and E. W. McFarland, *Ireland and Scotland in the Age of Revolution: Planting the Green Bough.*

9   Peter Berresford Ellis and Seumas Mac A' Ghobhainn, *The Scottish Insurrection of 1820* (Edinburgh: J. Donald, 2001).

10   Tom Johnston, *History of the Working Classes in Scotland.*

11   William Cobbett, *Cobbett's Complete Collection of State Trials and Proceedings for High Treason and Other Crime and Misdemeanours from the Earliest Period to the Present Time.*

12   HO 102/15/78-9 referenced in Roger Wells, *Insurrection: The British Experience 1795–1803*, p. 96.

CHAPTER 13: FOREIGN ARMIES AND THE DUTCH INVASION

1   Henry Meikle, *Scotland and the French Revolution*, p. 163.

2   Ibid., p. 165.

3   Ibid.

4   William Theobald W. Tone (ed.), *Life of Theobald Wolfe Tone* (General Books LLC, 2012), p. 432, referenced in C. J. Woods, 'A plan for a Dutch Invasion of Scotland 1797', *Scottish Historical Review* (1974), vol. 53, no. 155, p. 108.

5   Henry Meikle, *Scotland and the French Revolution.*

6   C. J. Woods, 'A plan for a Dutch Invasion of Scotland 1797'.

7   Ibid.

8   Roger Wells, *Insurrection: The British Experience 1795–1803.*

9   C. J. Woods, 'A plan for a Dutch Invasion of Scotland 1797', p. 110.

10   In December 1798 the *Caledonian Mercury* published a poem that lauded Admiral Duncan and reported on a public thanksgiving that was announced by a royal proclamation, which stated that radical plots had been uncovered involving the United Irishmen.

11   Murray Armstrong, *The Liberty Tree: The Stirring Story of Thomas Muir and Scotland's First Fight for Democracy.*

12   Henry Meikle, *Scotland and the French Revolution*, p. 173.

13   Ibid., p. 173.

14   Ibid., p. 174.

15   Ibid., p. 175.

16   Ibid., p. 176.

17   Ibid., p. 177.

CHAPTER 14: A LEGACY REMAINS AND THE FATE OF THE OTHER MARTYRS

1   Henry Meikle, *Scotland and the French Revolution*, p. 214.

2   Ibid., p. 214.

3   Ibid., p. 215.

4   Bob Harris, *The Scottish People and the French Revolution*, p. 209.

5   Ibid., p. 213.

6   Ibid., p. 214.

7   Ibid.

8   National Records of Scotland, RH/2/4/76.

9   Henry Meikle, *Scotland and the French Revolution.*

10   Henry Cockburn, *Memorials of his Time*, (Edinburgh: A. & C. Black, 1856), p. 183.

11   Michael Roe, 'George Mealmaker, the Forgotten Martyr', p. 294.

12   Ibid.

13   Ibid., p. 292.

14   Ibid, p. 294.

15   Ibid., p. 295.

16   HO102/22, F537, referenced in Gordon Pentland, 'Radical Returns in an Age of Revolutions', *Études écossaises* (2010), vol. 13, pp. 91–102.

17   Ibid., p. 96.
18   Ibid.
19   Ibid.

CHAPTER 15: RADICALISM REIGNITED

1   Roger Wells, *Insurrection: The British Experience 1795–1803*, p. 305.
2   Ibid.
3   E. W. McFarland, *Ireland and Scotland in the Age of Revolution: Planting the Green Bough*, p. 224.
4   Roger Wells, *Insurrection: The British Experience 1795–1803*, p. 305.
5   Henry Meikle, *Scotland and the French Revolution*, p. 193.
6   National Records of Scotland, RH2/4/92.
7   National Records of Scotland, RH2/4/98.
8   Ibid.
9   John Brims, 'The Scottish Democratic Movement in the Age of the French Revolution', p. 576.
10   Ibid., p. 577.
11   'Scot Corr', vol. xxvii, referenced in Henry Meikle, *Scotland and the French Revolution*, p. 222.
12   'Scot Corr', vol. xxvi, 25 December 1816, referenced in Henry Meikle, *Scotland and the French Revolution*, p. 222.
13   Tom Johnston, *Our Scots Noble Families*, p. 235.
14   Peter Berresford Ellis and Seumas Mac A' Ghobhainn, *The Scottish Insurrection of 1820*, p. 109.

CHAPTER 16: EVENTS IN ENGLAND

1   'Scot Corr', vol. xxviii, referenced in Henry Meikle, *Scotland and the French Revolution*, p. 226.
2   Charles Tennant, *The Radical Laird: A Biography of George Kinloch, 1775–1833* (Kineton: Roundwood Press, 1970).
3   Sylvia Clark, 'The Crime of Rebellion', Paisley Library.
4   Peter Berresford Ellis and Seumas Mac A' Ghobhainn, *The Scottish Insurrection of 1820*, p. 128.
5   Élie Halévy, *The Liberal Awakening* (London: Ark, 1987).
6   John Parkhill, *The History of Paisley* (Paisley: Robert Stewart, 1857).
7   Charles Tennant, *The Radical Laird: A Biography of George Kinloch, 1775–1833*.
8   Sylvia Clark, 'The Crime of Rebellion', Paisley Library.
9   Peter Mackenzie, *Reminiscences of Glasgow and the West of Scotland*, p. 63.

CHAPTER 17: THE 1820 RISING

1   Peter Berresford Ellis and Seumas Mac A' Ghobhainn, *The Scottish Insurrection of 1820* and Peter Mackenzie, *Reminiscences of Glasgow and the West of Scotland*.
2   F. K. Donnelly, 'The Scottish Rising of 1820: A Reinterpretation', *Scottish Tradition* (1976), vol. 6, pp. 27–37.
3   Tom Johnston, *Our Scots Noble Families*, p. 240.
4   Ibid.
5   National Records of Scotland, PRO HO 102/32.
6   Tom Johnston, *Our Scots Noble Families*, p. 240.
7   Gordon Pentland, *The Spirit of the Union: Popular Politics in Scotland, 1815–1820* (London: Pickering & Chatto, 2011), p. 106 and Sylvia Clark, 'The Crime of Rebellion'.
8   Ibid.
9   F. K. Donnelly, 'The Scottish Rising of 1820: A Reinterpretation'.
10   Peter Berresford Ellis and Seumas Mac A' Ghobhainn, *The Scottish Insurrection of 1820*.
11   Ibid., and Peter Mackenzie, *Reminiscences of Glasgow and the West of Scotland*.
12   Ibid.
13   Letter from Boswell to Lord Sidmouth, DEO 152M, Gordon Pentland, *The Spirit of the Union: Popular Politics in Scotland, 1815–1820*, p. 106.

14 John Parkhill (ed.), *The Life and Opinions of Arthur Sneddon, an Autobiography* (Paisley: James Cook, 1860), referenced in Gordon Pentland, *The Spirit of the Union: Popular Politics in Scotland, 1815–1820*, p. 106.

15 Peter Berresford Ellis and Seumas Mac A' Ghobhainn, *The Scottish Insurrection of 1820*.

16 James Halliday, *1820 Rising: The Radical War* (Stirling: Scots Independent, 1993), p. 22.

17 Peter Berresford Ellis and Seumas Mac A' Ghobhainn, *The Scottish Insurrection of 1820*, p. 221.

18 F. K. Donnelly, 'The Scottish Rising of 1820: A Reinterpretation'.

CHAPTER 18: AFTERMATH AND EPILOGUE

1 Peter Berresford Ellis and Seumas Mac A' Ghobhainn, *The Scottish Insurrection of 1820*, p. 274.

2 Ibid.

3 Ibid., p. 257.

4 Henry Meikle, *Scotland and the French Revolution*, p. 229.

5 Tom Johnston, *History of the Working Classes in Scotland*, p. 243.

6 Charles Tennant, *The Radical Laird: A Biography of George Kinloch, 1775–1833*, p. 235.

7 Gordon Pentland, 'Radical Returns in an Age of Revolutions', p. 97.

8 Ibid.

9 Tom Johnston, *Our Scots Noble Families*, p. xxxiii.

10 Ibid., p. xxxi.

INDEX

Abercromby, Lord 81, 82–3
Aboyne, Earl of 164
Act of the General Assembly 31
Adam, John 185–6, 190
Aitken, James 168
Aitken, John 138–9
American Revolution 19
Amiens, Treaty of (1802) 242
Anderson, David 176
Anderson, James 68–9
Arniston, Lady Anne 40, 41
Arnot, Robert 221
Association against Levellers and Republicans 59–60
Atholl, Duke of 154, 160–61, 163

Baird, John 281–2, 294–6
Baird, Thomas 254–5
Bantry Bay, Ireland 123, 150, 196, 200–201
Batavian Republic (Dutch) 201–5
Berresford Ellis, Peter 127, 132, 161, 255, 267, 275, 287
Berry, Walter 69
Black, David 146
Black Watch 45
Blackie, John 187
Blair, Adam 185–6
Bligh, Capt. William 234
Bonnymuir, Battle of 282, 284, 292, 294
Boswell, Alexander 285–6
Botany Bay 5, 226–8, 273, 296
Braxfield, Lord 71, 78–9, 80, 100, 166–8
Brims, John 247–8
British Empire 14–15
Brotherstone, Stephen 183
Brown, Mathew 90–91

Brown, Walter 139–40
Buccleuch, Duke of 153–4
Burdett, Sir Francis 251
Burgh Reform Organisation, Aberdeen 36
Burke, Edmund 25
Burns, Robert 26, 45–6, 122–3

Cadell, John 175–6, 177, 180, 188, 191
Caledonian Mercury 9, 25, 49, 209, 210
Callender, James Thomson 18
Calvinism 31, 34
Cameron, Angus 132, 161–4, 167–9, 193–4, 213
Campbell, Christopher 167
Campbell, Ilay 99–100
Campbell, James 67, 70, 75
Campbell, Thomas 105, 243
capital punishment 224–5
Carnochan, Thomas 168
Cartwright, Maj. John 238, 248
Castle Hill Rebellion 236
Cato Street Conspiracy (1819) 272–3
Chartism 6, 10, 298–9, 301
Christie, John 167
Church of Scotland 30–32
Clelland, James 296
Clouston, David 146
Cobbett, William, Political Register 250
Cockburn, Lord Henry 25, 78, 215, 216, 222, 256
Colquhoun, Archibald 246–7
Combination Laws 247
conscription 149–74
Convention Act (1793) 95
Corn Laws (1815) 247
Craig, Malcolm 68–9
Craig, William 131

Craigdallie, James 132, 143, 192
Crookston, Joan 181, 192
Culloden, Battle of 8, 16
Cunningham, Thomas 190

Daendels, Gen. Herman 201–2, 203
Declaration of Independence, American 32
Defenderism 242, 245
dissenting churches 31–3, 34
Donnelly, F. K. 275, 287
Dorr, Capt. Ebenezer 206–7
Douglas, David 139
Douglas, Rev. Neil 255–6
Downie, David 113–14, 116–17
Drennan, William 62
Drummond, John 168
Duncan, Adm. Adam 40, 205
Duncan, Alison 189
Duncan, David 189–90
Dundas family 92, 99, 106
Dundas, Henry 22–4
    on conscription 150, 151–2
    demonstrations against 38, 52–3
    letter from Margarot 237
    memo to R. Dundas 192, 194
    monument 7
    and the Pike Plot 125, 130
    political control 221, 222–3
    support for new laws 125
    and trials 100
Dundas, Robert 54–5
    and Braxfield 100, 114, 117
    on conscription 155
    and H. Dundas 223
    letter from Arnot 221
    and Lord Sidmouth 260
    and Mealmaker 136, 142–3
    memo to H. Dundas 132, 190, 195
    memos to London 165, 167
    on Muir 77
    and reform 32
    Solicitor General 23
    and Tytler 66
Dutch Navy 204–5

Easter Rising, Ireland 24
Edinburgh Gazetteer 61, 69, 71, 97
Edinburgh Review 223
    1820 Rising 275–89, 291, 319–21, 323
Elder, George 181
Elder, John 69
Ellis, James 230–31

Emmet, Thomas 120
England 259–73
Enlightenment 30
Erskine, Henry 121–2
Eskgrove, Lord 81, 101, 141

First National Convention of the Scottish
    Friends of the People 4, 52, 54–5, 57, 61–2
    delegates 307–11
    political aims 63
    resolutions 64–5
Fox, Charles 87
France 17, 197–9, 201, 202
Fraser, Robert 167
French Revolution 6, 16–17, 24–6, 197, 244, 250
Friends of Liberty, Society of the 51, 81, 82, 130
Friends of Man 70
Friends of the People, Society of the 47–55
    Canongate 86
    conventions 89–97, 198, 311–14
    cooperation with other organisations 18–19,
        88
    demands of 63, 249
    meetings 6
    members 4

George I, King 8
George III, King 7, 37–9, 106
George IV, King 7, 8–9, 253, 255
George Street, Edinburgh 7
Gerrald, Joseph
    arrested 97
    background 4
    colony life and death 228–9, 229
    and Convention Act 95
    Friends' conventions 90–91
    and Friends' meetings 106–7
    illness 206
    LCS member 49
    memorial 2
    on prison ship 224
    trial 104–5
Gillies, Lord Adam 254–5
Glasgow Advertiser 190–91
Glasgow Courier 59, 128, 134–5
Glasgow, Peter 166
Glen's Inn 177–9
'Glorious Revolution' (1688) 25
Goldsmiths' Hall Association 60, 64–5, 76, 117
Gordon, Lord Adam 53, 57, 58, 155, 156, 176
Gould, John 182
Gray, Archibald 145, 146, 192

Gray, Benjamin 249
Greig, Sarah 168
Grenville, William 222

Halévy, Élie 267
Hamilton Rowan, Archibald 62, 73, 91–3, 95, 120
Hamilton, Thomas 11
handbills 38–9, 42, 63, 82, 110, 153, 171
Hardie, Andrew 281–6, 300
Hardie, Keir 301
Hardy, Thomas 49, 98, 106, 120, 141, 142
Harris, Bob 33, 59, 152–3
Hastie, Archibald 237, 248, 269
Hawkesbury, Lord 177
Henderson, David 168
Highland Clearances 15, 45, 304
Highland Society 9
Hoche, Gen. Lazare 201, 202, 204
Hood, Janet 188
Hope, Lord Charles 267, 292
Hume Brown, Peter 36, 76
Hume, David 1
Hume, Joseph 11
Hunt, Henry 262
Hunter, John 228

Industrial Revolution 6, 216–17, 245
Inglis of Cramond, Sir John 60
Irish rebellion (1798) 171–2

Jacobites 8, 9, 16, 58, 287, 299–300
Johnston, Alexander 296
Johnston, John 146
Johnston, Tom
    and Militia Act riots 193
    on Pike Plot 118–19
    on riots 152
    on strikes 275
    The History of the Working Classes in
        Scotland 16
    Our Scots Noble Families 23, 303
Johnston, Capt. William 69

Keane, Fergal 24
Kemp, William and D. 184
Kennedy, John 146
Kerr, Christopher 166
de Kersaint, Armand 197–8
King, Capt. Philip 232–3
Kinloch, George 261, 264, 270, 300–301

Laidlaw, William 183–4

Laing, Malcolm 104
Lang, John 297–8
Lang, William 249
Lauderdale, Earl of 80
Lawson, William 183, 190
Leslie, Alexander 127, 143–5
Little, Robert 166
Logue, Kenneth 26, 152, 168
London Corresponding Society (LCS) 4, 49,
    87–8, 106–7, 124, 145
Lord Advocate, office of 20
Lord Lieutenant, office of 112
Louis XVI, King 25–6, 67, 70

Mac A' Ghobhainn, Seumas 127, 132, 161, 193,
    255, 267, 275, 287
McAllister, Theophilus 129, 146
McArthur, John 249
Macarthur, John 233
McCulloch, Thomas 296
Macdonald, Gen. Jacques 204
McFarland, Elizabeth (E. W.) 119, 152, 193
McFarlane, Thomas 301
McIntosh, James 169
Mackenzie, Peter, Reminisces of Glasgow and the
    West of Scotland 10–11, 21, 275
McKinlay, Andrew 255
McLaggan, John (Duke Lennox) 169
MacLaren, Alexander 254–5
McLeod, Gilbert, The Spirit of the Union 270,
    287, 299
McLeod, John 249
Maconochie, Alexander 260
Manchester Patriotic Union 262
Margarot, Maurice
    arrested 97
    background 4
    colony life and death 232, 235, 239
    Friends' conventions 90–91, 93, 95
    and Friends' meetings 247
    LCS member 49
    memorial 2
    on prison ship 224, 226
    returns to Britain 237–9
    trial 102–4
    writes to Hardy 106
Masonic groups 129
Mathieson, W. L. 21
Mealmaker, George 129–32, 134–43
    arrested 130, 192
    background 5
    church elder 33

Mealmaker, George *cont.*
colony life and death 229, 231–5
Friends' conventions 95
letter to London reformists 122
and palmer 81–2
reputation 111, 126, 205–6
sermon 124
The Moral and Political Catechism of Man
136, 138
Meikle, Henry, *Scotland and the French*
Revolution 121, 200, 221
Members of Parliament, Scottish 20–21, 23, 100
Mengaud, Citoyen 200–201
Menzies, James 161, 162, 164, 167, 169, 170
Menzies, Sir John 162
Menzies, John 69–70
Militia Act riots 143, 149–74
Miller, Walter 111
Mirabeau, Comte de 67
Mitchell, Robert 189
Moderate faction 31–2
Moffatt, William 237
Moffatt, William (lawyer) 11, 12, 66, 248
Moffatt, William (servant) 184–5
Moniteur Universel, Le 209
Montgomery, William 187
Morton, John 68–9
Muir, Thomas
colony life 225–6, 228
convicted 86
First National Convention 63
and France 67, 70–72, 199, 206–14
Friends' figurehead 54–5
and Friends' meetings 48
in Ireland 72–3, 75
and Irish counterparts 62, 106
lawyer 43, 66, 224
legacy 16
memorial 2, 3, 11
questioned 66–7
speeches 5, 76
support for 87–8, 90, 92
trial and conviction 75–81, 304
Munro, Robert 297
Murray, James 298

Napoleon Bonaparte 17, 123, 206, 213, 215, 244
Napoleonic Wars 244
National Assembly, French 36
Neil, John 271–2, 297
Neilson, William 146
Nelson, Admiral 1, 13

Nelson, William 191
Ness, Peter 182–3
New Town, Edinburgh 7
Nicholas, Isaac 235
Nicholson, John 189

O'Connell, Daniel 11
Ogilvie, John 249
Outerside, Nicholas 188

Paine, Thomas
background 33–4
convicted 65–6
effigies burned 59
in France 67
writing 36
The Age of Reason 34
Common Sense 33
Rights of Man 6, 69, 76
Palmer, Thomas Fyshe 80–87
background 3–4
colony life and death 229–31
and friends 206
memorial 2
on prison ship 224–6
support for 90
Unitarian minister 32, 54
Paterson, James 146
Pentland, Gordon 238, 239
Perthshire, Sheriff Clerk of 110
Peterloo massacre (1819) 13, 18, 175, 261–3
Phillip, Capt. Arthur 226
Pike Plot (1794) 113–20
Pitt the Younger, William 7, 23, 222
Pittock, Murray 15–16
Political Martyrs' Monument 1–3, 10–12
Popular faction 31–2
population 27
prison ships 105–6, 224–5

Rae, Sir William 292
Ramsey, James 167
Red Clydesiders 33, 303
Reform Acts (1832, 1867, 1884) 7, 221, 300, 303
Reformation 34
Reformed Church 30, 31
Reformers' Gazette 10
Reidpath, Neil 189
religion 30–33, 63, 129, 173, 220–21
Richardson, James 166
Riot Act, reading the 40, 41, 180, 265
Ritchie, Alex 190–91

Robertson, Alexander 184, 186–7
Robertson, James 69
Robespierre, Maximilien 34, 67
Roe, Michael 234
Roger, Archibald 191
Roger, Isabel 181, 191
Ross, Robert 188
Royal Company of Archers 8
Royal Martyr, The (play) 110
Royal Navy 123, 199, 204–5, 208
Russell, John 249

St Andrew's House 1
Sands, Robert 143
Sands, William 132, 139
Scots Magazine, The 25
Scott, Alexander 69, 97
Scott, Sir Walter 8, 270
Scottish Labour Party 303
Scottish National Party 303
Scottish songs 172
Second Great Awakening 220
Second National Convention 84–5
Seditious Meetings Act (1795) 125
sheep, year of the 44–5
Sheffield Constitutional Society 107
Sidmouth, Lord 260, 269–70
Sinclair, Charles 90–91
Six Acts (1819) 267
Skirving, William 33
    arrested 97
    background 4
    colony life and death 228, 229
    and Friends' meetings 48, 50, 55
    illness 206
    and Irish counterparts 62
    leadership 86–7, 88
    memorial 2
    on prison ship 224–6
    trial 98, 101–2
Smith, James 69–70
Smith, William 181, 296
Sons of Liberty 70
Spain 208
Speirs, James 297–8
Spence, Thomas 272
Sprott, Andrew 167
Stewart, John (alias McCulloch) 169
Stewart, William 69
Stirling, James 38
strikes 36, 57, 246–7, 277–80
Symington, John 188

Tait, William 185–6
Tandy, James Napper 213
Tayler, Wat 15
Taylor, Alexander 265, 266
Thistlewood, Arthur 273
Thomas the Rhymer 109–10
Tillans, George 187, 189
Tolpuddle Martyrs 15
Tone, Wolfe
    and the Dutch 202, 204
    in France 199, 206, 213
    suicide 173
    United Irishmen founder 73, 127
    and United Scotsmen 195
Tory Party 7, 23, 85, 222, 223
trade unionism 6, 28–9, 247, 298–9
Tranent, Massacre of (1797) 175–96, 272
Treason Acts (1708, 1795) 114
Treaty of Union 30, 63–4, 249
Tree of Liberty 52, 54
Turner, James 250
Tweedale, Marquis of 176–7
Tytler, James 66, 68

Union Society, British 145
United Irishmen, Society of 171–4
    disbanded 120
    flee to Scotland 128
    and Muir 73, 212
    and Scottish counterparts 52, 76, 96, 195,
        242
    success of 62
United Scotsmen, Society of the 125–8, 143–7
    and Irish counterparts 18, 242
    members 162, 170, 192–6, 212, 241–2
    Resolution and Constitution 131, 136, 315–17
    and union societies 268
United States of America 19–20, 216
Unlawful Oaths Act (1797) 133

Van Diemen's Land 297, 298
vote, right to 7, 20, 300, 304

Watson, Robert 210–11
Watson, William 249
Watt, Robert 113–18, 126
weaving industry 27–8, 36, 126, 233–4
Wellington, Duke of 1, 13
Wells, Roger 17
Whig Club, Dundee 36
Whigs 48–9, 87, 222
White, Andrew 301

Whitelaw, James 190
Williamson, Ann 168
Williamson, Robert 168
Wilson, Elizabeth 166
Wilson, Francis 189
Wilson, James 283, 284, 292–4, 295
Wilson, Thomas 241, 243
de Winter, Adm. Jan Willem 205
Witherspoon, Rev. John 32
Wright, Major 178